The Distributed Smalltalk Survival Guide

Advances in Object Technology Series

Dr. Richard S. Wiener,
Series Editor and Editor of
Journal of Object-Oriented Programming
SIGS Publications, Inc.
New York, New York

and

Department of Computer Science
University of Colorado
Colorado Springs, Colorado

Additional Volumes in Preparation

The Distributed Smalltalk Survival Guide

Terry Montlick

PUBLISHED BY THE PRESS SYNDICATE OF THE UNIVERSITY OF CAMBRIDGE
The Pitt Building, Trumpington Street, Cambridge CB2 1RP, United Kingdom

CAMBRIDGE UNIVERSITY PRESS
The Edinburgh Building, Cambridge CB2 2RU, UK
  http://www.cup.cam.ac.uk
40 West 20th Street, New York, NY 10011-4211, USA
  http:www.cup.org
10 Stamford Road, Oakleigh, Melbourne 3166, Australia

Published in association with SIGS Books

First published in 1999

Design and composition by David Van Ness
Cover design by Tom Jezek

Printed in the United States of America

A catalog record for this book is available from the British Library.

Library of Congress Cataloging-in-Publication Data is on record with the publisher.

ISBN 0-521-64552-2   paperback

For Charlotte

≡Contents≡

Chapter 8: AN EXAMPLE: The Stock Market Project . . 119

Chapter 9: Building Complex Distributed Systems . . 159

Chapter 10: Whither the Internet?

Notes

Index

≡Figures≡

═══Acknowledgments═══

Many people helped in the writing of this book. I'd like to thank Yen-Ping Shan and John Kellerman of IBM for their help on the IBM Distributed Feature. Thanks also to Jeff Eastman, of Windward Solutions, for his perspectives on both ObjectShare Distributed Smalltalk and DNS SmalltalkBroker. Jay Almarode of GemStone Systems was invaluable in providing his technical expertise on GemStone. Paul Windward and John Mullen at DNS Technologies helped me with important information about SmalltalkBroker. And David Whiteman of Applied Reasoning Systems taught me the fine points of Classic Blend.

My thanks to Mike Piscotty of Lawrence Livermore National Laboratories for arranging for me to visit, and to spend time with his fine staff. And thanks to all the Smalltalkers I know who have shared their knowledge over the years.

≡Introduction≡

The days of the monolithic computer program are giving way to a new era. *Distributed computing* is coming of age. The major technical roadblocks that prevent different systems from freely exchanging information will disappear forever. The computing environment of tomorrow is a shared one.

Why is this important? Aren't there PCs everywhere running all manner of spreadsheet, accounting package, project manager, and report writer? Well, that's just the problem. Everyone has their own private PC world, with only minimal communication with other computers. Simple network interconnection software, such as for workflow and messages, has already had a major impact on the business enterprise. But computers, both personal and mainframe, still remain their own little islands of computing, with at best a few ferry boats chugging between them. Even the Internet, with its browsers and their new Java interpreters, doesn't really solve the problem on its own.

There is not yet true *interoperability* — the ability of different programs on diverse computer systems to access each other's information and functionality. Without interoperability, individual programs running on different machines cannot be leveraged by the entire business enterprise. The whole cannot become anything more than the sum of its parts. Because strategic business partnerships face a polyglot of incompatible software and systems, such partnerships cannot function in a tightly coupled manner to act swiftly and efficiently to meet increasingly competitive challenges.

Why now? Hasn't interoperability through distributed computing been a desirable goal in the past? What makes the difference today? The answer is simple. *Objects.*

Objects encapsulate both data and behavior. They are self-contained units of computing. Objects are like individual programs, but with a natural programmatic connection built right in. As such, they are perfect candidates for distribution. All you need to do is define the interfaces to objects, and a means for referencing those objects and passing arguments to them.

Of course, this is not as easy as it sounds. You have to create a solid infrastructure for distributed computing that must deal with many issues, including network communication, serialization of objects, common information protocols, and a myriad of other technical problems.

Ironically, Smalltalk itself is the ultimate monolithic solution. It's a completely self-contained development and execution environment, with its own virtual machine. An editor, various types of browsers, and an execution engine are all integral parts of Smalltalk.

But the objects from which everything in Smalltalk is built are also its salvation. Because Smalltalk objects maintain a strict separation between interface and implementation, their internal operations are hidden. This makes it relatively straightforward, at least conceptually, to place their implementation somewhere else.

Smalltalk has come of age as a distributed computing environment. There are several commercial, off-the-shelf choices available today to a designer of a distributed Smalltalk project. Smalltalk is a pure object-oriented language and also a commercially successful one, so it's natural for software companies to develop products that allow Smalltalk objects to be distributed. This book will go into some detail on those choices, to teach you what you need to know to move into the exciting new age of distributed Smalltalk.

═Chapter 1═

What Is Distributed Smalltalk?

In this book, "distributed Smalltalk" is any software that allows Smalltalk objects residing in different Smalltalk images to communicate with each other.

Picture an international investment firm with offices in New York, London, and Tokyo. The company has built its own distributed Smalltalk application to track the prices of its investments and do sophisticated financial modeling for them. At 9:00 AM Eastern time, the New York Stock Exchange opens for business. But the London exchange has already been operating for five hours. When the New York office opens, it can view the trades that have occurred so far that same day in London because its local report objects have already communicated with the company's London trading objects. The New York part of the distributed Smalltalk program becomes very active as trading starts. Many new objects get created there.

A restless executive from the Japanese office can't sleep, and logs onto the Tokyo computer from home. She's interested in some American holdings, and begins checking some financial modeling objects that are resident on the New York computer, and that have access to New York's up-to-the-minute trades.

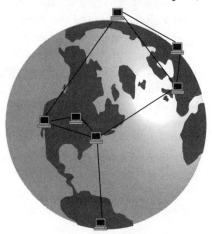

Figure 1-1. Global distributed computing

Sound like futuristic pie-in-the-sky? The fact is, the tools to readily build such a system are available right now. And even more sophisticated distributed Smalltalk applications are under development.

Ask Federal Express (FedEx). It is using distributed Smalltalk today to turn its centralized shipment status database into a distributed, intelligent information system. FedEx constantly feeds routing information for each package into its main database at various steps in the delivery process. There are literally millions of shipments to sort through to determine the status of a given package. This is a challenge for even the most powerful mainframe, so Smalltalk-based distributed computing is way forward.

The new system being built both captures and maintains data at the local level. A local version of the entire database allows a local system to intelligently communicate with the rest of the distributed system only as required. The new system is designed to enable real-time shipment analysis, and to improve overall system efficiency, performance, and flexibility.

Continental Power Exchange, in Atlanta, Georgia, is using distributed Smalltalk to do complex, mission-critical transactions. Its main product, CPEX, serves as an electronic trading system of electricity between buyers and sellers. The deregulation of electric power in the U.S. is what has created this market opportunity. According to Stan Stasiak, Executive Director of Marketing at Continental Power Exchange: "In order to yield the promise of deregulation, a way must be found to provide both liquidity and reliability in the electric industry."

As of 1997, CPEX was the largest electronic wholesale marketplace for electricity trading. Over 60 participants had a combined generating capacity of more than 190,000 megawatts. These participants include utility companies, municipalities, marketers, and government agencies. They are distributed throughout the United States and Canada.

CPEX is actually a commodities futures marketplace. But unlike other commodities futures, which trade months or years in advance, CPEX trading is done for product which is delivered within hours. And the service runs 24 hours a day, seven days a week. Reliability and real-time performance are major requirements.

The CPEX server is implemented with CORBA-complaint distributed Smalltalk. In addition, client software is written in Visual C++. The Smalltalk architecture will scale up via CORBA, expanding to more servers as growth requires.

Another electric power player, Florida Power and Light (FP&L), continues to build its distributed Smalltalk infrastructure for information management. FP&L has been using GemStone client/server Smalltalk, with a team of over 100 Smalltalk developers.

It is now leveraging distributed Smalltalk to move to CORBA-based business objects. FP&L's approach is server-oriented, using what it calls Inter-application Enablers (IEs). Using IEs, applications request services, rather than data directly. A business logic layer arbitrates among these service requests. A federation of as many as 30 GemStone servers will provide system-wide distributed object access, supporting as many as 5,000 users.

Building distributed Smalltalk applications is not a cookbook procedure—not yet, anyway. But this is true of building any type of complex software system. And we are still on the edge of the object-oriented software technology frontier in general. We still strive to build high-level object components that we can plug together freely.

So, like much of software engineering, using distributed Smalltalk is as much of an art as it is a science. But general patterns are emerging. This book seeks to discover and analyze those patterns, and illustrate them with practical examples wherever possible.

And while multiple and diverse vendor implementations are available for doing distributed Smalltalk, much commonality exists. Exploring that commonality teaches much about general principles. It permits us to view distributed Smalltalk at a high level. In turn, analysis of the implementation differences helps guide you in choosing a distributed Smalltalk.

The Basic Principle

With distributed Smalltalk, objects in one Smalltalk image can utilize objects in other Smalltalk images. Compare Figure 1-2 with Figure 1-3. Typically, the remote objects remain on the remote machine, and they receive messages from the local sender.

The local machine actually talks to a **proxy** for the remote object. A proxy is a stand-in for a remote object. It is a special kind of object that has little behavior of its own. The sole purpose of this local proxy object is to automatically forward messages to its corresponding remote object.

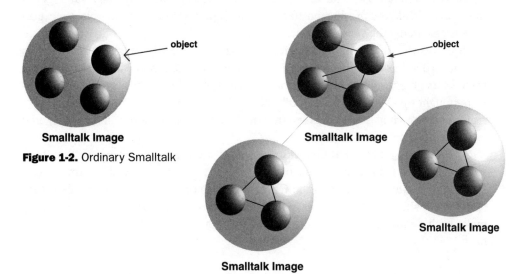

Smalltalk Image

Figure 1-2. Ordinary Smalltalk

Smalltalk Image

Smalltalk Image

Smalltalk Image

Figure 1-3. Distributed Smalltalk

The proxy exists on a client. The real object, or **object implementation**, is on a server. But distributed Smalltalk can go way beyond tradition client/server computing, as we'll see in Chapter 3. Here, client and server are simply roles played by objects. In one situation, an object may act as a server to another object, but at some other time, the roles may be reversed. A true peer-to-peer relationship is possible between distributed Smalltalk objects. But in each individual message interaction, the sending object is considered to be the client, while the receiving object is the server.

The Different Distributed Smalltalks

You face a number of choices in using distributed Smalltalk. One of the most important is selecting which commercial implementation to use. There are four products that meet our definition of distributed Smalltalk. Two are from Smalltalk vendors. The two others are from third parties.

The Smalltalk vendors: ObjectShare and IBM

Both major commercial Smalltalk language vendors, ObjectShare (formerly ParcPlace-Digitalk, formerly ParcPlace) and IBM, ship their respective versions of distributed Smalltalk. ObjectShare sells what used to be Hewlett-Packard Distributed Smalltalk (HP-DST), which it bought from Hewlett-Packard. It has been renamed simply Distributed Smalltalk (DST). Note the capital "D" which distinguishes this from generic distributed Smalltalk. This book is about distributed Smalltalk with a small "d," but it also explores the ObjectShare product as well as some others.

ObjectShare Distributed Smalltalk is an add-on product to the flagship VisualWorks Smalltalk. And IBM has the Distributed feature for its VisualAge for Smalltalk. While the products differ very much in operation and details, their purpose is essentially the same.

IBM was the first Smalltalk language maker to sell a distributed feature for its product. IBM has pursued an aggressive move into the Smalltalk market. Within three years of getting into the Smalltalk business, it had released its third major version, bought up OTI, the supplier of ENVY, the Ferrari of team Smalltalk development tools (which had been bundled into the Professional version of its product), and released the Distributed feature.

So it's not surprising that ObjectShare would want its own distributed Smalltalk product to sell. DST is a mature product that has been deployed in commercial applications. And it adheres to the **Common Object Request Broker Architecture (CORBA)**, which you'll hear lots more about in this book. That ObjectShare would make such a move is an indicator of the importance of distributed Smalltalk to its future.

Third-party options: SmalltalkBroker and GemStone

There are also a couple of important third-party options. DNS Technologies has created **SmalltalkBroker (STB)**, which runs not only with both the ObjectShare VisualWorks dialect of Smalltalk and IBM VisualAge, but VisualSmalltalk Enterprise, the Digitalk dialect in the ObjectShare line. SmalltalkBroker is one of the CORBA-compliant distributed Smalltalks. IONA Technologies, Ltd. has been a distributor of SmalltalkBroker. IONA is at the forefront of CORBA commercialization. IONA's own C++-based product, Orbix, was the first complete implementation of the CORBA specification. IONA Technologies no longer resells SmalltalkBroker. This is no reflection on the product, which has been used successfully in commercial applications.

GemStone Systems has a client/server Smalltalk known best as a powerful Smalltalk-based **Object-Oriented Database Management System (OODBMS)** . But it is a distributed Smalltalk in its own right, because it meets the definition in this book. GemStone has been successfully deployed in what are probably the largest commercial distributed Smalltalk projects to date. Because most distributed applications need a database anyway, if you choose GemStone for its distributed Smalltalk capabilities, you get an industrial-strength OODBMS "free." And as you will see, there is a CORBA connection for GemStone, as well.

Rolling your own

It's also possible to create your own custom distributed Smalltalk solution, instead of using one of the ready-made distributed Smalltalks discussed in this book.

Why create a custom solution rather than use an off-the-shelf one? Why build when you can buy? When you can get away with a quick-and-dirty solution, which typically isn't very often. This is only recommended for the simplest of systems; for example, where two machines running Smalltalk need to exchange a single type of object over a network connection.

For example, if you are using ObjectShare VisualWorks, you can start with an example demo called "CANDO," which should be available from your ObjectShare technical representative.

This demo uses TCP/IP sockets (see "TCP/IP Communication" in Chapter 3) to establish a point-to-point connection between a Smalltalk client and a Smalltalk server. VisualWorks comes with a library of classes to do low-level TCP/IP socket communication. The demo is built upon "Transport Interface" classes, written by Tony White and Dwight Deugo, which use the standard VisualWorks Binary Object Stream Service (BOSS) to serialize objects so they can be sent between Smalltalk images. The connection is seen as an ordinary Smalltalk Stream, but it utilizes the VisualWorks socket library. The standard Smalltalk message **nextPut:** is used by the client to send an object, while the message **next** is used to receive an object.

IBM Smalltalk also gives you access to low level communication facilities, such as TCP/IP, token ring, and their MQ Series message-oriented middleware product. You could create your own software which uses the Swapper, the IBM equivalent of VisualWorks' BOSS. The Swapper serializes and unserializes objects, using the classes ObjectDumper and ObjectLoader. You can use these classes to convert objects to and from arrays of bytes. These byte arrays can be shipped across serial links that you have established.

These are no-frills solutions, but may be useful in simple cases. If you run into problems, though, you're on your own. Without using a full distributed Smalltalk, support and maintenance are your problems.

CORBA or not?

IBM's approach was to create a custom Smalltalk distributed environment. ObjectShare's was to comply with the industry standard for distributed, object-oriented computing, **CORBA.** You learn a lot about the details of CORBA later in this book.

CORBA is a public standard from the **Object Management Group (OMG)**. It specifies how to distribute all kinds of objects, not just Smalltalk objects. However, two of the four distributed Smalltalks comply with CORBA: ObjectShare's Distributed Smalltalk (DST) and DNS Technology's SmalltalkBroker (STB). Interestingly enough, one person, Jeff Eastman, was the architect of both of these products. Jeff developed the earlier product when he was at Hewlett-Packard.

CORBA, HP, and the OMG

Hewlett-Packard (HP) was one of the original four founding members of the OMG. Back in 1987, HP got together with three other major computer manufacturers: Data General, Sun, and Prime Computer.

At their meetings, these companies realized that they had a common need to develop comprehensive object-oriented systems for business computing. And they understood that a very significant effort would be required to do this. Cooperation would achieve this ambitious goal more effectively than each party developing their own proprietary system.

By late 1989, the computer vendors had created an ad-hoc group named the Object Management Group (OMG), and installed Chris Stone of Data General as its president. There were two basic approaches: a static model and a dynamic model. The static model was backed by Sun and HP, while the dynamic model was supported by DEC. In the end, a synthesis of both models was realized in CORBA. (See "What's in an ORB?" in Chapter 5.) The OMG has steadily moved towards setting a powerful, flexible standard for the distributing computing environment of the future. The version of CORBA that has so far been implemented by most vendors, version 2.0, was released in July, 1995. Currently, the OMG is up to version 2.2. The CORBA specification is terse and elegant, a cohesive synthesis of the best ideas on distributed object technology.

CORBA services

CORBA was designed so that major new features can be added to it transparently. These features, called **services**, can be automatically inherited by distributed objects. For example, there is a service called the Life Cycle Service, which is how objects are created, deleted, copied, and moved. This and a host of other services necessary for real-life distributed objects have been defined, and are called the Common Object Services[1]. These are currently 16 in number:

- **Naming Service:** This associates names with objects so they can be looked up by name. The Naming Service provides the ability to bind a name to an object relative to something called a **naming context**. A naming context is an object that contains a set of name bindings in which each name is unique. The naming service resolves a name by determining the object associated with the name in a given context.

- **Event Service:** This facilitates automatic communication between objects. The service supports asynchronous events (decoupled event suppliers and consumers), event "fan in," notification "fan-out,"—and through appropriate event channel implementations—reliable event delivery. Both push and pull event delivery models are supported; that is, consumers can either request events or be notified of events. Suppliers can generate events without knowing the identities of the consumers. Conversely, consumers can receive events without knowing the identities of the suppliers. There can be multiple consumers and multiple suppliers of events.

- **Persistent Object Service:** This allows object states to be long-lived, as in a database. It provides a set of common interfaces to the mechanisms used for retaining and managing the persistent state of objects. The object ultimately has the responsibility of managing its state, but can use or delegate to the Persistent Object Service for the actual work. There can be a variety of different clients and implementations of the Persistent Object Service, and they can work together. This is particularly important for storage, where mechanisms useful for documents may not be appropriate for employee databases, or the mechanisms appropriate for mobile computers do not apply to mainframes.

- **Life Cycle Service:** This service defines how objects are created, deleted, copied, and moved.

- **Concurrency Control Service:** This mediates concurrent access to objects. The Concurrency Control Service enables multiple clients to coordinate their access to shared resources. Coordinating access to a resource means that when multiple, concurrent clients access a single resource, any conflicting actions by the clients are reconciled so that the resource stays in a consistent state. Concurrent use of a resource is regulated with locks. Each lock is associated with a single resource and a single client. Coordination is achieved by preventing multiple clients from simultaneously possessing locks for the same resource if the client's activities might conflict. Hence, a client must obtain an appropriate lock before accessing a shared resource. The Concurrency Control Service defines several lock modes, which correspond to different categories of access. This variety of lock modes provides flexible conflict resolution.

- **Externalization Service:** This defines how to record an object's state in a stream of data. The Externalization Service defines the means for externalizing and internalizing objects. Externalizing an object is to record the object state in a stream of data (in memory, on a disk file, across the network, etc.) and then be internalized into a new object. The externalized object can exist for arbitrary amounts of time, be transported by means outside of the ORB, and be internalized in a different, disconnected ORB. For portability, clients can request that externalized data be stored in a file whose format is defined with the Externalization Service Specification.

- **Relationship Service:** This service allows entities and relationships to be explicitly represented. Entities are represented as CORBA objects. The service defines two kinds of objects: **relationships** and **roles**. A role represents a CORBA object in a relationship. The Relationship interface can be extended to add relationship-specific attributes and operations. In addition, relationships of arbitrary degree can be defined. Similarly, the Role interface can be extended to add role-specific attributes and operations. Type and cardinality constraints can be expressed and checked: exceptions are raised when the constraints are violated.

- **Transaction Service:** This supports a transaction which can be committed or rolled back. The Transaction Service supports multiple transaction models, including the flat model, which is required, and a nested model, which is optional. The Transaction Service supports interoperability between different programming models. For instance, some users want to add object implementations to existing procedural applications and to augment object implementations with code that uses the procedural paradigm. To do so in a transaction environment requires the object and procedural code to share a single transaction. Network interoperability is also supported, since users need communication between different systems, including the ability to have one transaction service interoperate with a cooperating transaction service using different ORBs.

- **Query Service:** This allows selection of objects which satisfy arbitrary criteria. It allows users and objects to invoke queries on collections of other objects. The queries are statements that include the ability to specify values of attributes, to invoke arbitrary operations, and to invoke other Object Services. The Query Service allows indexing. It maps to the query mechanisms used in database systems and other systems that store and access large collections of objects. The Query Service provides an architecture for a nested and federated service that can coordinate multiple, nested query evaluators.

- **Licensing Service:** This allows application producers to control access to their products. Producers can implement the Licensing Service according to their own needs, and the needs of their customers, because this service does not impose its own business policies or practices. A license in the Licensing Service has three types of attributes that allow producers to apply controls flexibly: time, value mapping, and consumer. Time allows licenses to have start/duration and expiration dates. Value mapping allows producers to implement a licensing scheme according to units, allocation, or consumption (for example, metering or allowance of grace periods). Consumer attributes allow a license to be reserved or assigned for specific entities; for example, a license could be assigned to a particular machine.

- **Property Service:** This provides the dynamic equivalent of object attributes. It defines operations to create and manipulate sets of name-value or name-value-mode tuples. The Property Service was designed to be a basic building block, yet robust enough to be applicable for a broad set of applications. It provides "batch" operations to deal with sets of properties as a whole. The use of "batch" operations is important for systems and network management (SNMP, CMIP, etc.).

- **Time Service:** This service provides a unified notion of time and event ordering. The Time Service enables the user to obtain current time together with an error estimate associated with it. It determines the order in which events occurred and computes the interval between two events.

- **Security Service:** This provides for secure use of objects. It specifies the identification and authentication of principals, both human users and objects, to verify they are who they claim to be. There is also authorization and access control, which decides who can access an object. Security auditing makes users accountable for their security related actions. Secure communication is also provided. This requires trust to be established between the client and target, which may require their mutual authentication. The Security Service also provides integrity protection to assure that messages are not tampered with.

- **Trading Object Service:** This lets one ORB determine what is available on another ORB. It provides a matchmaking service for objects. The service provider registers the availability of the service by invoking an export operation on the trader, passing as parameters information about the service being offered. The export operation carries an object reference that can be used by a client to invoke operations on the advertised services, a description of the type of the offered service and information about the distinguishing attributes of the service.

- **Collection Service:** This offers Smalltalk-like collection classes and methods. The Collections Service provides a uniform way to create and manipulate the most common collections generically. Collections are groups of objects which, as a group, support some operations and exhibit specific behaviors that are related to the nature of the collection rather than to the type of object they contain.

- **Change Management Service:** This provides version control.

This is an impressive list! It illustrates just how complex and extensive general-purpose distributed computing needs to be in order to work over the range of real-life, commercial applications. Only a modest subset of these services are available in the commercial CORBA-based distributed Smalltalks, but new ones are being added. CORBA Common Object Services have evolved rapidly, and their details have been agreed upon by CORBA members at different times. So some time is required for the commercial implementations to catch up, particularly for the later services to be defined.

CORBA pluses

CORBA has a number of advantages. It was designed from the ground up to be a universal, distributed object computing standard. It goes beyond any vendor-specific solution, and provides a high level of interoperability.

An open standard

Because CORBA is an open, vendor-neutral standard, there is minimum risk in committing to it. The OMG has over 800 industry members and counting. Members generally regard CORBA as the only infrastructure powerful enough to meet both the current and future needs for distributed computing. Large-scale commercial projects are currently under development that will link hundreds of computers via the CORBA distributed object infrastructure.

Every year, the OMG holds a show and conference called ObjectWorld. It has become a major industry event at which vendors display their CORBA wares and services.

And CORBA, despite its existing power, is growing and evolving. International groups of experts from the OMG member organizations meet every two months to focus on new standards for specific capabilities not yet defined in CORBA, and to apply it to specific industries, such as telecommunications and medical services.

Smalltalk dialect interoperability

With CORBA compliance, you automatically get the ability to communicate between different Smalltalk dialects. The Smalltalk language mapping for CORBA is based on a core of classes found in all Smalltalks. It is defined in the IBM document *Smalltalk Portability: A Common Base*[2], which is also the basis for the ANSI Smalltalk standardization effort.

Of course, the different Smalltalks are still confined to separate images, and can only talk to each other via CORBA-supplied object proxies, called references in

CORBA. This is much less direct and transparent than object communication within the same image. But CORBA acts as a universal translator to map a message sent from say, IBM VisualAge for Smalltalk, to an object written in ObjectShare Visual Smalltalk.

Multi-language interoperability

With either Distributed Smalltalk or DNS SmalltalkBroker, you can mix and match Smalltalk with other software written in C, C++, Java, COBOL, or any other language for which there is a CORBA mapping. Multi-language interoperability is one of the key features of CORBA. In this book, we stick to Smalltalk-to-Smalltalk.

However, the future possibility of talking between objects implemented in other languages may be something to bear in mind when designing your system. If you create CORBA-compliant Smalltalk objects, they can be used transparently by programs written in other programming language.

This could be a big internal selling point for your distributed Smalltalk project, particularly if your management is wary of committing to the Smalltalk language for a large project. The CORBA approach doesn't lock you into Smalltalk for the entire life history of the project. You can, at any time in the future, add software components which are written in other programming languages.

CORBA minuses

In trying to be all things to all object-oriented languages and environments, CORBA makes some inevitable compromises. This can make CORBA-compliant distributed Smalltalks somewhat complex.

You have to write IDL

For a Smalltalk object to receive messages via CORBA, it must conform to a standard interface. This is written in a universal interface language called **Interface Description Language (IDL)**. You learn this language later in this book. It looks like C++, not Smalltalk. A CORBA distributed object must always have an IDL description. You have to write this if you are using one of the CORBA compliant distributed Smalltalks.

It's possible to automatically generate "stubs," empty Smalltalk methods to be filled in by the programmer, from IDL, using tools provided in the CORBA-compliant distributed Smalltalks. You can also automatically go from IDL to Smalltalk to some extent. But even if you use such tools, there is still hand work to be done.

A least common denominator?

The authors of CORBA tried their best not to limit language capabilities when using distributed objects. And they succeeded, even though very disparate computer languages are involved. There is support for dynamically bound languages like Smalltalk, as well as statically bound languages such as C and C++. But with complete interoperability, some compromises are inevitable. What's natural in one language can be awkward in another. But fortunately, CORBA was very cleverly designed. Everything is possible, although sometimes some effort is necessary. For example, every possible Smalltalk class is not automatically mapped to IDL. You can, however, explicitly map Smalltalk classes to CORBA by adding your own IDL.

You can choose to automatically generate the IDL from either of the CORBA-compliant distributed Smalltalks. But then you loose the ability to easily inter-operate with other languages because all your parameters are untyped.

Smalltalk has no typing of parameters. You are free to send absolutely any object as a parameter in a message, so long as the messages that may subsequently be sent to that parameter will be understood. But in a statically-compiled language like C++, this is simply not feasible. It's possible to use all untyped parameters, but creates significant overhead for typed languages. So you are greatly encouraged to type the parameters in IDL.

Typing is not very natural in Smalltalk. But if you want Smalltalk objects to be readily CORBA distributable, their public messages must confine themselves to parameters of known type.

There are ways around the CORBA typing problem, however. In Chapter 5, the section "Smalltalk IDL secrets" describes how to tame CORBA so that it is more Smalltalk-friendly. One way is to use the CORBA "any" type. With this type, you can pass absolutely any defined CORBA type. So as long as the Smalltalk objects you pass can be mapped to CORBA types, you can use the "any" type.

But what about statically-typed languages? How can they handle the "any" type? Code written in such languages must explicitly determine what type was actually passed in the "any" parameter. CORBA defines how to do this in each of its language mappings. So using the "any" type with impunity causes no problems for Smalltalk, but it can create extra code overhead for other languages.

Smalltalk inelegance

The CORBA language mapping makes sharable Smalltalk server classes harder to write. Fortunately, the Smalltalk clients who call upon instances of these classes can look standard. But for the distributed server objects, you must think in terms of IDL.

Before you write a distributed Smalltalk class, you typically have to write its IDL interface. DST, for example, has a tool that then generates the "stubs" for the corresponding Smalltalk methods. These stubs are empty methods, which give you a place to start in writing the Smalltalk code.

You can also take an existing Smalltalk application and distribute it using CORBA. Then, you must identify those classes that will be distributed, and write IDL interfaces for them. This can require modification to the Smalltalk classes if they take non-CORBA liberties. This generally means writing IDL interfaces for those classes whose instances are used as arguments to or answer objects of your interface classes.

The Microsoft factor

For a long time, Microsoft was conspicuously absent from the many member companies of the OMG. Microsoft has been promoting its own proprietary standard called **Component Object Model (COM)**. COM is the object communication system for **Object Linking and Embedding (OLE)**, Microsoft's popular desktop solution for linking applications together.

If you look at COM, it has little of the power and simplicity of CORBA. There are no high-level language bindings, such as to Smalltalk. Instead, it uses a large set of **Application Program Interface (API)** calls. COM is only supported within a single machine, not between multiple machines on a network. Only recently has the distributed version, **Distributed Component Model (DCOM)**, been available.

But Microsoft is the proverbial 800-pound gorilla. It is a potent force in the marketplace which simply cannot be ignored. And to some degree, choosing CORBA is a choice against Microsoft. It is possible to encapsulate OLE objects so they can work with CORBA in addition to COM. However, it is in the interest of any company promoting a private standard to forestall the widespread adoption of a public standard.

Microsoft has given in to some degree on CORBA. It has finally become a member of the OMG. It has announced that it will provide a link from DCOM to CORBA. This grudging acknowledgement of and interoperability with the CORBA standard has come as a relief to many organizations who have been on the fence about CORBA.

The OMG did not sit idly by while Microsoft made up its mind to join the game. It issued a **Request For Proposals (RFPs)** in 1995 to specify how CORBA and COM would interoperate. As part of the CORBA version 2.0 specification, issued in July of 1996, it formally defined how to map between COM and CORBA. The spec has been tweaked some since, to keep it current and to address DCOM interoperability.

Where deficiencies exist in COM, the OMG has outlined what to do. For example, COM exception handling is nonexistent. Instead of throwing an exception, COM provides error information as a system error code returned by an operation. There is no provision for user defined exceptions. However, the OMG has described the exact translation of COM system errors to CORBA exceptions. And user exceptions are mapped to COM interface and structure, and are communicated back to the CORBA client as an optional COM output argument.

Using CORBA with other distributed Smalltalks

A CORBA-compliant distributed Smalltalk does not rule out another distributed option. In fact, you can combine a commercial CORBA Smalltalk implementation with either the IBM Distributed feature or with GemStone Smalltalk.

IBM encourages the combined use of the VisualAge Distributed feature and its own **System Object Model (SOM)**, not to be confused with Microsoft's Component **Object Model (COM)** and **Distributed System Object Model (DSOM)** CORBA-compliant ORBs. DSOM is a separate API framework within SOM that extends SOM across multiple machines.

IBM is no stranger to CORBA technology. Its OS/2 operating system has used SOM internally since 1992. Because SOM can handle light-weight, fine-grained objects, it was used as the infrastructure for the OS/2 Workplace Shell which interconnected objects on the desktop.

IBM sees this combination of architectures, Distributed feature and SOM/DSOM, as providing the best of both worlds: transparent distributed Smalltalk communication, while allowing Smalltalk objects to communicate with programs written in other languages. For this reason, IBM sees no need to have its Distributed feature conform to the CORBA standard.

In order to access SOM or DSOM objects, IBM VisualAge for Smalltalk must utilize Smalltalk wrappers classes that represent SOM classes. These wrapper classes behave just like the SOM classes. Smalltalk objects can interact with them as you would any ordinary Smalltalk objects, given the restrictions of a typed CORBA interface. The SOM wrapper object communicates with the SOM DDL (dynamic link library), which relays messages to and from the actual SOM (or DSOM) object. These wrappers can be used as components by VisualAge's visual component glue tool, called the Composition Editor, where they can be interconnected with other components. The SOM wrappers appear in the Composition Editor as non-visual parts.

In addition, IBM VisualAge for Smalltalk can utilize DNS SmalltalkBroker as a CORBA-compliant ORB. So there are three ways (potentially, in combination) to distribute a VisualAge for Smalltalk application: the VisualAge for Smalltalk Distributed feature, SOM/DSOM, and DNS SmalltalkBroker.

GemStone has support for CORBA as well, via its GemORB product. GemStone utilizes DNS SmalltalkBroker for this system. This means that an additional layer of distribution, Gem to Gem (GemStone server to GemStone server), is available. GemStone combined with CORBA extends the limited client/server model provided by GemStone alone. Key ORB components, such as the Interface Repository, are stored in the robust, persistent data store of the GemStone server.

Company	Standard	Implementation
GemStone	CORBA	GemORB
ObjectShare	CORBA	Distributed Smalltalk
IBM	CORBA	SOM/DSOM
DNS	CORBA	SmalltalkBroker
Microsoft	COM	COM

═Chapter 2═

Who Needs It, and What It Can Do

How do you know if you need distributed Smalltalk? Ask yourself the following simple question:

"Could my Smalltalk software benefit significantly from being distributed over more than one computer?"

If the answer is yes, then you should at least consider distributed Smalltalk. A "yes" does not mean you should automatically choose it. It may still not be right, for a variety of reasons that I discuss later.

Examples

Here are some typical systems where distributed Smalltalk may be beneficial:

- A customer service system spanning different departments, where specialized databases exist in different places.

- A product data system for a high-tech manufacturer. Multiple off-the-shelf software packages, running on different computers, need to be integrated into a single coherent system.

- A payroll system where business rules are kept secure by being on a corporate server, while other activities reside on local machines.

- Inter-library loan software, where each library maintains its own electronic card catalog of books. One library can ask all the others for the availability of a particular title.

- A manufacturing environment, where process control software runs on a few large servers, but graphing and spreadsheet software must runs on PCs.

Large systems

Large Smalltalk systems that require flexible communication between separate computers are prime candidates for distributed Smalltalk. There are other means for doing this, of course: the computers could be linked to a central database, and all information which these machines need in common could be placed there. However, this could make it cumbersome to exchange information. Perhaps it would be better if each Smalltalk computer had its own database, and when they needed to exchange data, they could simply request objects from each other.

Distributed servers

Clients do not necessarily have to be written in Smalltalk. You can use distributed Smalltalk to implement distributed servers which cooperate by sending messages to each other's objects. This strategy does not lock you into using a Smalltalk GUI. So long as your clients can communicate effectively with their servers, you have freedom to use the GUI tools and languages of your choice.

If you use a CORBA-compliant distributed Smalltalk, then your user clients can be written in any language which maps to CORBA: C, C++, Cobol, and others to come. GemStone supports multiple client languages as well.

A useful technique when using multiple distributed servers in a complex business domain is to create a relatively simple, high-level interface from the client. The client can deal in large-grained objects, and messages to those objects. They can send messages to server process objects, making requests for functions such as "get me all of today's new orders for branch offices in New York, Los Angeles, and Seattle." The servers can break such a message down into smaller steps, in turn dispatching messages to servers residing in these locations.

This technique has many advantages: it simplifies the messages between clients and servers; it encapsulates complexity that is irrelevant to the client. It provides a clean, API-like model for requests to the server, which enables implementation details to change and evolve over time without impacting the client. It even provides a simple synchronous message model for the client into processes that are inherently asynchronous on and between servers.

The Plain Brown Wrapper

There is one huge category of potential applications for distributed Smalltalk: rejuvenating and giving new life and purpose to legacy systems.

Legacy systems

Legacy systems are fertile ground for reengineering client-server software. In the process of rearchitecting legacy systems, many organizations are seeking to move to distributed objects in order to provide flexible, more scaleable software.

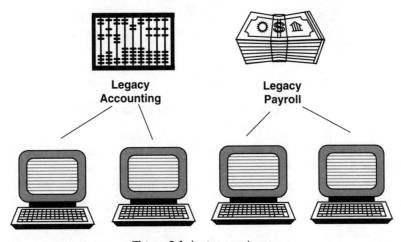

Figure 2-1. Legacy systems

    We've all come across legacy systems. How about that 20-year old accounting program that requires a team of 6 COBOL programmers to change 60 lines of code and not have the whole thing crumble into incoherent bits? Or the factory control module that only one person understands—and she retired last year?

    It's all very well and good to want to throw away all your old software and replace it with brand spanking new Smalltalk code that will be much easier to maintain and modify. But in practice, few companies can afford to rewrite the hundreds of thousand lines of code that runs all of their operations. And managers have a hard time justifying this, to say the least.

    There's a way out, though, an intermediate step which moves in the right direction, while leveraging your existing investment in software. One way to transform a legacy system into an object-oriented one is by placing it inside a **wrapper**. A wrapper is a layer of software that makes the entire legacy system appear from the outside to be one or more objects. This gives the legacy system the interface you need without having to rewrite its code.

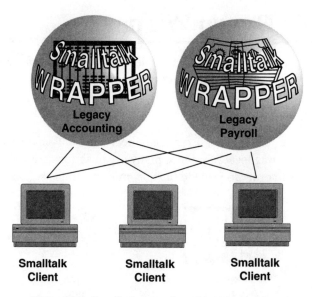

Figure 2-2. Smalltalk wrapping of legacy systems

Depending on how flexible the interface to the legacy system is, writing the object wrapper may be simple or difficult. Many legacy systems have no straightforward programming interface, because nobody had ever foreseen the day when they would need to be anything but self-contained (or if they did, they chose to look the other way—does this sound suspiciously like the year 2000 problem?). Such systems have only a user interface, usually based on a primitive text terminal display such as an IBM 3270 screen. In this case, one must resort to **screen-scraping**, which is the practice of creating a sort of "virtual user," a piece of software that reads the characters from the fields intended for a display terminal, and packages those fields into objects.

This particular architecture is an example of a three-tiered one. This approach is discussed in detail later in this chapter.

The important thing to notice is that the wrappers are implemented in distributed Smalltalk, as are the clients. This enables them to communicate using the common currency of objects. Later, if it is deemed economically feasible and advantageous to rewrite one or more of the legacy systems, the wrapper can be transparently replaced, and the client interface can remain exactly the same.

You could also add another layer. The clients could be dumb **Graphical User Interfaces (GUIs)**, and between the client GUIs and legacy wrappers could reside in another layer possessing some intelligence. This is called a **business logic layer**. More about that in the section "Beyond Plain Old Client/Server."

Still another approach to renovating legacy systems is to upgrade them incrementally. This can be a mandate from top management, so that the risk associated with deploying an entirely new system is lowered. An incremental approach is easiest where there is an API available for the legacy systems.

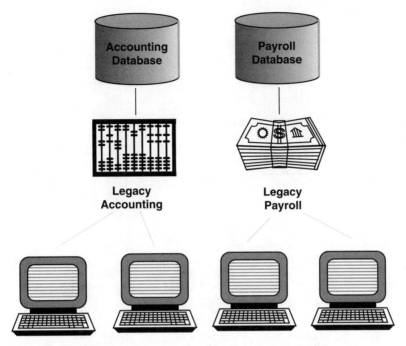

Figure 2-3. Legacy systems with their databases

For example, Smalltalk clients could be written so that they can implement the API to a legacy system. But they can also talk to a new, replacement system written in Smalltalk, thereby utilizing distributed Smalltalk at least partially.

Consider the legacy systems, with their databases, shown in Figure 2-3. Here, we have access to the APIs for both the legacy accounting and legacy payroll systems. Furthermore, we know how the data is stored in the databases, so there is the flexibility to replace the functionality of the legacy systems incrementally.

This sort of functional replacement is an incremental migration to a new architecture. Figure 2-4 shows how we can replace the legacy payroll system with a new one written in Smalltalk. This new Smalltalk payroll system talks to Smalltalk clients. But these Smalltalk clients continue to use the old legacy accounting system by getting in directly at its API. Of course, in order to do this, the legacy accounting API must be directly accessible from the network. If not, a communications layer will have to be added.

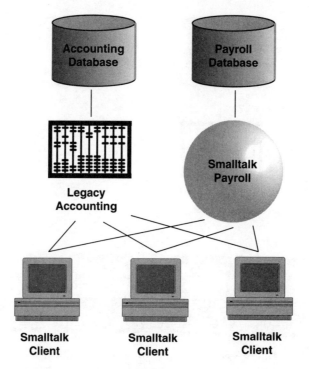

Figure 2-4. Incremental migration of legacy systems

Notice also that the new Smalltalk payroll system continues to use the old database. This could be migrated to another database as necessary in another phase. No change is required to the Smalltalk client, since its interface to the Smalltalk payroll system will not change.

A second phase of migration can now be done (see Figure 2-5). The accounting system can be rewritten in Smalltalk. At this stage, you could choose to better integrated the user interfaces of the two systems. Also, a common, Enterprise database has been added. This might be designed to lay the groundwork for a future migration to real business objects.

With phase 2 of this legacy system migration, the middle tier in a three-tiered architecture has been added. More about this in the following section. But we have obviously made the overall system more flexible.

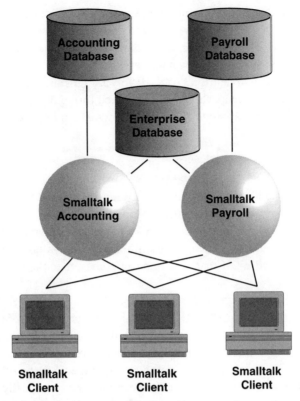

Figure 2-5. Incremental migration of legacy systems, phase 2

The Down Side

Nothing comes for free in this world. The hurdles in moving to distributed Smalltalk are not insignificant. Anyone seeking to use distributed Smalltalk should do a risk/benefit analysis to assure that the decision makes sense.

Cost

Cost is a factor which can't be ignored. Distributed Smalltalk is an add-on product, which typically carries a significant price tag. In addition to development licensing, it may be licensed on a per-machine basis. Overall, the cost of adding distributed Smalltalk may in some cases approach the licensing costs of ordinary Smalltalk alone. It may simply be too expensive to use for a project with a large number of workstations, each running distributed Smalltalk. But the distributed computing world is becoming more and more competitive.

Software prices can often change, or be a function of the scale of your deployment, so we can't quote any here. The best thing is to check with vendors for their current pricing policies.

The cost of additional servers machines must also be considered. Distributed Smalltalk images have to live somewhere, and this is somewhere is typically a beefy, multi-CPU server machine. Furthermore, network performance analysis and redesign could be required to support the new hardware.

Don't forget about workstation costs. If you are currently using Smalltalk "fat clients," you probably have all the power you need for your workstations. But even the ultimate "thin client" approach, the Web browser, can impose demands on your workstations.

Reliability

Another factor is reliability. If one machine running distributed Smalltalk goes down, will that bring the entire system to a halt? Communication in distributed Smalltalk is, by default, **synchronous**, meaning that once a message is sent to another machine, an answer is expected. The current Smalltalk process waits until the answer is received before proceeding. If that answer never comes, then the Smalltalk process is hung, or **blocked**.

However, IBM VisualAge Distributed, ObjectShare Distributed Smalltalk, and DNS SmalltalkBroker support CORBA-compliant **Event Services**. Smalltalk images can send **events** to each other, which are objects that do not need answers. Events support asynchronous operation. The sending Smalltalk process is not held up until an answer is received. Events may be automatically queued up if the other computer is not available. But the calling of Event Services must be specifically added to your code. It is not transparent to your program. The CORBA Event Service is discussed in more detail in the section in Chapter 7, "Events and Asynchronous Communication." Another non-transparent "non-synchronous" strategy is possible with CORBA. This is using so-called **deferred synchronous** operations. It is not synchronous, because it required polling, but neither is it truly asynchronous. This is described in detail in Chapter 5, in the section "Dynamic Invocation Interface and Deferred Synchronous Operations."

It's also possible to architect your application so that a synchronous operation received by the server calls a Smalltalk method which spawns one or more asynchronous operations. Setting a watchdog timer allows the server-side synchronous operation to be "woken up" so that retries or error recovery can take place, and the client does not get hung.

Still another approach is to use one-way messages; that is, messages which do not wait for replies. This is a similar approach to deferred synchronous messaging. However, you can delegate some other object than the original sending object to handle the ultimate disposition of the message. This was the approach taken by Lawrence Livermore National Laboratories for its Data Warehouse system. See the section in Chapter 4 named "Helper classes."

Complexity

There is no doubt that distributed Smalltalk can add significant complexity to a development project. Such complexity typically scales with the size of the project. For a large project, distribution may not result in any added complexity. It may, in fact, reduce complexity because it provides a structure that simplifies large-scale granularity.

But for small and medium-sized projects, there is an initial "hit" to add distribution to Smalltalk. This varies with the particular brand of distributed Smalltalk. The IBM Distributed feature imposes the least amount of added complexity. CORBA-based distributed Smalltalk impose a relatively large amount of complexity.

If a project is properly architected, this complexity can buy much additional flexibility. Flexibility and malleability allow a system to grow more smoothly. While more future growth may not be what upper management wants to hear, it is a fact of life for software projects. There is an adage which says that "software is not written; it is rewritten." Better it be rewritten in a clean and incremental fashion.

Performance

Because Smalltalk method invocation can now result in a large amount of network overhead, significant performance issues may arise. You must now be aware of which objects are on the same machine, and which are on different machines. This will be discussed in more detail in Chapter 7.

No amount of good, up-front architectural design can guarantee high performance. Bottlenecks always exist, and the only way to find them is to actually run your software under real-world conditions.

End-to-end stress tests are important before you deploy a distributed Smalltalk application. Be prepared to do a significant amount of tuning, and to budget time in a project for this.

There are actually two components to message processing and communication performance. One is raw speed, as you might expect. The other is latency, which is not the same thing. Latency is the time delay between two events, often a round-trip time. High latency may limit interactivity. It may also reduce overall processing, even though you are moving information as fast as it will go. This can happen when you must wait for a reply between messages.

In a computer network, you may have very high speed, but also high message latency, which you observe as poor performance. A classic example of this is in satellite communication. If your network is distributed over such a distance that a satellite "hop" is required, this will add half a second of delay for a round-trip. Geosynchronous telecommunications satellites orbit at a fixed distance of 22 thousand miles above the earth. So that at the speed of light, the delay is necessary to bounce a message off a satellite, even if it doesn't have to travel any addition distance.

If you implement a user interface that is tightly coupled with a domain model a satellite hop away, you will not have very satisfied customers! This is, of course, a partitioning issue, which will be covered in Chapter 7. Proper partitioning is critical to the performance of a distributed application.

Beyond Plain Old Client/Server

The line between distributed computing and client/server computing is very blurry. The terms tend to get used interchangeably, especially when there's a customer involved.

"Yes, of course. You're looking for client/server? That's what we specialize in! Oh, you need distributed computing? We do that just as well!"

So to avoid confusion, I'm going to adopt a very restrictive definition of client/server. I'll call it **Plain Old Client/Server (POCS)**. This is where a client program running on one machine directly communicates with a database server on another machine. Period.

This book is not about Plain Old Client/Server. There are Smalltalk objects that act as clients to other Smalltalk objects acting as servers, but we're still going to call this distributed Smalltalk, not Client/Server.

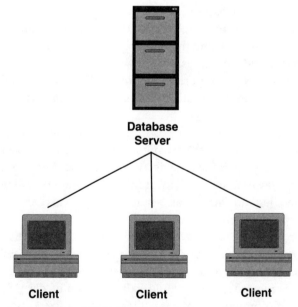

**Database
Server**

Client   **Client**   **Client**

Figure 2-6. Plain Old Client/Server (POCS)

Why Plain Old Client/Server isn't enough

In Plain Old Client/Server, most of the intelligence must reside on the client. In complex, networked software, this is often the wrong thing to do. It puts a substantial and unnecessary computing burden on the client machine.

But more importantly, it means that the rules a business follows, its **business logic** (also called **application logic**), must be on the client machine. If the rules the business objects follow change, then all the software on every last client machine needs to be updated with the new rules. This discourages change in a business, and is not the best way to remain dynamic and competitive. Also, putting too much on the client machine makes it a "fat client," and this is often not the best way to divide up software. The fat client approach can place higher demands on CPU and disk resources from a client machine, and mean that more expensive desktop computers may be required throughout a company. Furthermore, such clients do not provide fault tolerance, or scale to support a very large number of objects, or a smaller number of very large object.

But where else can business logic go in POCS? Relational database vendors resort to a feature called "stored procedures" to allow preset queries and a limited amount of logic to on the server. While this provides more value to RDBMS products, it's not the ideal and most flexible thing to do, particularly when objects are ultimately enveloped.

Three-tiered architecture

In an object-oriented system, business logic should ideally be encapsulated in business objects. Business objects may be placed in a middle layer between client and server, and the resulting architecture is then dubbed **three-tiered**. So Plain Old Client/Server can be given another name: two-tiered architecture. To build real business objects, you need to go beyond simple two-tiered client/server.

Distributed Smalltalk makes building a three-tiered system much easier. It gives you all the infrastructure you need. You're free to partition the classes that constitute your business logic, and place them anywhere you like. Put them on the database server, or off-load them onto one or more machines that talk to your server.

When you add a middle tier, you also add flexibility to the inner tier. It may now be more than just a database server. It may include other services beyond persistence, such as printing or e-mail.

Here's a caution. Beware of the "three-tiered" buzzword! Not all three-tiered software accommodates Smalltalk. And a three-tiered system is not even guaranteed to be object-oriented. A good example is the **Distributed Computing Environment (DCE)**, which is a standard from the **Open Software Foundation (OSF)**. This allows you to build a solid middle layer for distributed computing; but DCE is based on remote procedure calls (RPCs), not objects. IBM's MQSeries Three Tier is closer because it's "object-based"—it uses entities which have some object-like characteristics. But because it does not allow inheritance, one of the requirements for full-fledged objects, it is not object-oriented either.

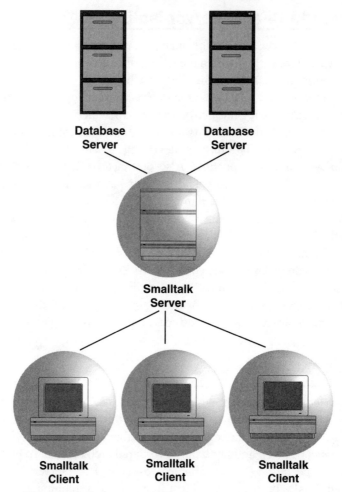

Figure 2-7. Three-tiered distributed Smalltalk architecture

Do not confuse the middle layer of a three-tiered architecture with "middleware." They are not necessarily the same thing. Middleware means just about any high-level software that sits between client and server and provides almost any useful service. For example, **message-oriented middleware (MOM)** provides sophisticated messaging features, such as asynchronous queuing, priorities, and message filtering. But this doesn't, by itself, allow you to code arbitrary application logic.

Even Smalltalk-based **Object-Oriented Database Management Systems (OODBMS)** do not necessarily require distributed Smalltalk. Though they can potentially filter a large number of Smalltalk objects and only return the ones that were asked for, they don't (except for GemStone) provide remote object-to-object communication. They can, however, work very well together with distributed Smalltalk, and provide long, healthy lives to objects by providing persistence.

≡Chapter 3≡

How Does It Work?

Distributed Smalltalk must use some mechanism to communicate between Smalltalk images on different machines. Fortunately, this is one area where distributed Smalltalk doesn't have to invent anything new: all distributed Smalltalks make use of an existing, pervasive standard. This is the networking standard that is used to carry more computer information more miles than any other.

TCP/IP Communication

Who in the computer field hasn't heard these magic letters? TCP/IP is none other than the network protocol that carries the Internet. And being very long-established, it's one of the most common schemes used to interconnect computers within companies. So it's not surprising that TCP/IP is the one type of network supported by all types of distributed Smalltalk.

TCP/IP stands for Transmission Control Protocol/Internet Protocol. It was developed back in the early 70s with funding from the U.S. Government's Defense Advanced Research Projects Agency (DARPA) to support the ARPANET. This was a computer network linking military agencies, defense contractors, and universities doing military research. It was the original Information Superhighway, and has in fact evolved, nearly unchanged, into what we know today as the Internet.

TCP/IP is actually two separate layers: TCP sits on top of IP. TCP is responsible for breaking up information into packets, called **datagrams**. TCP passes these datagrams to IP, and it is IP's responsibility to find a route for datagrams, and get them delivered to their destination.

IP

IP is a "connectionless" service, where just a source and destination address for each datagram are given. So not all the datagrams between source and destination need to travel the same route. This means that they may arrive out of order. Fortunately, they have sequence numbers, and this enables the destination TCP to reassemble the datagrams into their original order.

Each IP datagram has a header that carries an address for both the sender and the receiver. An IP address is 32 bits long, broken up into 4 8-bit **octets**. The term byte isn't used. Old and venerable communications protocols such as TCP/IP predate the time when computers standardized on 8-bit bytes, so octet is the name always used in telecommunications. But this is also more accurate, because it reminds you that network communication is virtually always **serial**, or one bit at a time, so that a byte is not transferred as an indivisible unit, as it is within a single computer. Networks deal in a series of bits, which are blocked into octets.

An IP address is written as four decimal numbers (each an octet between 1 and 254, with the numbers 0 and 255 reserved for special use) separated by periods. If you are on a TCP/IP network, then your computer has its own unique IP address to identify it on the network. The computer at each end of a TCP/IP connection has a special name. It's called a **host**. So an IP address is also a **host address**.

A host is identified on its particular network by a host number. The four numbers of a host address can be divvied up in three different ways, called **classes**:

Network class	Numbers for network	Numbers for host
class A	1	3
class B	2	2
class C	3	1

There are a few class A networks, where each can have many hosts. There are a moderate number of class B networks, where each can have a moderate number of hosts. The majority of networks are class C, where each can have a small number of hosts.

The value of the first number of a host address determines the network class. A small number means a class A network, a moderate number a class B network, and a high number a class C.

A key feature of an IP datagram header is its checksum. This is used to verify that the datagram got through uncorrupted. If it didn't, it gets retransmitted, so all the data flowing through a TCP/IP network is guaranteed to be error-free.

TCP

Because IP datagrams are connectionless, TCP provides "virtual circuit" service between the two communicating programs. It encapsulates IP into a connection-oriented service. Although the datagrams may go on their merry way across multiple networks, TCP makes it look as though they all traveled down a single pair of wires. It also manages flow control, so that a fast sender does not overwhelm a slow receiver.

TCP adds a header of its own, and this header provides some important information. The TCP header extends the 32-bit IP address with two 16- bit **port addresses**, one for the source and one for the destination. Because TCP provided end-to-end service, it's necessary to identify which logical port, also called a **socket** or **Berkeley socket** (after the university folks who developed this feature), is at each end. After all, a single computer may have several TCP virtual circuits connected at any one time, each devoted to a different application. The port numbers uniquely identify the application running at each end of the TCP virtual circuit. The port number serves an additional purpose. When a virtual circuit connection is established, the receiver uses the destination port number to determine which application to "wake up" and connect to. Or, you can think of each application as "listening" on a particular port number. For example, File Transfer Protocol (FTP) always listens on port 21.

Hosts can also be referred to by name in addition to IP address. Internally, TCP/IP always uses IP addresses, but when you want to connect to a particular host computer, it's much easier to remember a name than a number. **Host names** are stored in a central database that is called a **name server**. The name server looks up a host name and returns its corresponding host address. You will encounter a different type of name server later that is specific to distributed Smalltalk, so I will call a TCP/IP name server by its proper technical name, a **domain name server.**

Host names are unique on a network. If that network happens to be the Internet, host names must be issued by a central authority (the Internet Network Information Center, or InterNIC), which guarantees that each is unique worldwide. You've seen host names before: they have names like **www.ibm.com**, and **telnet.compuserve.com**.

TCP/IP is everywhere!

One of the great virtues of TCP/IP is that it is equally at home on a Local Area Network (LAN) as on a Wide Area Network (WAN). If you are familiar with the 7-layer OSI standard (which is illustrated in Figure 7-5) for communication protocol, IP sits at the third, or Network Layer. TCP is right above it at the fourth layer, the Transport Layer. Below IP is the second layer, the Data Link Layer, and below this, the first, which is the Physical Layer. The Data Link Layer specifies the low level networking scheme, such as Ethernet, Token Ring, X.25, etc. The Physical Layer is the actual transmission medium: a twisted pair of wires, coaxial cable, or fiber optics, for example.

TCP/IP specifically avoids defining the Data Link Layer or the Physical Layer. This means that virtually any low-level network can carry TCP/IP. It can cross many different types of networks. Datagrams get relayed automatically by IP routers that are called **gateways**. IP datagrams can ride the X.25 Public Data Network just as easily as they do a standard T-1 interoffice telephone line.

A testament to TCP/IP's versatility is the fact that it runs the entire worldwide Internet, composed of around 100,000 individual computer networks. TCP/IP is available on over 150 different computer platforms, ranging from an IBM XT PC to a CRAY2 supercomputer!

Distributed Object Spaces

TCP/IP is the most-used communications protocol to interconnect computers. But what does this mean to the Smalltalk programmer? TPC/IP interconnects not only different computers, but different Smalltalk **object spaces**.

When you're programming with ordinary Smalltalk, you don't need to think about object spaces. There's only one object space, and all your Smalltalk objects live in it. Within one object space, objects address each other directly. An object space is a single logical piece of computer memory in which all active objects reside. It's really just the place for objects in a single executing Smalltalk image. It's also the subset of a computer's memory space that one Smalltalk memory manager controls.

With distributed Smalltalk, objects in different object spaces can send messages to each other. It doesn't matter on what machines the object spaces are located, or how far away they are physically. TCP/IP network communication handles all that for you automatically.

Client and server object spaces

Originally used to describe the IBM Distributed Feature, the concept of **client object spaces** and **server object spaces** are applicable to all distributed Smalltalks. The distinction between these two types of object space is whether or not an object space can accept a connection from other object spaces.

If an object space can listen for a connection from another object space, it is called a server object space. A client object space, on the other hand, can establish connections to server object spaces, but cannot accept connections from any other object spaces. So in order for distributed Smalltalk to work, you need at least one server object space.

IBM Distributed Feature
Using the IBM Distributed Feature, object spaces can be either client object spaces or server object spaces. If you like, you can make all your object spaces server object spaces.

Once a connection is established, communication between object spaces with the IBM Distributed Feature is peer-to-peer. Objects in either object space can freely send messages to each other. Client and server object spaces are only distinguished when a connection between object spaces is first established.

You can put more than one object space on a single computer. Each one corresponds to a separate Smalltalk image in memory. This is particularly useful for debugging. You're not forced to work on two machines at once to use distributed Smalltalk. You just have to keep track of which screen windows correspond to which object spaces; that is, if you have multiple windows. A server object space's image does not necessarily need any windows. It can operate "headless." And with this approach, you don't even have to worry about having a network connection. Remember, though, you've got to have sufficient memory for all the images you intend to have active on one machine!

CORBA-compliant distributed Smalltalks

For the CORBA-compliant distributed Smalltalks, DST and STB, a Smalltalk object space is a server object space if it has an **Object Request Broker (ORB)**. An ORB is the software that makes distributed objects available to the rest of the world. You learn lots more about ORBs later in this book. Server object spaces can talk peer-to-peer. But unlike IBM Distributed, where all objects in an object space are implicitly distributed, CORBA requires you to make explicit interfaces in order to distribute each class of object.

CORBA ORBs provide all the machinery necessary to talk to CORBA objects, either locally or remote. They know how to send operations to ORB objects, marshalling their arguments as necessary. In the language of distributed computing, creating a serialized version of the arguments for a request is called **marshalling**, while reconstructing the arguments on the other end is called **unmarshalling**.

You use an ORB on a local computer to communicate with an ORB on a remote machine. So CORBA communication is ORB to ORB. This means all CORBA Smalltalk object spaces are server object spaces.

For the CORBA-compliant distributed Smalltalks, object spaces allow peer-to-peer communication. There's one catch, though. In order for objects to be distributed, they must have explicit CORBA interfaces. Until you provide a CORBA interface for a Smalltalk class, it cannot be shared because it is invisible to other object spaces.

GemStone

GemStone has a more complex structure than the other distributed Smalltalks because it includes an object database. This database is managed by a single process called the **Stone**. The Stone handles database login and logout, concurrency, and all the other functions you'd expect from a powerful commercial database. The Stone is also responsible for allocating the objects in the shared server object space.

GemStone has other processes, called **Gems**, which interact with the Stone. Each Gem is a multi-user Smalltalk virtual machine that runs in same object space as the

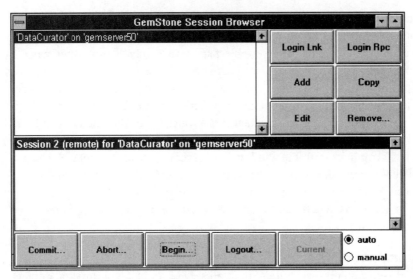

Figure 3-1. GemStone Session Browser

Stone. The Gem Smalltalk dialect is distinct from all others; however as of version 5.0 of GemStone, it conforms to the proposed ANSI Smalltalk standard. Each user application program in GemStone must communicate with at least one Gem. An application connects to the GemStone server by logging in to GemStone. Each logged-in connection is called a **session**, and is supported by one Gem process. See Figure 3-1.

A user application program in GemStone can be written in C, C++, or Smalltalk. When it's written in Smalltalk, then it can qualify as distributed Smalltalk because the Smalltalk application and the Smalltalk Gem may be on different machines.

So in GemStone, there are two kinds of object spaces: client object spaces and server object spaces. The Gem processes share a common server object space. There is no peer-to-peer communication. A GemStone client cannot share its objects.

When the Smalltalk application is on a client machine and the Gem process is on a server machine, the GemStone session is called an **RPC** session. RPC stands for Remote Procedure Call, the low-level mechanism that handles the communication between the two computers. There is another type of GemStone session called a **linked** session. Here, an application and a Smalltalk Gem run on the same machine and share the same operating system process, though they maintain separate object spaces. While this is faster because it needs less network traffic, it is also less flexible, and does not qualify as being distributed Smalltalk. In this book, distributed Smalltalk using GemStone always means using RPC sessions.

Client/server object space summary. The following table outlines object space features.

Features:	IBM	CORBA	GemStone
Server object spaces	✓	✓	✓
Client object spaces	✓		✓
All object spaces are server		✓	
Peer-to-peer with client object space	✓	N.A.	
Distributed objects for all object spaces	✓	✓	
Objects implicitly distributed	✓		

How do you make a connection between object spaces?

For the IBM Distributed Feature, there is nothing special you need to do to make the connection between two object spaces. It is created implicitly, the first time an object in one object space tries to send a message to any object in the other (a server) object space.

For the CORBA-compliant distributed Smalltalks, a client object space must somehow get a reference (a proxy) to a server space object. It's something of a chicken-and-egg situation. To reference a distributed object, you need a reference to a distributed object.

There are a couple of ways of getting this reference. The brute force way is to generate what's known in CORBA as a **"stringified" Interoperable Object Reference (IOR)**. This is an ordinary character string that uniquely identifies an object. Any CORBA object is capable of generating a stringified IOR for itself by sending it the appropriate message.

Both Distributed Smalltalk and SmalltalkBroker have class methods in the ORBObject class that support this. Both use the method referenceToFile:, the argument of which is a filename. This method creates a "stringified" IOR and writes it to that file. Once this string is created from a client, it can be read by the server from a file using the class method referenceFromFile:.

This may sound cumbersome, but you only really need such a stringified IOR for the one server object, one which can access other server objects. This first server object will "serve up" all the other object references you need.

Another more sophisticated way to get object references is to use the CORBA Naming Service. This is supported by both CORBA-compliant distributed Smalltalks. The Naming Service is one of the most important Common Object Services of CORBA. It provides a way to bind a name to an object, and to look up that name binding.

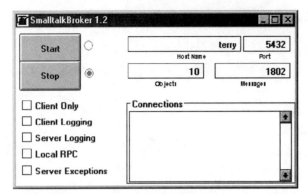

Figure 3-2. SmalltalkBroker's ORBControl window

For example, in DNS SmalltalkBroker, you can, on the server, create an object named myCorbaServer from a class called AServerClass:

    myCorbaServer := AServerClass new.

Then register this object with the CORBA naming service, giving it a name:

    CorbaORB default namingService bind: 'Joe' obj: myCorbaServer.

On the client, you must first get a reference for the server's Naming Service by specifying the host name and port number for the server. Remember that for all distributed Smalltalks, a specific port number is used to distinguish that application from other TCP/IP applications. A port number for SmalltalkBroker is can be found in the ORBControl window, as shown in Figure 3-2.

    aNamingService := CorbaORB default namingService: <aHost> port: <aPort>.

You can now ask the naming service to give you the reference for the server object from its name by sending it the resolve: message:

    aCorbaServer := aNamingService resolve: 'Joe'.

IBM Distributed Feature: the server object space daemon

A server object space using the IBM Distributed Feature has a special background program, or **daemon**, to listen for anyone trying to establish a Smalltalk connection via TPC/IP. When it hears such a connection, it routes it to the correct server object space on the machine. If the Smalltalk image corresponding to that object space is not running, it can automatically start it up.

You only need one daemon for all the server object spaces on a single machine. Since a daemon will be listening for an incoming connection via TCP/IP, you need to configure it to tell it which TCP/IP port number to monitor. You also typically tell it how long to wait before "timing out;" that is, how long to wait for a server object space to start up after it is requested by the daemon.

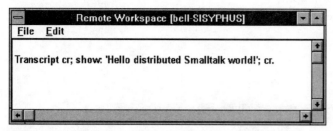

Figure 3-3. IBM Distributed's Feature Remote Workspace

CORBA-compliant distributed Smalltalks: the ORB

An ORB uses a daemon, too. But a Smalltalk object space must already be running. An ORB is started in each object space, and each ORB has a daemon listening on a particular TCP/IP port. If no such daemon has been started, then any attempt to communicate with the corresponding ORB will fail. If you try to send a message to an object in a non-running ORB, you will generate a CORBA Smalltalk exception.

Remote windows

Remote windows allow you easy access to a remote object space. They are very useful tools in developing distributed applications.

Not all the distributed Smalltalk support the various types of remote windows. The CORBA-compliant distributed Smalltalks, SmalltalkBroker, and PP-D Distributed Smalltalk do not support remote windows. A remote window would provide visibility into the internal machinery of remote object space, and as such, is contrary to the design and intent of CORBA.

Remote workspace

A remote workspace enables you to execute Smalltalk code in remote object space, not your local one. IBM and GemStone provide remote workspace windows, however they differ in implementation.

IBM Distributed Feature.   To start a Remote Workspace window using the IBM Distributed Feature, do the following:

Select the **Browse Name Servers** from the IBM Distributed **Distribution tools** menu. This opens a browser which lists the names of all name servers in the local object space. From within this browser, select the object reference pointing to the object space you want to open a remote workspace window on. Then, select **Referenced Object Space**→**Open Workspace** from the pop-up menu. A remote browser window opens, as shown in Figure 3-3.

Now, type the following into the remote workspace window:

    Transcript cr; show: 'Hello distributed Smalltalk world!'; cr.

See Select this text, and execute **do it** from the pop-up menu. Where does this text show up? Not in your local object space's transcript! You have to look at the transcript window for the remote object space, wherever (and on whatever machine) that is.

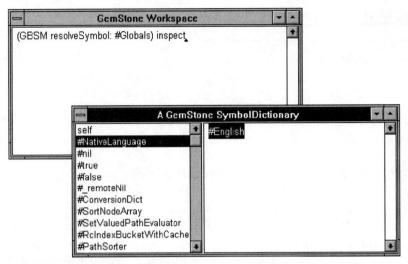

Figure 3-4. GemStone workspace

GemStone. Gemstone supports a type of remote workspace called a GemStone workspace. To open a GemStone workspace, select **Workspace** from the **GemStone Tools** menu, or click on the GemStone Workspace icon, which looks like a stack of pages. A typical Gemstone workspace is shown in Figure 3-4.

A Gemstone workspace is a combination of a client workspace and a remote workspace. It has all of the standard Smalltalk workspace menu commands, plus three more which are specific to Gemstone:

- GS-do it
- GS-print it
- GS-inspect

These are identical to their ordinary Smalltalk namesakes. The difference is that the operations are sent to the remote system for execution, and the results returned in the GemStone workspace window.

Remote browser

A remote browser works just like an ordinary Smalltalk browser, except that its classes are within a remote object space.

GemStone. GemStone offers a remote browser, which you can use to inspect classes, and add classes and methods on the GemStone server.

To open a remote browser, select **Browse** → **All Classes** from the GemStone menu. Or click on the GemStone launcher's Class Browser icon, which looks like a magnifying glass inspecting a tree of classes. You will then see a Gemstone remote browser like the one in Figure 3-5.

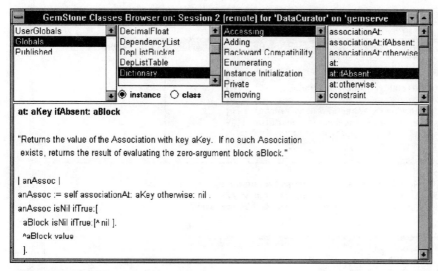

Figure 3-5. GemStone remote browser

Remote inspector

A remote inspector is a tool to inspect an object in a remote Smalltalk image. Remote inspectors are not supported in the CORBA-compliant distributed Smalltalks.

GemStone. A remote inspector in GemStone is called a **GemStone Inspector**. This is displayed when you execute the **GS-inspect** command from a GemStone workspace. This creates and displays an inspector on the particular remote object instance you have chosen to inspect. See Figure 3-6.

IBM Distributed Feature. You can open a remote inspector using the IBM Distributed Feature in three different ways.

One way is using a tool called the Name Servers browser. To access this tool, choose the **Browse Name Servers** from the IBM Distributed **Distribution tools** menu.

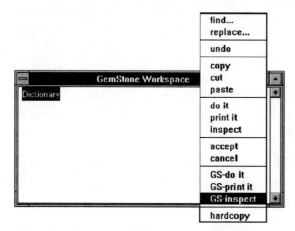

Figure 3-6. Opening a GemStone Inspector

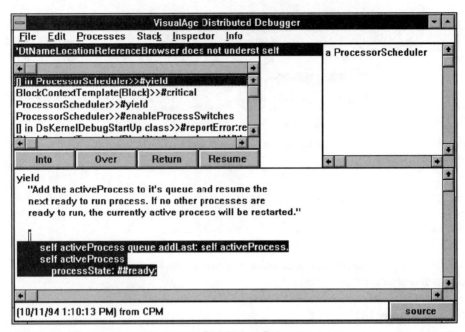

Figure 3-7. IBM Distributed's Feature Distributed Debugger

This opens a browser which lists the names of all name servers in the local object space. From within this browser, select the object reference pointing to the object you want to inspect. Then, select **Referenced Objects**→**Inspect Object** from the pop-up menu in the **Name Server Keys** list.

Another way to open a remote inspector is through a local workspace. Select a shadow representing the object you want to inspect, and then select the **Inspect** choice from the pop-up menu.

Finally, you can select an object you want to inspect from a remote workspace, and select the **Inspect** choice from the pop-up menu.

Once a remote browser is open, messages can be sent to remote objects via this browser. If an exception occurs, a Distributed Debugger window is opened (see Figure 3-7).

Remote transcript

A remote transcript window mirrors everything displayed in the transcript window that belongs to a remote object space. As long as this window is open, all messages sent to the transcript for the remote object space also appear in the remote transcript window.

Only the IBM Distributed Feature supports a remote transcript. Note that opening a new remote transcript window will not display anything that is already present in the transcript for the remote object space.

To start a remote transcript window, do the following:

Select the **Browse Name Servers** from the IBM Distributed **Distribution tools** menu. From within this browser, select the object reference pointing to the object space you want to open a remote transcript window on. Then, select **Referenced Object Space→Open Transcript** from the pop-up menu. A remote transcript window opens.

Now, repeat the example used in the remote transcript. The message now appears in both the transcript for the remote object space, wherever it resides, *and* the remote transcript window.

Using Your Proxies

In this book, a **proxy** is the generic term for a local object which stands in for a remote object. Messages sent to the proxy object are automatically forwarded to the remote object.

CORBA-compliant distributed Smalltalks

In CORBA, a proxy is called a **reference**. Once you have obtained a reference, all messages to that reference are automatically forwarded to the remote object. The answered object from the message send is, in general, also a reference. But in the case when the answered object is one of CORBA's Basic Types, such as an Integer type, floating point type, char, or boolean, the result is a local Smalltalk object, not a proxy for a remote object.

Because CORBA supports any mix of programming languages, the implementations of object are **opaque**. You are not allowed to see inside an object, other than through the methods for that object which have been made public (i.e., have a CORBA interface). Because the implementation must be handled in the remote object space, you must always work through a CORBA reference.

IBM Distributed Feature

When using the IBM Distributed Feature, the terminology can get a little confusing. What is a single proxy object in other distributed Smalltalks is split into two components in the IBM Distributed Feature. There is an object reference and a **shadow**.

A shadow is actually the proxy for the remote object. But in order to get the shadow, you first have to get the reference. The reference tells where to find the remote object. It's simply a description. But it doesn't let you interact with the remote object. For this you need a shadow. If you have an object reference, you send it the message shadow, and you get a shadow as the answer.

Explicit references are only necessary when you don't use a **distribution matrix**. This is a powerful facility within the IBM Distributed Feature that allows you to

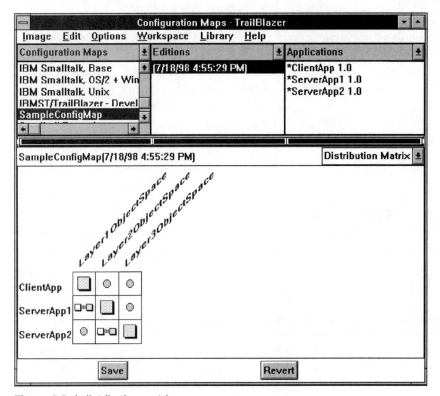

Figure 3-8. A distribution matrix

specify which pieces of your distributed application should be placed in which object spaces. A distribution matrix is a table that describes which classes are found in what object spaces (Figure 3-8), and also whether objects for such classes are real objects or shadows.

When you distribute your application via a distribution matrix, shadows are automatically created for you and appear locally. This is a very powerful feature of the IBM Distributed Feature. You don't have to go through the intermediate step of retrieving references and then asking them for shadows.

In the example of Figure 3-8, three object spaces are shown. These are called Layer1ObjectSpace, Layer2ObjectSpace, and Layer3ObjectSpace, and are the columns in the distribution matrix.

Object classes are grouped by being in the same **Envy** application. Envy is the team Smalltalk development tools bundled into the Professional version of VisualAge for Smalltalk, and used the Distributed Feature. An Envy application is a group of classes that should be treated as a logical unit for development. But an Envy application also plays a key role in partitioning VisualAge distributed programs. Three Envy applications, each containing a group of classes, are shown as rows labeled ClientApp, ServerApp1, and ServerApp2.

A single box icon in a distribution matrix cell indicates that the application in that row is to be loaded into the object space for that column. An icon with two interconnecting small boxes designates that a shadows for the objects in the row application are to be created in that column's object space.

So Figure 3-8 shows that ClientApp is to be loaded into Layer1ObjectSpace, ServerApp1 is to be loaded into Layer2ObjectSpace, and ServerApp2 is to load into Layer3ObjectSpace.

Now comes the interesting part. A double box "shadow" icon says to shadows for ServerApp1 objects within Layer1ObjectSpace. This means that the objects in Layer1ObjectSpace, namely those if ClientApp, will automatically be able to see the objects of ServerApp1.

Similarly, the other "shadow" icon causes ServerApp2 objects to be shadowed in Layer2ObjectSpace. This, in turn, gives the Layer2ObjectSpace objects, namely those of ServerApp1, automatic access to ServerApp2 objects. With one simple distribution matrix, a three-tiered Smalltalk architecture, with one client tier and two server tiers, has been specified!

GemStone

GemStone has two standard ways of distributing its Smalltalk objects: through replicates and forwarders. There is also another class of GemStone object called a GbsObject.

Replicates

Objects in Gemstone can be configured in a number of different ways. There can be a one-to-one mapping of classes between the client Smalltalk object space and the GemStone server (Gem) object space. When it is used as an OODBMS, objects are typically replicated this way in both spaces. A client Smalltalk object that is mapped to a duplicate GemStone object is called a **replicate**.

It is GemStone's job to keep the corresponding objects in sync. If a client Smalltalk replicate is modified, this object is marked as "dirty" until its out-of-date GemStone counterpart can be updated. If a GemStone object is modified, its client Smalltalk counterpart is out-of-date, which makes the GemStone object "dirty."

The term **faulting** is how a dirty GemStone object is copied into the client Smalltalk. The term **flushing** describes the process of copying dirty client Smalltalk objects into GemStone.

You can select policies for automatically instantiating local objects that correspond to remote server objects.

For example, if objects are large and have a few levels of hierarchy, it is often not a good idea to locally replicate all the objects. Instead, object **stubs** can be present in the local object hierarchy which are stand-ins for their remote objects. Stubs reduce the amount of space taken up in the client, because a stub consumes a bare minimum amount of memory. Only when the stub is accessed by your application program is its remote state automatically fetched. The client Smalltalk code does not have to explicitly check for stubs. When a stub is accessed, it is transparently "unstubbed." Furthermore, a replicate can be sent a message to stub itself, freeing up space in the client.

Forwarders

When using GemStone as a distributed Smalltalk, there is another way to use a local representation of a remote object. This is by using a **forwarder**. A forwarder acts as a stand-in for a remote object. It knows which GemStone server object it represents, and responds to all messages by passing them to this server object.

A forwarder is designed to be transparent in the client Smalltalk. This means that GemStone forwarders respond to messages differently than the proxies of other distributed Smalltalks. By default, sending a message to a forwarder answers an object which is a client Smalltalk replicate of an object. If that object doesn't already exist in the client Smalltalk object space, it is created. To get the message to answer a forwarder instead, you must preface the message with the two characters "fw."

For example, to get the third object in an OrderedCollection called aCollection-Forwarder, which is a forwarder, you write:

    aCollectionForwarder at: 3

This returns a local object. To get a forwarder for the third object, you write:

    aCollectionForwarder fwat: 3

Forwarders can be created in different ways. One way is to send the message asForwarder to a local object. Another is to specify that a **connector** create a forwarder as part of its initialization. A connector is an object that defines a relationship between a client Smalltalk object and a corresponding GemStone object.

GbsObjects

Because GemStone was originally designed as an object database, it implicitly uses the notion of synchronizing local client objects with remote server objects. While this makes object persistence very painless and transparent, it isn't always the ideal model for a general distributed application. Typically, we want to distinguish between sending messages to local objects and sending messages to remote objects. It is not necessarily desirable to keep local and remote object hierarchies in sync.

This means that in some cases, neither a replicate nor a forwarder is appropriate. At first, a forwarder looks very much like a proxy in other distributed Smalltalks. But there is a crucial difference: because a forwarder is designed to completely supplant a local object, it isn't possible to maintain both a forwarder for a remote object and a distinct local object.

There is a way around this. You can choose to work at a lower level than either replicates or forwarders, sidestepping the transparency built into GemStone. You can use the client Smalltalk class called **GbsObject**. This class is very useful in GemStone because an instance of it is a pure, local proxy for a remote object. It does not implicitly synchronize client and server objects. And sending a message to a GbsObject for remote execution answers another GbsObject object, rather than a local object copy. So it is a much better match to our notion of a proxy than a forwarder.

To get a GbsObject from a local replicate object, you send it the message "asGSObject." The class "GbsObject" used to be called "GSObject," hence the message name. However, this terminology was changed with version 5.0 of GemStone, which uses the term "GemBuilder" for the client software. GemBuilder classes start with "Gb," so this is where the name "GbsObject" comes from.

You can also get a GbsObject proxy for an object on the server by asking for it by name from client Smalltalk. Do this with the following messages sent to the current client Gemstone session, obtained from the class GBSM, the GemBuilder session manager:

> GBSM currentSession resolveSymbol: <objectName>
> GBSM currentSession resolveSymbol: <objectName> ifAbsent: <exceptionBlock>

There is one inconvenience when sending messages to GbsObjects. To get the message sent to the remote object rather than have the message sent just to the local proxy object (which is not very useful), you have to either send it a clumsy "remotePerform:" message, or prefix each message with the two letters "gs," which get stripped off for execution on the GemStone server.

In Chapter 8, I implement an example program in GemStone, using GbsObjects to distribute it. There, I show you a trick you can use to get around the "gs" prefix requirement, and make a more seamless and transparent distributed Smalltalk application.

Which should you use?

For a distributed Smalltalk application, you should carefully think through what objects should exist on just the client, on the server, or on both. To gain access to an object on the server, you must use a forwarder or a GbsObject. You should compare the functionality of forwarders with that of GbsObjects to see which is a better match for your needs. Remember that in order to use GemStone as the middle tier in a three-tiered architecture, Smalltalk messages must be forwarded to the GemStone for execution, not performed locally, within client Smalltalk. GemStone makes server object access so automatic that it is often easy to get confused as to whether you are using client objects, server objects, or both.

≡Chapter 4≡

CASE STUDY: The LLNL Data Warehouse

In 1994, Larry Snyder approached Mike Piscotty to lead the development of a new system. Larry is Technical Support Division Leader in the Administrative Information Systems (AIS) Department within Lawrence Livermore National Laboratory (LLNL), which is operated by the University of California for the Department of Energy. A demonstration prototype of the "Community Services Network," a collaborative case management system for Health and Human Services, was to be developed.

This prototype was a system integration effort involving videoconferencing over ISDN lines. It would utilize off-the-shelf packages bundled together with object technology and be funded from a Cooperative Research and Development Agreement with Community Services Network, Inc. (CSN), a health and human services consulting company. It had to be put together in a very short time.

But Larry had seen what Mike Piscotty, Client Laison for Special Projects, had done before. He and his team of object-oriented developers had just finished deploying Media Star, a document imaging system written in VisualWorks Smalltalk and Gemstone. The "Community Services Network" would be built using distributed object technology and incorporate real-time video teleconferencing.

With the skills of Smalltalk developer Christine Broadway and GemStone DBA Brad Calderon, plus a host of other technical team members, another sophisticated software system was constructed. CSN took this system on the road, demonstrating the state-of-the-art software in America's inner cities.

The AIS management was very impressed by the rapid pace of this development. So, in 1996, AIS chartered Mike to apply his group's expertise to undertake its most ambitious project yet: the new Data Warehouse system.

All the while, Mike had been quietly laying the groundwork for more widespread use of object-oriented technology in the development of business information systems at Lawrence Livermore National Laboratory. And this was just the right opportunity for him to move object-oriented technology into department-wide use. Ever since attending the 1992 OOPSLA conference, he was convinced of the great potential of object-oriented technology in general, and of Smalltalk in particular. "We have taken the 'Field of Dreams' approach," said Mike. "Build the components and infrastructure via a few pilot applications, and they will come."

And he's made at least one convert. "Its been a learning curve," said Larry Snyder about Smalltalk. "I still think it's the right answer."

Scope

It was the answer for a major, high-profile undertaking. The Data Warehouse Project was slated to replace an Amdahl mainframe-based reporting application known as ASSIST. By 1986, a team of over 20 programmers had worked for 18 months, writing in the Nomad 4GL to create the first release of ASSIST. In fact, the new Data Warehouse was familiar territory for both Mike and Christine. They had been project leaders for the original ASSIST program. New development continued on ASSIST right up until 1996, occupying an average of three full-time developers every year since its original release.

With an average of around 10,000 people working on-site, Lawrence Livermore National Laboratory, in Livermore, California, is one of America's premier government science and technology labs. The myriad R & D efforts at LLNL include The National Ignition Facility, which will build the world's most powerful laser, and the Accelerated Strategic Computing Initiative's (ASCI) High Performance Computer Support project, that will allow ASCI scientists using teraflop computers to generate, store, access, and manipulate terascale amounts of data.

A lot of business data is managed by the AIS Department in support of the LLNL business processes. Over 12,000 financial reports must be generated every month, within the space of only three days. Managers throughout the lab have to be able to access their project data on an ad-hoc basis. Business domains such as Procurement and Human Resources need to be included. Fiscal year-end reporting, for accountability to the Department of Energy, must also be done. See Figure 4-1.

All LLNL financial reporting was done using the ASSIST system, developed using the Nomad 4GL. And now it would be rewritten, almost exclusively in Smalltalk. The scope of the Data Warehouse project was extended to include additional LLNL business data. It would build infrastructure to be leveraged by applications such as

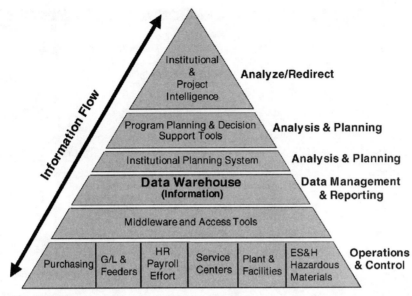

Figure 4-1. The role of the Data Warehouse at LLNL

the Institutional Planning and Pricing System (IPPS), which supports comprehensive project planning and analysis.

Before version 3.0 of the Data Warehouse project could be released by mid-1999, a whopping 1600 individual tasks would need to be completed. And by that time, LLNL's intrepid team of software developers would make themselves experts in distributed Smalltalk.

Capabilities

The Data Warehouse was to deliver LLNL business data with reporting functionality similar to the ASSIST mainframe system it was replacing. It would be the primary reporting vehicle for the LLNL enterprise user. Part of the required functionality was support for high-volume batch reporting, ad hoc queries, on-line drill down reporting, and general lookups.

An ad hoc reporting framework needed to exist that would support access to every warehouse business object. A user needed to be able to generate general-purpose lookups using a straightforward UI. Drill-down to finer levels of object detail would also have to be provided (see Figure 4-2). In addition to displaying the data on the screen, printing and Excel-compatible downloading of report data was necessary. Because batch reports were needed on a regular basis, automatic scheduling would also be required.

The Data Warehouse needed to support a variety of business data. Costs and obligations, at both the summary and detailed levels, needed to be maintained and

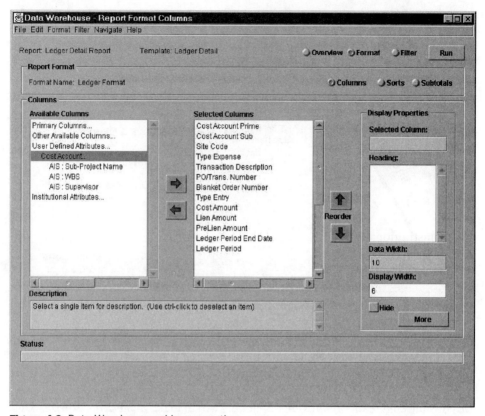

Figure 4-2. Data Warehouse ad hoc reporting

reported on. Effort for both LLNL and supplementary labor had to be tracked. The Data Warehouse would be the primary information resource for institutional planning. Funding, procurement, human resources, property, and Environment, Safety & Health (ES&H) data would be supported.

With the overnight blossoming of the Internet, a Web browser user interface was mandated for the Data Warehouse. It was realized that Web-based deployment would reduce application rollout costs. In addition, on-line, Web-based help would aid in documentation efforts. A browser interface would also provide the cross-platform portability that VisualWorks had previously delivered. And with the Web browser deployment strategy, users would need to be authenticated over LLNL's intranet.

A capability known as User Reporting Attributes (URA) was defined. This would provide a level of user customization beyond anything that ASSIST had ever delivered. With URAs, users would have the ability to create, maintain, and report using their own data associated with key institutional data objects such as accounts, people, and purchase orders (see Figure 4-3).

URAs may be used for report data filtering. They could select a subset of data to be reported. Example URAs might include sub-project name, Work Breakdown Structure (WBS), and supervisor. A key capability of the URA concept is the ability

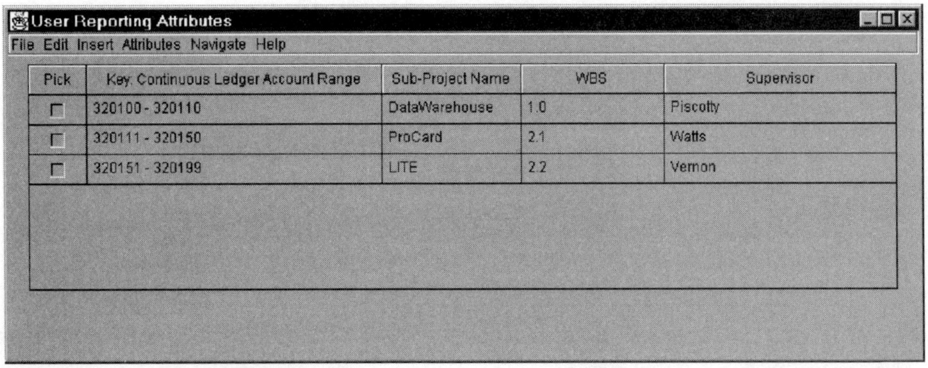

Figure 4-3. URA Maintenance UI

to join institutional business data with user-maintained data (see Figure 4-2). This makes effective use of the server-processing capabilities by processing the join operation at the server tier, rather than at the client tier.

Architecture

To come up with an architecture, an extensive analysis process was begun. The System Object Modeling Team was assembled to identify the key objects of the system. They took the existing ASSIST functionalities that needed to be replaced, such as ad-hoc reporting, drill-down reporting, and data loading, and gave them to different developers to analyze and build use cases. They used the Paradigm Plus O-O design tool.

Development of the architecture

A core set of designers was chosen to participate on the Data Warehouse System Object Modeling Team. These designers included Christine Broadway, Craig McChesney, Sean Felten, Dave Biggers, and Mike Piscotty. Larry Wichter would be the Technical Project Leader for middleware. Sean Felten was selected as Enterprise System Object Architect, and Neda Gray as Enterprise Business Object Architect.

All developers who wrote the use cases presented them to the System Object Modeling Team for review. From these, the team developed object-interaction diagrams to refine the details of the use cases, and object models emerged.

From the object models, major components were identified by their behavior. The team found the places where they needed data brokers for all business objects. They realized that they needed components such as output services and scheduling. These components were defined and then assigned to developers, who did more analyses to develop the detailed models and build the components.

From this overall process, the need for an explicit middle tier of architecture emerged. People had been originally thinking of a two-tiered client/server approach.

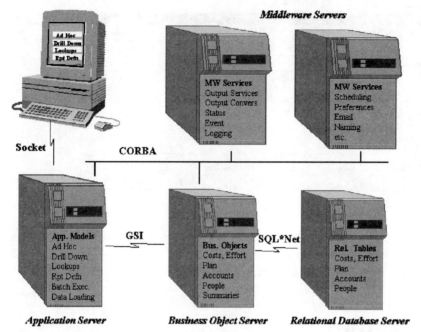

Figure 4-4. Data Warehouse system architecture

Many were used to dealing with a monolithic application talking directly to an Oracle relational database, and didn't at first understand what was to be gained with a multi-tiered architecture. Many on the team had little experience with an object-oriented approach. Through the analysis, the advantages of a middle tier to implement business rules and business logic emerged. Collectively, the team came around to thinking that this was the right approach, and that it would work.

In addition to the overall multi-tiered architecture, it was decided to have a set of Middleware Services distinct from Enterprise Business Objects. These services would use a CORBA interface. See Figure 4-4. Most would be written in Smalltalk and use the DNS SmalltalkBroker ORB. Several Java services were written and deployed using the Visigenics Java ORB. This was done in order to gain experience with inter-language interoperability and to act as a hedge toward language diversity.

On the other hand, Enterprise Business Objects would be exposed as GemStone objects by the Data Warehouse reporting framework, regardless of whether they were persistently stored in GemStone as objects or stored in Oracle tables. Initially, the Gemstone business objects would be accessed only from GemStone Smalltalk clients. In the future, GemOrb will be explored to CORBA-enable the business object server, so that Enterprise Business Objects have a CORBA interface as well.

There was considerably more experience at LLNL with GemStone than with CORBA, so that the GemStone approach was viewed as the safest. Therefore a backup plan was devised for critical CORBA-based middleware services, such as the output services which would generate the reams of monthly reports in a short time

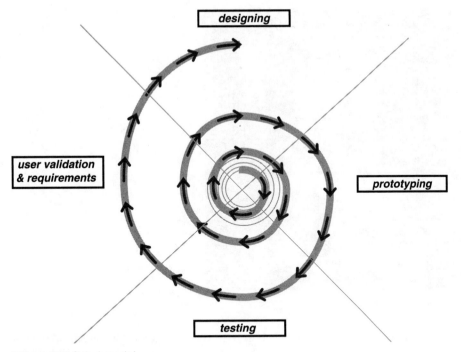

Figure 4-5. Spiral model

window. An alternate GemStone "back door" route was created in order to hedge bets. This middleware service was readily moved from VisualWorks, where it had resided on a middleware server, to GemStone Smalltalk. It turned out that output services needed to have persistence. It needed to know about the requests it was given and the status of those requests. So, moving these services to GemStone was a good choice. However, CORBA performance was up to the challenge, so that the "back door" route plan of communicating via the GemStone client/server route rather than CORBA never had to be used.

LLNL developers do object modeling from the start of each Smalltalk project, and the Data Warehouse was no exception. Christine Broadway said, "We start with a model and then we build a prototype based on the model. Then we would refine that model. So it's an iterative process.

"We found that sometimes the requirements don't come out until you show the UI to the user. We found that the users were then able to better articulate the actual requirements. With Smalltalk, you can develop a lot of functionality in a short period of time. It's been really useful to mock up screens in VisualWorks and get some initial impressions from the client," says Christine.

This is a typical "spiral" development process, which is very effective in implementing user requirements (see Figure 4-5). It works well with the rapid prototyping environment that VisualWorks Smalltalk provides. With each iteration around the spiral, progressively more complete versions of the software are built. And with each revolution, prototyping and customer feedback are used to reduce risk.

Figure 4-6. Waterfall model

This approach has proved more useful than the traditional "waterfall" development process (see Figure 4-6), where only a single pass is made through the requirements phase. Real projects rarely follow the sequential flow that the waterfall model proposed. Iteration always occurs, as LLNL found. And as Christine pointed out, it is often difficult for the customer to state all requirements explicitly, as the waterfall model requires.

But a prototype does not an architecture make. It's important to realize that the spiral model does not by itself generate a good architecture. That issue must be addressed separately. You must be vigilant about evolving a good architecture as part of the spiral model iteration process. The more up-front thought put into designing an appropriate but flexible architecture, the better off you will be. Notice that LLNL started off on the right foot, with a model. A prototype was built from the model, and not vice-versa.

Putting the client on a diet

Up until the Data Warehouse project, the "thick client" Smalltalk approach had been used. But the thick client had to go. Different applications were requiring different desktop system resources. "If we got one application to work on the desktop, we were pretty happy," said Mike Piscotty. "Getting two was a virtual impossibility, and three applications to work on the desktop together required divine intervention. There were different drivers with different versions. Everything was incompatible. You'd kind of reach a deadlock, so either you'd run this application or you'd run that one."

LLNL software developers used two different approaches to Web-enable the Data Warehouse. The first, simpler approach used ObjectShare's VisualWave product, which is available for VisualWorks Smalltalk. VisualWave gives developers the ability to run applications on the server side and have their interfaces served up as automatically-built HTML pages to a Web browser. This works well for many applications, where relatively static, forms-oriented HTML browser windows will suffice.

The second approach used more powerful technology. It utilized a product called Classic Blend, from Applied Reasoning Systems Corporation in Raleigh, North Carolina. Classic Blend runs on top of ObjectShare VisualWorks. It allows standard Smalltalk applications to present their graphical user interfaces (GUIs) as live Java applets. Smalltalk application GUIs run inside a Web browser and function just as they do on a standalone workstation. Every VisualWorks window is automatically translated on-the-fly to a Java window. Likewise, VisualWorks widgets are automatically translated to their Java GUI class equivalents.

Classic Blend implements a "mini-ORB" to manage communications between the Java client-side objects and Smalltalk server-side objects. Both Java and Smalltalk objects send messages to each other via these ORBs. A single TCP/IP connection is maintained for each active Classic Blend application, and objects are streamed between Java and Smalltalk over this connection.

The interesting thing about both of these Web Smalltalk tools is that they automatically generate a thin client. The Smalltalk application exists on a server machine, and only its UI is present on the client. In fact, an extra tier of architecture is created. In the case of the Data Warehouse, a three-tiered architecture, using Gemstone Smalltalk business objects as its middle tier, automatically becomes a 4-tiered architecture (see Figure 4-7).

Of course, thinning the clients shifts the processing burden to servers. LLNL uses an 8-CPU Sun Ultra Enterprise server for running GemStone and Oracle. Another 8-CPU Sun Ultra Enterprise machine acts as a Web application server. A 4-CPU Ultra runs Middleware Services.

The architectural strategy for the Data Warehouse did not end with a Web client layer. There was an intentional effort to architect the system from independent software components. Extensible frameworks were built wherever possible in order to provide future leverage. Common frameworks were used for both the Data Warehouse proper and the first application, called Institutional Planning and Pricing System (IPPS), to utilize the Data Warehouse's business objects.

Application partitioning

"Application partitioning is the hardest part of developing a system of distributed objects," says Framework Developer Craig McChesney. "Sometimes the correct architecture is obvious. Sometimes you have to build and study a number of prototypes to produce a solid design."

LLNL developers faced numerous decisions about partitioning system functionality. They had to determine whether to deliver Java user interfaces or Smalltalk ones using Classic Blend. For each business object, they decided whether to use Oracle or

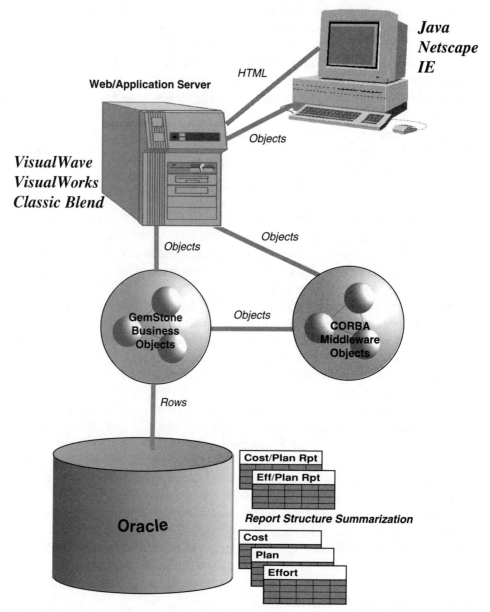

Figure 4-7. Data Warehouse layered architecture

GemStone for persistence. They had to optimally partition business object functionality between the application and database tiers. They designed a broker framework
to de-couple the application tier from the persistence implementation. Finally, they
had to determine which tier would contain the report execution engine, a crucial
piece of the Data Warehouse.

They had agreed that in general, user interfaces would be developed in VisualWorks and delivered to Web browsers via Classic Bend. But there were some exceptions. Some interfaces required custom widgets that could not be delivered using Classic Blend. For example, a full-featured spreadsheet interface was desired for the report result viewer. It would have to provide capabilities beyond the standard VisualWorks table or dataset widgets. The designers found a Java widget that provided the desired functionality. They had two implementation choices for using custom Java widgets: They could hook the custom widget into the Classic Blend framework with some proprietary Java and Smalltalk coding, or they could write a Java user interface containing the widget that communicated with the Smalltalk server via CORBA. The latter alternative was chosen because it didn't tie the report result viewer to a vendor's proprietary messaging framework.

Although GemStone is a critical piece of the Data Warehouse architecture, the system architects realized that most of the Lab's operational business systems used Oracle for data storage. For each business object, they determined whether the data were available from Oracle or from some other source. If so, would GemStone load and maintain the data or access it from the source system? They based this decision on a number of factors, including frequency of access, data volume, special benefits of making the object persistent in GemStone, and end-user performance requirements.

The application tier required fully functional business objects for use by other application objects and by users. The database tier also needed functional business objects to support interactions with Middleware Services, the pricing calculator, and the report engine. The system architects wanted to take full advantage of the active nature of the GemStone database, so GemStone class definitions were created for each business object. Data could be retrieved from Oracle and then instantiated into GemStone objects, allowing behavior to be defined for objects stored in the relational database. GemStone replication allowed VisualWorks class definitions to be mapped to database objects. GemStone's forwarder mechanism was also used to allow the application tier to send messages directly to objects in the database tier.

A business object broker framework was developed to de-couple the application and database tiers. A **broker** allows the application tier to store and retrieve business objects without any knowledge of the underlying persistence implementation. This makes changes in the persistence method (i.e. Oracle vs. GemStone) for a particular business object transparent to the application tier.

Broker functionality itself may be partitioned using GemStone replication between the application and database tiers. This minimizes the network traffic between the two. The broker framework is abstracted away from the GemStone implementation, enabling brokers to be created for virtually any data source. For Oracle data, it was decided that brokers would use GemStone's Gem Connect tool to retrieve data and then instantiate Gemstone objects using that data. This arrangement allowed specification of database tier behaviors for those objects—something that would not have been possible had the brokers been connected directly to Oracle.

Finally, system architects had to decide exactly which tier should house the report execution engine, Reportoire by DNS. This product was originally implemented in VisualWorks. Because business objects were managed by GemStone, they would need to be dynamically copied ("faulted") into the application tier during report execution. This situation concerned the system architects, who knew that a given report might touch literally thousands of business objects. LLNL worked with the vendor to port the report execution engine to the GemStone server. This eliminated network traffic and made better use of GemStone's persistence tools.

Business objects

Enterprise Business Objects were developed for the Data Warehouse. Business objects for such fundamental entities as cost, effort, plans, accounts, people, and procurements were required.

All of these objects were implemented as subclasses of an abstract GemStone Smalltalk class called LLNLPersistentObject. Since they were implemented on the GemStone server, they were automatically distributed and persistent.

Developers also created a subclass of LLNLPersistentObject called LLNLDynamicallyAttributedObject. This class had an instance variable called dynamicAttributes, which was a Dictionary that mapped symbols to arbitrary objects. Dynamic attributes were the means by which the URA facility was implemented. A user could add her own custom attributes to an object for reporting, and these attributes would be entered into the dynamic attributes dictionary for that object. The implementation of LLNLDynamicallyAttributedObject overrode the standard doesNotUnderstand: message in the object class, so that a message that referenced a dynamic attribute would be automatically sent to the attribute object as defined in the dynamicAttributes Dictionary. This implementation allowed dynamic attributes to have parity with "real" object attributes and to behave exactly the same way.

The need for metadata

It was soon discovered that not everyone at LLNL thought of these things in the same way. The business community thought of them in terms of business processes, functional relationships, and business data. But the user community of scientists, engineers, and project managers viewed these same things in terms of their own laboratory business processes and used a different nomenclature that was relevant for their projects.

Something was needed to resolve the two different views. An Enterprise Data Alignment Process was needed (Figure 4-8). This brought key individuals together from both the user community and business community at LLNL.

Members were identified representing each Directorate area of LLNL. Dave Biggers, who was familiar with providing end user support for the ASSIST application, led this effort and was responsible for establishing the meetings, setting the agenda, facilitating the discussions, and interfacing with the Data Warehouse development team.

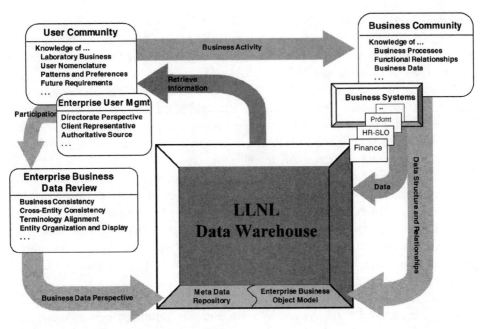

Figure 4-8. Enterprise Data Alignment Process

An important concept emerged from this process. The information about Enterprise Business Objects that users required was not a property of the business domain objects themselves but was something else. It was metadata and should be represented in the object model as such. **Metadata** is data that describes other data. An object's class is an example of metadata, because it describes the object.

So the metadata objects were not the same as domain objects. Their classes were subclassed from a GemStone Smalltalk class that LLNL developers called DNSBusinessEntity. These objects had an association with their respective domain objects and collectively formed a Metadata Repository.

In addition, one of these object had attribute objects, supplied from class DNSEntityAttribute. Such metadata attributes had associations with attribute objects of a domain object. The metadata attributes encapsulated information needed to generate user reports, information such as what the user wants to see as the name of a reporting attribute, as well as the printing format used to display it.

On the surface, giving report formatting information the fancy name of metadata might seem a bit overblown. After all, it is just extra description information. Why not just stick this information into the domain model somewhere? Because the information is not part of the data itself. It describes the data, and is therefore metadata.

The presence of correctly modeled metadata paves the way for more sophisticated capabilities. For example, introspection could be added to the Metadata Repository, such that users could ask questions about the structure and relationships between the domain models themselves. I revisit metadata later in this book (Chapter 9), where it will be shown as a key to the development of reusable components.

Sharing business objects with IPPS

A key goal in building business objects is to be able to readily share them among all the application programs that need to use these objects. As the first such application beyond the Data Warehouse, IPPS required such access.

IPPS is an internal system for LLNL. It handles all the details of planning for new projects within LLNL. Users can create financial plans and submit them to their management for higher level approval. The manager can make changes to a project plan and in turn submit the plan to the next management level for approval. The process could continue for as many levels as were required.

IPPS also contained its own business objects. A complex set of business rules determines rates for calculating various charges and burdens for pricing a project. These rates and rules change frequently. A Calculator Services domain model was created for this purpose. It contains the business objects that drive the calculator engine. It specifies the calculations to be performed via formulas that are implemented as Smalltalk blocks. This model interacts with Enterprise Business Objects such as Accounts and People, provided by the Data Warehouse.

IPPS' Calculator Services business objects, and their very intelligent pricing abilities, formed the core of the system. When a user was building a new financial plan from the ground up, these business objects collaborated to automatically add prices to the appropriate fields on the screen.

Like all good objects, the Calculator Services objects could be readily reused. IPPS provides a "Quick Pricer" screen for doing quick calculations outside the context of specific projects (see Figure 4-9).

Like the main IPPS system, the Quick Pricer is implemented in VisualWorks Smalltalk as a GemStone Smalltalk client and talks to the calculator services objects that are distributed on the GemStone Server. The Quick Pricer provides its UI layer to the Web user via VisualWave, while the rest of IPPS uses Classic Blend. The Quick Pricer has a simple, fixed form screen that VisualWave handles quite easily. But if this changes, the UI could be readily implemented with the more powerful Classic Blend, with minimal impact on the software. This is just one example of the implementation that a flexible, multi-tiered architecture provides. The Calculator Services business objects are safely two tiers away from the user interface, not knowing or caring how they are being invoked.

Middleware services

In addition to the Enterprise Business Objects was a set of middleware objects that provided common services. These would be deployed via CORBA so that all AIS applications could use them. Several Middleware Services were rolled out, including e-mail services, status services, event services, output services, and logging services.

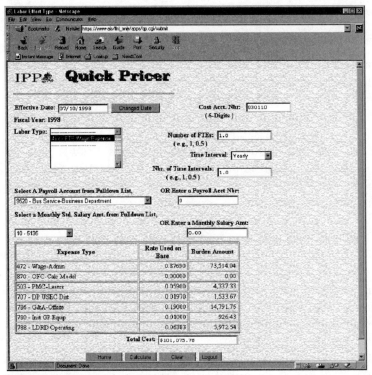

Figure 4-9. IPPS Quick Pricer screen

Services locator

The Middleware Services use a Services Locator. This locator dispenses services as they are requested from client objects. Services register themselves independently with the Services Locator, allowing redundant services. The client object does not have to know or care where the service served up by the Services Locator resides.

The Services Locator can handle load distribution to redundant services via an arbitration policy. This arbitration policy can be one of three standard ones: first available (the default policy), round-robin, or random selection. Furthermore, the Services Locator protocol included an "arbitrator" interface. If an arbitrator is supplied, an arbitration request is delegated to this arbitrator object, and it is that object's responsibility to decide on the service to supply.

Service Locators are federated. **Federated** means that multiple Services Locators can collaborate together but appear to the client object as if they were a single Services Locator. As each Services Locator comes up, it contacts the others via CORBA and goes through a handshaking protocol which federates all of them.

Helper classes

An important architectural approach used by the Middleware Services team was the use of what they termed "helper" classes. The team learned that it was one thing to be the user of a service, but quite another to be the provider of that service. A significant amount of work was required to provide Middleware Services. Helper classes, built as part of Middleware Services, helped!

A helper object is a wrapper for a remote object's proxy. This wrapper insulates the distributed Smalltalk client objects from all behavior that is specific to the proxy. In addition, Middleware Services requests could be bundled in via the helper classes.

Ideally, a proxy would act exactly like an ordinary object, and no special treatment would be required. Its use would be completely transparent. But in practice, a proxy needs to handle specific distributed Smalltalk behavior.

One example of such behavior is the handling of exceptions that can be raised from a particular distributed Smalltalk implementation. LLNL uses both GemStone and the CORBA-complaint SmalltalkBroker. Each can raise its own types of exceptions in case something goes awry, such as a server connection being lost. It's obviously undesirable to scatter exception-handling code throughout Smalltalk clients, let alone distributed Smalltalk implementation-specific exception handlers.

The client application talks to a "helper" wrapper, as though it were an ordinary object. One such wrapper would form a layer between each proxy object and a Smalltalk client application, effectively encapsulating distributed Smalltalk behavior. In addition to passing messages to the real proxy, the helper object would, unbeknownst to the Smalltalk client, handle all other behavior necessary and useful to being a distributed object.

Exception handling was just one such behavior. Invoking Middleware Services as necessary brings in a whole new and powerful set of behaviors.

For example, logging services could be turned on, so that distributed Smalltalk messages sends were automatically logged to a file. This proved invaluable to the LLNL team during debugging. With their logging facility, they could also do performance monitoring and tuning.

Helper objects can provide client-side behavior that is key to properly utilizing Middleware Services. A client can make a Middleware Services request which happens to be implemented through CORBA. But as far as the client is concerned, it is using a service that is local to him. Helper objects can even make decisions about whether to pass requests on to Middleware Services at all. A helper can utilize local caches, so that in some cases, it does not have to use a CORBA message send at all. If requested information happens to be in a local cache, there is no need to redundantly issue a CORBA Middleware Services request.

"We also built what we called the 'test class' for each service," said Larry Wichter, Technical Project Leader on Middleware Services. "The test class was intended to be two things. It was an example of how to use the service from a coding point of view. And it was also supposed to exercise all of the behavior of the component. It could be run with other test classes to do benchmarking."

Middleware Services had to be lightweight from the client object's point of view. A service could not tie down a client application while it was being performed. This was another feature that helper objects enabled.

An example of such a lightweight implementation can also be found in logging services. The helper object sends a message to logging services such that the message does not wait for a reply. This is a done via the CORBA "oneway" message, which is discussed in Chapter 5, in the section "Operations do all the work." The level of logging may be controlled so that different degrees of logging are enabled. The log could be set, for example, to log every message, or to just log "debug" messages. Having the client-side helper object do the filtering of messages, rather than passing everything to the remote CORBA logging services only to have some these messages thrown away there, makes a lot of sense.

Helper objects can even do "hot swapping" of Middleware Services. If one such service goes down, another equivalent service could potentially be found via the Services Locator and substituted for the original service. The helper object could accomplish this transparently, without its client object knowing.

It was important to LLNL that Middle Services be 100-percent CORBA compliant. That way, they would be utilizing standards-based technology, rather than relying on a particular vendors' proprietary solutions. Some of the software facilities required for Middleware Services were in fact available from some of the vendors, but as proprietary implementations. They would not inter-operate with other brands of CORBA ORBs. So the decision was made to exclude such vendor-specific solutions and to create standard CORBA interface-based implementations instead.

Lessons Learned

As early adopters of Web-centric distributed computing, the Data Warehouse group went through their share of pain and suffering. They found that the promise of Java's platform independence was somewhat of a myth, at least at this juvenile stage of Java's life. Products were immature and had quality and performance problems. "Write once, debug everywhere" was indeed their experience.

Because of this product immaturity, tight cooperation between the developer community and the LLNL infrastructure providers, the Administrative Information Systems organization's systems programmers and DBAs, was essential. These systems folks found that they had to function as their own systems integrators. Products did not work together without considerable effort to eliminate interface problems. Difficulty in getting Smalltalk and Java CORBA ORBs to inter-operate was one such problem.

They also found that all Web browsers are not created equal. It became essential to test applications on all target browsers and platforms: PC, Mac, and Unix workstations. There was a significant variation in performance between different Java virtual machines. They also found that end-to-end stress tests were critical to determine response time and scalability.

Another lesson was learned within the Middleware Services group. In the scramble to get their software written and working and available to their internal clients, not enough effort was devoted up-front to creating a reusable framework.

Sean Felten, the Enterprise System Object Architect, said that they should have created a framework and architecture that said, "If you are making a service, here is how it will act. Here is what it will conform to. Here is common service behavior that services will exhibit. Here is an abstract component which implemented such common services behavior."

According to Larry Wichter, "We were aware of what we should have been doing. But there was this real-world 'driver' of having a client who wants something useful delivered in a reasonable amount of time. So when deadlines started to get placed on the calendar, you had to make decisions about what you were going to implement today."

Does this sound familiar? Struggling with a short-term reward provided by a quick solution, versus laying the groundwork for long-term needs, seems to be a constant theme in software engineering.

But all in all, the Lawrence Livermore National Laboratories Data Warehouse project was highly successful in building both a solid distributed computing infrastructure and in delivering a flexible, high-performance product. The widespread use of the Smalltalk language enabled agile responses to software needs, and rapid, "spiral model" development cycles. A commitment to good object-oriented analysis and design was instrumental in successful distributing Smalltalk objects throughout the enterprise. And via industry standard CORBA interfaces, these Smalltalk objects can be leveraged and put into widespread use, independent of a client's programming language.

≡Chapter 5≡

All About CORBA

CORBA is the public standard that provides a uniform way for objects to receive and respond to requests. CORBA specifies the structure of a request, how that request is delivered to a receiving object, and how results are returned to the client, the issuer of the request.

An Object Request Broker, or ORB, is the central machinery of CORBA[3]. An ORB enables objects to transparently make and receive requests and responses in a distributed environment. The objects receiving the requests are termed **server objects**, and actually reside in black boxes called **object implementations**. One object acts as a client to another object's implementation. A server object is also called a **CORBA object**.

Clients and server objects may use the same ORB, or different ORBs. For distributed Smalltalk, both the CORBA implementations use a separate ORB for each object space, as shown in Figure 5-1.

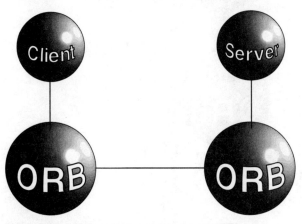

Figure 5-1. Client and server objects on ORBs

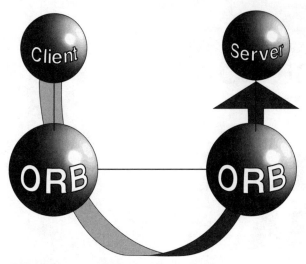

Figure 5-2. A request to a server object

The most important thing a client object can do is to issue a request to a server object. A request is an operation with zero or more arguments. A CORBA request is equivalent to a Smalltalk message. The CORBA-compliant distributed Smalltalks automatically translate the sending of an appropriate Smalltalk message into a CORBA request. This is illustrated in Figure 5-2.

A request returns results to the client that must be marshaled and unmarshaled, as shown in Figure 5-3. These results may include values, as well as status information indicating that exception conditions were raised in attempting to perform the request.

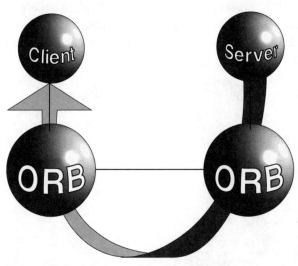

Figure 5-3. Result returned to client object

What's in an ORB?

A client deals with a CORBA object by using its **object reference**. This is an "opaque" value that uniquely identifies the object to an ORB. Everything a client does with a CORBA object, it does via an ORB.

Both clients and server objects are connected to an ORB through a few different interfaces. In fact, an ORB is composed of only two things: an **ORB core**, and **components** that are attached to this core. The components are either **interfaces** or **object adapters**. See Figure 5-4 for an inside view of a CORBA ORB.

On the client side, interfaces connect directly to the ORB core. There are three types of client interface: a **stub**, a **dynamic invocation**, and a direct **ORB interface**.

A **stub** is a fixed interface tailored to a specific type of object. A single object can have more than one stub. Stubs provide the sum total of the static client interface to an object.

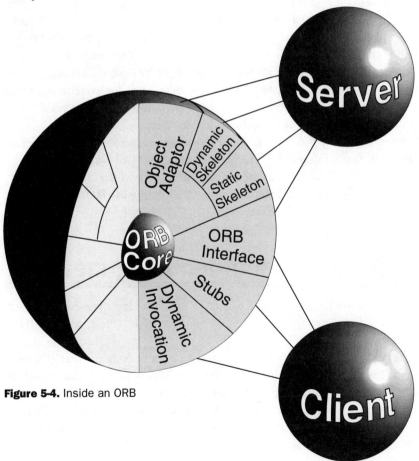

Figure 5-4. Inside an ORB

On the other hand, a single dynamic invocation interface to a client provides connections to all objects that are not hard-wired via stubs. Finally, the ORB interface provides a few functions that are outside the realm of either stubs or dynamic invocations, such as copying object references.

On the server object side, all but one interface—the ORB interface—is mediated by an object adapter that is connected to the ORB core.

An object adapter is an ORB component that provides basic services to an object implementation. And a server object's object implementation can talk directly to the ORB interface, or to an object adapter. Like a client, an object implementation can have a fixed interface, called a **static skeleton**, or a changeable one, called a **dynamic skeleton**. A dynamic skeleton enables new kinds of objects to be added at run-time and funnels all requests for such objects to one place.

You shouldn't be surprised to learn that the CORBA-compliant distributed Smalltalks use dynamic invocation and dynamic skeletons exclusively. This is a perfect match for Smalltalk's on-the-fly, dynamically defined objects.

You might think that a client-side stub can only talk to a static skeleton, and a dynamic invocation to a dynamic skeleton. No! That's one of the beautiful things about CORBA: the separation between client and object implementation is so clean that both kinds of skeletons appear identical to the client, who shouldn't really know or care anything about the "how" of its CORBA objects. So if you were to add some statically-bound C++ objects to your distributed Smalltalk system, they would have absolutely no trouble inter-operating with Smalltalk objects.

The ORB core is what provides the transportation between client and server object. If these reside on different ORBs, the ORBs automatically sends requests and results to each other. CORBA defines the interoperability by which ORBs communicate with each other. There is an **Internet Inter-ORB Protocol (IIOP)** that defines how ORBs communicate using TCP/IP.

IDL – Interface Definition Language

IDL, interface definition language, is the way CORBA object interfaces are specified. Readers with experience in C++ will find IDL very familiar. It follows a subset of ANSI C++ syntax.

But IDL is purely declarative. You cannot write program code in IDL. It is used only to specify exactly how to communicate with CORBA objects. It is not possible, nor desirable, to specify program operation semantics in IDL.

When you specify an interface to a CORBA distributed object using IDL, you are also implicitly specifying a Smalltalk class. The OMG has defined a Smalltalk language mapping, which spells out how IDL is mapped to Smalltalk.

For the IDL syntax descriptions, I'll use the following conventions:

Style:	What it represents:
Helvetica	Smalltalk language elements
Courier	IDL language and syntax elements
<user-supplied values>	What you must supply in formats and descriptions
*	Repeat the preceding syntactic unit zero or more times
+	Repeat the preceding syntactic unit one or more times
{ }	Group the enclosed as a single syntactic unit
[ ]	Optional syntactic unit _ may occur zero or one time
|	Alternatively

An object by any other name: the identifier

An identifier in IDL is used to give a name to something, such as a parameter or operation. IDL Identifiers can be any sequence of alphabetic, numeric, and the underscore (_) character. The first character must be alphabetic, and case is significant. Underscores are typically used to separate words for readability, such as in "my_variable," or "describe_contents."

Every IDL identifier has a Smalltalk mapping. Because some Smalltalk language implementations do not allow underscore characters, the Smalltalk mapping of IDL removes them. To convert an IDL identifier to a Smalltalk identifier, remove each underscore and capitalize the following letter, if it exists.

For example, the IDL identifiers:

```
my_variable
describe_contents
```

become the Smalltalk identifiers:

```
myVariable
describeContents
```

The IDL identifiers myVariable and describeContents are perfectly legal, and their Smalltalk language mappings are the same. For CORBA-based distributed Smalltalk, it is simpler to follow the Smalltalk identifier naming conventions for IDL identifiers. Then the two type of identifiers can have exactly the same names.

IDL's universal container: the module

At the top level of IDL "code" is the **module**. Modules group other IDL elements together, and give them a context.

```
module <module name> {
    { <@code-IDL>\module definition> } +
```

A *<module definition>* is one of the following, followed by a semicolon (;):

- Interface

- Type

- Constant

- Exception

- Module

Notice that a module can be recursively nested within a module. There is no equivalent in Smalltalk to a module. However, in both ObjectShare Distributed Smalltalk and SmalltalkBroker, a class knows how to answer a name that includes its module. The next section discusses this further.

For public consumption: the interface

Perhaps the most important elements in a module definition are its **interfaces**. An interface corresponds to a Smalltalk class. It has an interface name, one or more scoped names, and a body:

```
interface <interface name>  : <scoped name>{, <scoped name>}* {
    <interface body>
}
```

A scoped name is the fully qualified name of an interface. A scoped name consists of the name of the module in that the interface is defined, followed by two colons (::), and then the interface name. A scoped name identifies an interface, or any other CORBA entity, as being specific to a module. The same name may be used in different modules for different purposes, so that to unambiguously pinpoint it, a scoped name is used. The name is then said to be scoped to a particular module.

Though it's not part of the OMG mapping, every Smalltalk class that corresponds to an IDL interface in both DST and SmalltalkBroker classes has a special method that answers its scoped. This is the instance method **CORBAName**.

For example, suppose there is an interface called **MyInterface**, defined in module **MyModule**. The corresponding Smalltalk class would be called **MyInterface**, and would contain the following instance method:

```
CORBAName
    ^'MyModule::MyInterface'
```

Let's get back to the definition of an interface. In the above description, the scoped name is the interface from which this interface inherits. It is the equivalent of a Smalltalk superclass. But wait a minute: the definition of an interface says that you can have more than one scoped name, with each additional one separated by a comma. This is multiple inheritance!

Not surprisingly, C++ has multiple inheritance. So although Smalltalk itself doesn't have multiple inheritance, Smalltalk CORBA interfaces, which map into Smalltalk classes, do have multiple inheritance. They inherit from other CORBA interfaces.

This feature is particularly important for using CORBA services. To give an object the capabilities of a particular CORBA service, you simply inherit from its interface. CORBA services are orthogonal—you are able to freely mix and match them. So to give an object both persistence and concurrency, you declare its interface to multiply inherit from the interfaces for both the Persistent Object Service and the Concurrency Control Service.

An interface body consists of any number of the following types of declarations, each separated by a semicolon (;):

- Operation
- Constant
- Type
- Attribute
- Exception

Operations do all the work

An operation is equivalent to a Smalltalk method. There are some minor differences, though: an IDL operation can return a result or no result, called a void. When an operation is declared in IDL, its return type is specified as either void or a specific type, which is a parameter type spec. A parameter type spec is one of three things: one of the basic types, the string type, or a scoped name, which allows any IDL type to be used.

A Smalltalk method always answers an object. But with an operation that returns no result; the corresponding Smalltalk result object is undefined.

An operation's parameters can be individually passed in one of three modes: **in**, **out**, and **inout**. An in is a parameter that is only passed from the sender (client) to receiver (server). An out is a parameter that only passes from receiver to sender. An inout parameter is passed in both directions; that is, it can be passed from sender to receiver, and modified by the receiver.

But in Smalltalk, a message argument is generally thought of as only an "in;" that is, going from sender to receiver. This is because Smalltalk does not allow assignments directly to arguments within a method. In other languages, this is termed passing "by value," but that is a confusing term, both with reference to Smalltalk and CORBA. In Smalltalk, simple objects such as Integers are passed "by value," directly on the stack, while more complex objects are passed "by reference;" that is, pointers to those objects are placed on the stack. See the section named "'By value' techniques" for forcing "by value" semantics in the Smalltalk CORBA mapping.

CORBA defines objects "by reference" as utilizing the standard CORBA object reference. Hence, an object "by value" is a local copy, rather than a remote reference.

Smalltalk, however, *does* have an explicit mechanism for passing argument value back. This is by using a **value holder**. A value holder is a type of class that understands the value and value: messages. The value message answers the current value of a value holder. The value: message enables you to set a new value for it. A value holder provides a level of indirection, so an object can refer to another object using a simple protocol. ParcPlace-Digitalk's VisualWorks makes extensive used of value holders, which are of the class ValueHolder.

The CORBA Smalltalk language mapping has its own version of a value holder. It is a class that conforms to the **CORBAParameter** protocol. Such a class can understand the value and value: messages, just like any value holder. You can send any object the message **asCORBAParmeter**. This answers a CORBAParameter whose value will be the original object. The value of the CORBAParameter object can be subsequently changed by sending it a value: message.

To pass a CORBA **in** parameter, you use an ordinary Smalltalk object. But to pass a CORBA **out** or **inout** parameter, you must use an object that supports the CORBAParameter protocol.

Here's the formal definition for an IDL operation declaration:

```
[ <operation attribute> ] <operation type spec> <identifier> <parameter declarations>
        [ <raised expression> ] [ <context expression> ]
    <operation attribute> ::= oneway
    <operation type spec> ::= <parameter type spec>
                            | void
 <parameter type spec> ::= <basic type spec>
                         | <string type>
                         | <scoped name>
 <parameter declarations> ::= ( <parameter declaration>
                              { , <parameter declaration> }* )
                            | ( )
 <parameter declaration> ::= <parameter attribute> <parameter type spec>
                            <simple declarator>
 <parameter attribute> ::= in
                         | out
                         | inout
 <simple declarator> ::= <identifier>
```

The only possible operation attribute, oneway, specifies that the operation goes from sender to receiver, with nothing going from receiver to sender. Consequently, an operation declared to be oneway must specify a void return type, and it cannot have any output or inout parameters.

Constant

A **constant expression** is an expression that evaluates to a fixed value.

The CORBA Smalltalk mapping specifies that constants be stored in a Dictionary called CORBAConstants.

Type

Types are used to describe CORBA parameters, attributes, exceptions, and return values. They are much the same as the types you would encounter in C and C++.

IDL has a construction for naming types. That is, it provides declarations that associate an identifier with a type. The typedef keyword is used to associate a name with a data type. The structure, discriminated union, and enumerated types also associate names with data types, and declare data types with those names.

Where type declarator is any of the data types, other than structure, discriminated union, and enumerated types, a typedef declaration is defined as:

```
typedef  <type declarator>
```

Basic types

The **basic types** are:

- Integer types
  - **long**—integers in the range -2^{31} .. $2^{31} - 1$
  - **short**—integers in the range -2^{15} .. $2^{15} - 1$
  - **unsigned long**—integers in the range 0 .. $2^{32} - 1$
  - **unsigned short**—integers in the range 0 .. $2^{16} - 1$
- Floating point types
  - **float**—IEEE single-precision floating point number
  - **double**—IEEE double-precision floating point number
- **char** type—an 8-bit quantity, with conversion for different character sets
- **boolean** type—the values TRUE or FALSE
- **octet** type—8-bit quantities guaranteed not to undergo any conversion
- **any** type—permits the specification of any IDL type

The simple types map to Smalltalk as you would expect.

- The integer types map to Smalltalk objects of the **Integer** class.
- The floating point types map to Smalltalk objects of the **Float** and **Double** classes.

- The **char** type map to a Smalltalk object of the **Character** class.
- The **boolean** type maps to a Smalltalk object of the **Boolean** class (true or false).
- The **octet** type maps to a Smalltalk object of the **Integer** class.
- The **any** type maps to any Smalltalk object that has a mapping to an IDL type.

More about the "any" type

At first glance, you might look at the IDL **any** type and say, "Wait a minute. Forget about all this typing of data in CORBA. If I use 'any,' I can substitute any Smalltalk class I want."

Close, but not quite. Smalltalk objects used within CORBA are restricted to only those which have a corresponding IDL type.

This is not a problem for numbers, which can be mapped from IDL longs, floats, etc. But what about more complex Smalltalk classes? As you see in the next section, there are complex IDL types, the constructed types. You can freely use the any type, and I'll describe how in the section called "Smalltalk IDL secrets."

But if you haven't explicitly made an IDL type to correspond to the Smalltalk object you intend to substitute for an any, you're out of luck.

Structure type

A structure is the CORBA type that is a composition of other types. The definition of a structure type is:

```
struct <identifier> { <member list> }
    <member list>  ::= <member> +
    <member>  ::= <any type> <declarators>  ;
    <declarators>  ::= <declarator> { ; <declarator> }*
    <declarator>  ::= <identifier>
                    | <array type>
```

The array type is one of the CORBA types, and will be detailed a bit later. It allows fixed-size, multidimensional arrays of the given type to be declared.

The above formal definition of a structure type is a bit unwieldy, but some examples will make it clear.

```
struct fullName {
    string firstName;
    char middleInitial;
    string lastName
}

struct bankAccount {
    long accountNumber;
    fullName ownerName
}
```

Although the above examples make a structure type look a lot like a Smalltalk class, the two are *not* equivalent. A structure type is only data. It has no methods implicitly associated with it.

A structure type is a set of identifiers (excluding the case of an array for now), each of which has an associated type. When you instantiate a structure, each member in its member list is an instance of the designated type. Because an IDL structure type is "dumb" and without methods, it maps nicely to Smalltalk as an instance of the Dictionary class.

Remember that a Smalltalk Dictionary is a Collection of Associations, where each Association has a key and a value. To look up a value in a Dictionary, send it the at: message, with a key as its argument. The identifier for a structure member maps to the key for the Association. This key is an instance of Symbol, and has a value that is the member identifier, converted according to the standard Smalltalk identifier conversion rule given earlier. The value in each Association is an instance of the corresponding Smalltalk class for that member.

Here's an example of using the Smalltalk mapping for the fullName IDL structure given above:

```
aFirstName := aFullName at: firstName.
aFullName at: #middleInitial put: $E.
aFullName at: #lastName put: 'Newman'.
```

Enumerated type

An **enumerated type** declares a fixed choice of alternatives. The definition of an enumerated type is:

```
enum <identifier> {
    <enumerator> { , <enumerator>}*
}
```

where an enumerator is just an identifier.

An enumerated type is simply an ordered list of identifiers, which are called enumerators. The order in which the enumerators are named defines their relative order for comparison.

Here are some examples of enumerated types. They are defined in the module SomeEnums, for reasons that will be clear in a moment:

```
module SomeEnums {
    enum primaryColor { red, green, blue };
    enum digitName { zero, one, two, three, four, five,
            six, seven, eight, nine };
};
```

The CORBA Smalltalk mapping specifies that enumerators be String keys, and considers them constants. So they are stored in the Dictionary called CORBAConstants. Furthermore, these keys must be scoped names, which means you must include their module names. Note: there is no mapping done with the enumerators, as there is with an IDL identifier to a Smalltalk identifier.

To access particular enumerators, you must write Smalltalk code such as:

```
aColorEnum := CORBAConstants at: '::SomeEnums::red'.
anotherColorEnum := CORBAConstants at: '::SomeEnums::blue'.
```

One important thing about enumerators is that they are ordered. This means they automatically have all the Smalltalk comparison methods defined. These are "<", "<=", "=", ">", and ">=".

So given the above examples, the following expression is true:

```
(aColorEnum < anotherColorEnum)
```

Discriminated union type

A discriminated union declares a particular set of arbitrary CORBA types that can be equivalently passed to an operation, or returned by one. The definition of a discriminated unions type (or union type for short) is:

```
union <identifier> switch ( <switch type spec> )
                 { <switch body> }
<switch type spec>  ::= <any integer type>
                      | <char type>
                      | <boolean type>
                      | <enumerated type>
                      | <scoped name>  which evaluates to one of the above types
<switch body>  ::= <case>+
<case>  ::= <case label> <element spec> ;
<case label>  ::= case <constant expressions>:
                 | default:
<element spec>  ::= <any type> <declarator>
```

The basic idea in a discriminated union is to allow alternative data types to be passed. Each case is one alternative.

For example, this union uses an enum called myEnumType as the switch type spec:

```
enum myEnumType { aLong, aBoolean, aFloat };
union myUnion switch (myEnumType)
    case aLong: long l;
    case aBoolean: boolean b;
    case aFloat: float f;
};
```

A union type is the preferred way of returning a value of one of a limited number of data types. If an operation returns one of three types of variables, for example, use a union rather than the **any** type.

There are two Smalltalk bindings for union types: implicit and explicit. The implicit binding takes maximum advantage of the dynamic nature of Smalltalk, and is the least intrusive.

For an implicit binding, you simply use any type that matches the switch type spec in a discriminated union. In the above example, if a parameter of type myUnion is required, you can pass any Smalltalk instance that can be mapped into an IDL long, boolean, or float. Similarly, when a myUnion is returned as the result of an operation, the actual Smalltalk object that represents the value of myUnion is returned.

Use of the explicit union binding results in specific Smalltalk classes being accepted and returned. For Smalltalk-to-Smalltalk communication, there's really no reason to use explicit binding, so it won't be described any further.

String type

An IDL string is defined as:

```
string
| string < <positive integer constant> >
```

When the second form is used, the positive integer constant is the maximum size of the string. An IDL string maps to the Smalltalk String class. So if an IDL string is declared as the type for an argument, you pass it an instance of String.

Some examples of CORBA string declarations are:

```
string firstName;
string addressLine1 <32>;
```

The first IDL line declares that a string named firstName is unbounded. The second line declares that the string addressLine1 may be no longer than 32 characters.

Sequence type

An IDL sequence is simply a one-dimensional array. It is defined as:

```
sequence < <simple type spec> >
| sequence < <simple type spec>, <positive integer constant> >
```

When the second form is used, the positive integer constant is the maximum size of the sequence.

A simple type spec is limited to one of the basic types, the string type, or the sequence type.

The following are examples of IDL sequence declarations:

```
sequence <long> elements;
sequence <boolean , 8> flags;
```

In the first line, a sequence of longs called elements is declared. In the next line, a sequence of booleans called flags is declared, which has a maximum of eight elements.

A sequence maps to a Smalltalk OrderedCollection. When passing an OrderedCollection for a sequence, you must make sure that all the elements of the OrderedCollection map into the single IDL type declared for that sequence.

Array type

The array type is used to declare multidimensional arrays. An IDL array is declared as:

<identifier> { [<positive integer constant>] }+

The identifier declares the name for the array type. Each positive integer constant declares the fixed size of one dimension of the array.

An example of an array declaration is:

```
typedef long LongArray [4][5];
```

This declares a type called longArray, which is a two-dimensional array of longs where the dimensions are of size 4 and 5.

An IDL array maps to the Smalltalk Array class. Remember, though, that a Smalltalk Array is like a fixed-size OrderedCollection. It is one-dimensional, so multi-dimensional IDL arrays are mapped to Smalltalk Arrays whose elements are, in turn, Arrays.

So to access the last element of each dimension for a LongArray called aLongArray, write the following Smalltalk code:

```
value := (aLongArray at: 4) at: 5.
```

Attribute

An **attribute** is a shorthand way of declaring a pair of accessor functions—one to get the value of an attribute, and one to set its value. It is typically used to access a particular object that is part of the object defined by the interface (an "instance variable" in Smalltalk). However, no physical attribute needs to actually exist, because CORBA defines only an interface and hides the actual implementation details.

Accessors are very familiar to Smalltalk programmer. In Smalltalk, a CORBA attribute declaration automatically generates a pair of accessors, a "getter" and a "setter." These follow the standard Smalltalk convention, so that the declaration:

```
attribute string title;
```

generates the Smalltalk method title and title: to get and set, respectively, the value of the title attribute of the CORBA object.

There's one case, though, where only a get method is generated. This is when an attribute is declared as read-only, so it cannot be set through the IDL interface.

Here's the definition of an attribute declaration:

```
[ readonly ] attribute <parameter type spec> <simple declarator>
        { , <simple declarator> }*
```

Exception

An **exception** is a notification that an operation request was not performed success-fully. Each operation definition can include information about what kinds of run-time errors it may encounter. This is done via an IDL exception declaration. If an excep-tion is returned as the outcome of a request, then the value of the exception identifier is accessible to determine what sort of exception was raised.

Different Smalltalk dialects have somewhat different exception handling classes and messages. However, they all share a common theme. A block of code is sent as an argument in a message to an exception object. If that particular exception is raised anywhere inside this block, then another block argument to the message, a "handleBlock," is evaluated.

Because there are no standard Smalltalk classes and messages for exception han-dling, special CORBA-specific ones are defined. There are two such classes: one for exception objects and another for exception value.

A CORBA exception object conforms to the CORBAExceptionEvent protocol. This protocol has the following instance methods:

```
corbaHandle: aHandleBlock do: aBlock
corbaRaise
corbaRaiseWith:
```

The message corbaHandle:do: has two blocks as arguments. The aBlock is the Smalltalk block to be first evaluated. This block takes no arguments. The aHandleBlock is evaluated when the given exception occurs. It takes one argument, which is a Smalltalk object that conforms to the CORBAExceptionValue protocol. This protocol has a single instance method, corbaExceptionValue, which answers the Smalltalk Dictionary with which the exception was raised.

When code anywhere within aBlock wishes to raise an exception, it sends an exception object the corbaRaise or the corbaRaiseWith: message. If information should be sent about the exception, the corbaRaiseWith: message is used, with a Smalltalk Dictionary as the argument. This argument is passed as the argument to the aHandleBlock. If no information needs to be communicated beyond which type of exception occurred, the corbaRaise message is sent.

Wrapping code that may generate an exception within a block argument to a corbaHandle:do is optional. This message is used if you want to take some special action if an exception is raised. Otherwise, a standard Smalltalk error notifier win-dow will appear if CORBA exception is raised.

There is a set of standard exception definitions that may be returned by the invo-cation of any operation. They are automatically inherited by all IDL interfaces. Here are the standard exceptions.

Exception	Description
UNKNOWN	the unknown exception
BAD_PARAM	an invalid parameter was passed
NO_MEMORY	dynamic memory allocation failure
IMP_LIMIT	violated an implementation limit
COMM_FAILURE	communications failure
INV_OBJREF	invalid object reference
NO_PERMISSION	no permission for the attempted operation
INTERNAL	ORB internal error
MARSHAL	error marshalling parameter or result
INITIALIZE	ORB initialization failure
NO_IMPLEMENT	operation implementation unavailable
BAD_TYPECODE	bad typecode
BAD_OPERATION	invalid operation
NO_RESOURCES	insufficient resources for request
NO_RESPONSE	response to request not yet available
PERSIST_STORE	persistent storage failure
BAD_INV_ORDER	routine invocations out of order
TRANSIENT	transient failure – reissue request
FREE_MEM	cannot free memory
INV_IDENT	invalid identifier syntax
INV_FLAG	invalid flag was specified
INTF_REPOS	error accessing interface repository
BAD_CONTEXT	error processing context object
OBJ_ADAPTER	failure detected by object adapter
DATA_CONVERSION	data conversion error
OBJECT_NOT_EXIST	non-existent object, deleted reference

An exception declaration looks just like an IDL structure declaration. This is because the corbaRaiseWith: message is passed a Smalltalk Dictionary. Like an IDL structure, an exception structure maps to a Smalltalk Dictionary. The Exception declaration has the form of a set of exception type identifiers and their associated return value types.

Here's the definition of an exception declaration:

```
exception <identifier> { <member>* }
```

See the section "Structure type," for the definition of a member.

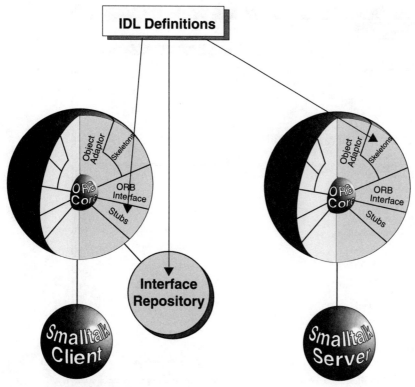

Figure 5-5. CORBA interface repository

Where to Find Everything— the Interface Repository

All the interfaces for an ORB are kept in its **interface repository (IR)**. The IR tells the ORB everything it needs to know about invoking operations on remote CORBA objects, and also handling invocations to local objects. The same IDL that is used to define what is placed in an interface repository also represents the client ORB's stubs and the server ORB's skeletons.

An interface repository is really just an active database of IDL declarations. In both varieties of CORBA-compliant distributed Smalltalks, they are kept in a class. When a Smalltalk image is saved, its current interface repository is also saved.

Distributed Smalltalk

In ObjectShare DST, the IR is in class DSTRepository. Actually, it IS the class DSTRepository. All publicly available CORBA objects are represented here. They are stored right in the class—each module is placed in its own instance method of the same name. You can open a browser on these instance methods, and you will see IDL.

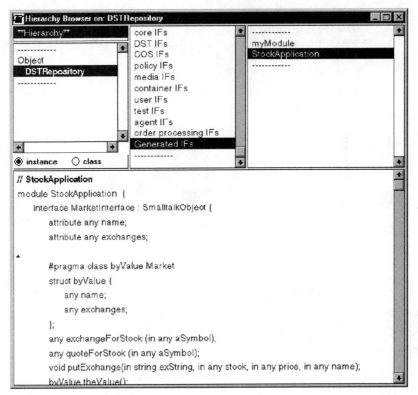

Figure 5-6. Distributed Smalltalk Interface Repository

For speed and efficiency, DST does not directly use the IDL representation of its IR, but a compiled version instead. This compiled version of IDL is to IDL source what bytecodes are to Smalltalk source. The internal, compiled version of the IR is stored as a Dictionary in the class variable InterfaceRepository of class ORBObject. A portion of the IDL in DST's interface Repository, as defined for The Stock Market Project example used later in this book, is shown in Figure 5-6.

How does DST manage to keep IDL in its instance methods, and have its own private compiler for IDL? A little-known fact: every class in Smalltalk can supply its own compiler, which can be something other than the standard Smalltalk compiler. In VisualWorks, the standard Smalltalk compiler class is the class Compiler, which is a subclass of SmalltalkCompiler. It is supplied by the method compilerClass in the Behavior method. But DST supplies its own compiler, class IDLCompiler, in its DSTRepository class compilerClass method. So it can compile the IDL in the instance methods of DSTRepository into its own data representation. This data is in the form of **metaobjects**. Metaobjects are higher level objects that describe ordinary objects. Smalltalk has its own metaobjects, such as instances of the class Class.

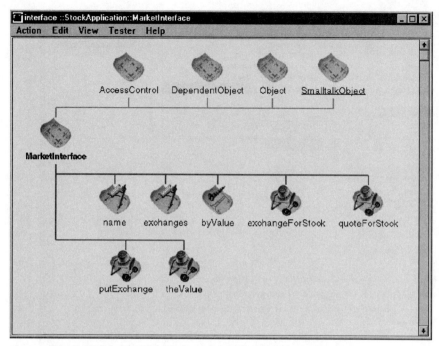

Figure 5-7. Distributed Smalltalk Interface Repository picture view

DST also has an alternate "sexy" Interface Repository picture representation that can also be displayed, as shown in Figure 5-7. Frankly, this representation is less detailed and useful then the simple textual one.

SmalltalkBroker

In DNS SmalltalkBroker, the interface repository is in the class ODLRepository. It is called ODLRepository instead of IDLRepository. This is because STB uses a superset of IDL called ODL, a proposed extension to IDL defined by the Object Database Management Group's ODMG-93 **Object Definition Language (ODL)** standard. But because ODL is a strict superset of IDL, you can ignore the OODBMS extensions and treat it just like any other IDL.

STB takes the same strategy as DST. It stores IDL (okay, ODL) modules as instance methods of class ODLRepository. The internal, compiled version of the IR is stored as a Dictionary in the ODLRepository class variable RepositoryDB. The compilerClass for ODLRepository is the class STBParser. Figure 5-8 shows SmalltalkBroker's representation of a portion of The Stock Market Project example.

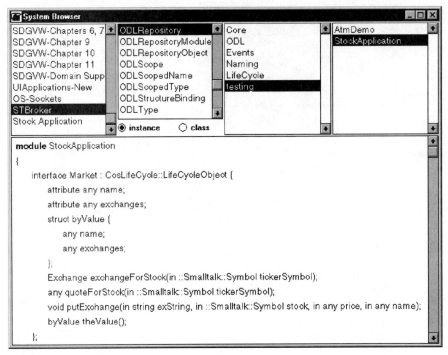

Figure 5-8. SmalltalkBroker Interface Repository

Interoperability

The CORBA 2.0 standard[†] defines how ORBs can communicate with each other. This is termed ORB interoperability. In CORBA terms, an ORB belongs to a single **domain**, which is equivalent to our object space. An invocation on a CORBA object, which is in another domain, must traverse a **bridge**. One of the neat things about CORBA is that the presence of bridges to other ORBs is completely transparent to client and server objects. A bridge effectively links ORB cores, acting as a sort of "wormhole" between them. You drop a request into your local ORB and, impervious to space (though not time), it magically appears on some remote ORB. This mechanism is very important for CORBA-compliant distributed Smalltalks, because the objects in different object spaces are on different ORBs.

Two protocols for bridges are specified: a **General Inter-ORB Protocol (GIOP)** and an **Internet Inter-ORB Protocol (IIOP)**. The IIOP is a special case of the GIOP. Other specializations of the GIOP may be defined in the future, but all CORBA 2.0-compliant ORBs must implement both the GIOP and the IIOP.

---

† As of this writing, CORBA 2.2 was the current standard level, however the existing CORBA-compliant distributed Smalltalks adhere to the 2.0 standard.

GIOP specifies a basic set of messages by which all ORB communication can be done. There are only seven message formats, but they are fundamental enough to handle everything. GIOP also specifies a **Common Data Representation (CDR)**, which maps the IDL data types to a canonical, low-level form. CDR automatically handles such things as byte ordering (whether bytes of native number types on a machine are ordered "big-endian" or "little-endian"), and data alignment (where some machine architectures required bytes of native number types to have a specific alignment in memory).

Via the IIOP, all ORBs can talk to each other using the Internet's protocol, TCP/IP. IIOP adds to the basic GIOP capabilities the functionality to deal with TCP/IP connections. It is the IIOP that is actually the ORB daemon that listens on a particular TCP/IP port.

Following a message through an ORB wormhole

Now that I've outlined all the basic structure and function of a CORBA ORB, let's follow a message that is sent to an object reference within a CORBA-compliant distributed Smalltalk.

First, the message is not immediately understood by the object reference because it is only a proxy, not the real object. Therefore, Smalltalk's standard "doesNotUnderstand:" method is invoked for the receiver. This method first checks that the ORB is running. If it is, it verifies that there is an interface defined for this object reference. If so, it does the following:

The method looks in its interface repository to make sure there is an operation defined for the interface that matches the Smalltalk message sent to the proxy. If there is a match, a header is first created by the GIOP. This header consists of some identifying information, such as the ASCII characters "GIOP" and a GIOP version number. Context information is passed (typically empty for Smalltalk), as well as the name string for the operation. Finally, the operation's "signature;" that is, its parameter and return value types, are used to marshal the Smalltalk arguments for the CORBA client request. The end result is a sequence of bytes, which are then shipped to the destination TCP/IP port ORB by the IIOP.

To accomplish the above, the GIOP uses the internal machinery of the dynamic invocation interface. It can cheat a little and be more efficient by not going through the interface explicitly, because it is integrated with the ORB core and knows how the dynamic invocation interface works internally. But the request object it creates is identical to the one resulting from using the dynamic invocation interface, and the invocation of this request is identical, as well.

On the remote CORBA ORB, the reverse happens. The byte stream is received and decoded. The header is read and verified, and the name for the operation is read. The operation is found on the remote ORB, and its signature is looked up. Then, the

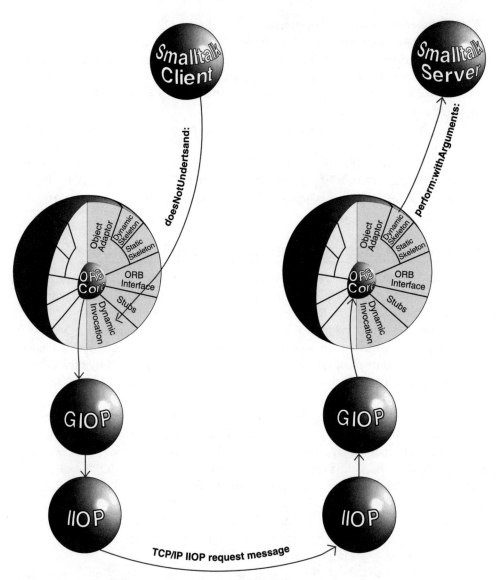

Figure 5-9. A Smalltalk message through CORBA ORBs

parameters are unmarshalled according to the signature. Finally, the standard Smalltalk message perform:withArguments: is sent to the remote object.

Similarly, on the remote ORB, the dynamic skeleton interface is used. This is, in fact, the only way that an operation can be invoked on a Smalltalk ORB, because Smalltalk is a dynamically bound language.

Smalltalk IDL Secrets

To take full advantage of CORBA-compliant distributed Smalltalks, you need to understand how Smalltalk classes translate to IDL types, and vice-versa. Even though Smalltalk is an untyped language, there is a mapping between the IDL types and the simplest built-in Smalltalk classes. Also, the notion of a completely general-purpose data type, a sort of "untyped" type, called "any," is provided in IDL. This can make life with CORBA much easier.

The amazing Any type

IDL typing was designed to accommodate statically typed languages such as C and C++. But if you are using it for distributed Smalltalk, you can take advantage of Smalltalk dynamic binding, and declare many arguments to be of type any. This gives you the flexibility to take full advantage of Smalltalk's polymorphism.

You can do this with impunity in DST, though not in STB. This will be discussed further in the section called "The common Smalltalk class mappings."

The built-in Smalltalk class mappings

Because all the IDL types are mapped to Smalltalk classes in some fashion, there is also a built-in mapping in the other direction, from these particular Smalltalk classes to IDL. This has important consequences for passing instances of these classes as CORBA parameters. It means:

1. These Smalltalk instances can be passed where an "any" is declared in the IDL interface for an operation.

2. The Smalltalk instances are passed "by value." That is, the state of the object is passed, and represented directly in a mapping from this IDL type to the destination implementation's language. Object references are not used.

Smalltalk class	IDL Type
Array	array
Boolean	boolean
Character	char
Float	float
Double	double
Integer	short, unsigned short, long, unsigned long, octet
OrderedCollection	sequence
String	string

What about the Smalltalk classes that have multiple IDL type mappings, namely Float and Integer? The Smalltalk object is automatically mapped to the appropriate IDL type, depending on its size. If it is an Integer that falls within the range of an IDL short, then that is what it is used.

Every CORBA parameter passed has a **TypeCode** associated with it. This TypeCode is one of the IDL types, and is automatically mapped back to an object of the original Smalltalk class. The TypeCode is what allows the server ORB and the object implementation to determine exactly what kind of parameter was passed.

Not every common Smalltalk class has a built-in CORBA mapping. There is no IDL concept of a Smalltalk Symbol, for example. But this situation can be easily remedied.

The common Smalltalk class mappings

Some standard Smalltalk classes beyond the ones defined by the OMG have corresponding CORBA IDL types. DST has a module called SmalltalkTypes that defines a large number of these. STB has a module called Smalltalk, which has fewer. IDL typedefs define IDL data types with the same names as their Smalltalk classes.

Another difference between DST and STB is that the mapping of these extra Smalltalk classes is automatic in DST. You can use the "any" type in place of these classes in their corresponding IDL usage. In STB, you must explicitly declare the scoped name, using the Smalltalk module in the IDL, as in `::Smalltalk::Symbol` to pass a Smalltalk Symbol.

This is an important distinction in philosophy between the two CORBA products: DST favors Smalltalk transparency over inter-language operability. If you try to pass one of these Smalltalk objects as an argument for an "any" to an ORB implementation that is anything other than DST, it generates an error. It has no IDL type declaration for this argument. What if you passed a Smalltalk Symbol where an "any" should go? A foreign language ORB wouldn't have a clue. DST, on the other hand, would handle it just fine because it has its own private knowledge, via an IDL interface, of this Smalltalk type.

STB could have chosen to do this as a special case, but then some degree of interoperability with other ORBs would be sacrificed. Because STB requires you to identify, in IDL, the interface for the common Smalltalk classes, the IDL is completely portable. The foreign language ORB would have explicit knowledge of the Smalltalk class mapping because it is told via an IDL declaration in exactly what interface it is declared.

Here are the Smalltalk classes that have mappings:

Smalltalk class	DST	STB
Association	✓	
Bag	✓	
ByteArray	✓	✓
ByteString	✓	✓
ByteSymbol		✓
ColorValue	✓	
Date	✓	
Dictionary	✓	
FixedPoint		✓
IdentityDictionary	✓	
OrderedCollection	✓	
Point	✓	
Rectangle	✓	
Set	✓	
Symbol	✓	✓
Text	✓	
Time	✓	

You are free to map any other Smalltalk classes, whether standard or custom, to IDL types. You are not limited to the ones in the table. The next section shows you how.

Moving between Smalltalk and IDL

There is a mapping between the above Smalltalk classes and IDL types. This means you actually get an object of the desired Smalltalk class, even though it may be passed by an IDL `struct`, which will, according to the CORBA Smalltalk mapping, always map to a Smalltalk Dictionary. A non-default mapping must be established between Smalltalk and IDL in each direction: Smalltalk to IDL, and IDL to Smalltalk.

To map a Smalltalk class to IDL, the class must have an instance method that answers its corresponding IDL interface. This method is called CORBAName. Once the mapping is established to IDL, the ORB can see the Interface Repository interface for this class, and all other information it needs to do the mapping.

Mapping IDL to Smalltalk is called **binding**. Binding from IDL to Smalltalk is performed two different ways in DST and in STB. DST puts binding information right into IDL. STB puts it into class methods. Its Binding Manager is used to load this into its binding database.

The DST way enables IDL to represent the binding information. This is both a negative and a positive. On one hand, it simplifies binding; on the other, it clutters the IDL with a lot of non-CORBA, DST-specific information.

DST does binding using its **class pragma**. A pragma is used to pass along implementation-specific information to a compiler; in this case, an IDL compiler. If another implementation doesn't understand a pragma, it simply ignores it. The following IDL tells DST to bind the Smalltalk class called OrderedCollection to the IDL type called OrderedCollection:

```
#pragma class OrderedCollection OrderedCollection
```

An IDL type called OrderedCollection also needs to be defined:

```
typdef sequence<any> OrderedCollection;
```

Passing an object "by value"

By default, CORBA ORBs pass distributed objects by reference, not by value. See Figure 5-10. Passing by value means that the receiver gets a local copy of the object. However, all IDL types are passed by value. So the basic types, plus unions, structures, strings, etc., are all passed by value. Any Smalltalk class you create your own typedef for may also be passed by value. An ORB knows how to pass a typedef by value because it has a language mapping between the IDL type and Smalltalk. However, a distributed object is generally defined by an IDL interface, not by a typedef.

The reason CORBA ORBs pass objects by reference is so that the objects remain opaque. This is by far the safest thing to do in a generic distributed environment such as CORBA. It means that the user of an object never needs to "peek inside." The only way to interact with an object is to send it messages.

An object is made up of both state and behavior. Behavior is defined by the operations an object knows how to perform. If there is no local implementation for this object, which would include its operations, then there is no way to do anything with the object. It's really only half an object, with state and no behavior. Besides, the internal state of an object defined by an interface is not, in general, available to an ORB. So as it is currently defined, CORBA couldn't pass such an object even if it wanted to.

This may seem confusing, especially because many languages freely pass arguments either by reference or by value with impunity. But in the *Object Management Architecture Guide*, the "strategy book" for the OMG that defines the Object Management Architecture (OMA), a sharp distinction is drawn between objects and non-objects. The combination of objects and non-objects constitute all denotable values.

According to the OMA, CORBA objects are by nature distributed and opaque. Non-objects are not. And all types, whether basic or constructed, are non-objects. This is in contrast to the Smalltalk environment, where all denotable values are objects.

While conceptually elegant, this "by-reference-only" strategy's shortcomings have been recognized by the OMG. The OMG issued a Request for Proposals (RFP) on

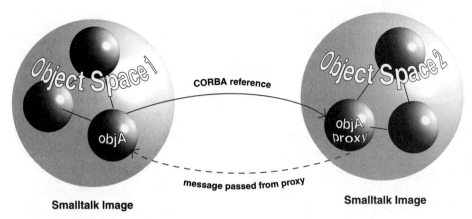

Figure 5-10. Passing by reference

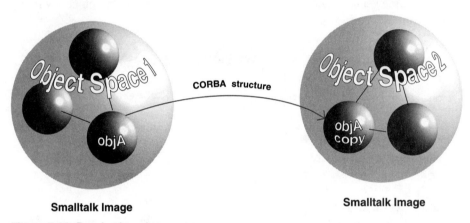

Figure 5-11. Passing by value

handling objects by value. This specification addresses the semantics of passing objects by value, including:

- The relationship between the identity of the object being sent and the object being received by value
- The relationship between the implementation of objects being sent and the object being received by value
- What happens when there is no appropriate implementation for an object

The Objects By Value Specification has completed, and only recent been approved by the OMG. Fortunately, we don't have to wait for the incorporation of this facility into existing distributed Smalltalks. There are ad-hoc techniques available right now for passing objects by value in both commercial implementations of CORBA distributed Smalltalk. I'll discuss these in the section "'By value' techniques."

Pros and cons

If you only have an object reference, and its implementation is in another object space, operations with this object can be expensive. They automatically create network traffic to and from the other object space when you perform operations on the referenced object.

If you are using distributed Smalltalk, you can have the same Smalltalk class represented in both object spaces. This is not readily possible, at least not yet, when using multiple languages via CORBA. You'd have to define implementations of the same class (IDL interface) in different languages to be able to inter-operate with object values.

Sometimes it's better to work with object references if the object implementation should be kept secure. If the object implementation is likely to change, and you don't want to have to update many client machines, passing by reference makes sense.

Here are some general guidelines for deciding whether to pass an object by reference or by value.

Situation	Pass by reference	Pass by value
many messages sent to object		✓
object used by other local objects		✓
secure server objects	✓	
implementation changeable	✓	
inter-language operability	✓	

"By value" techniques

To pass a Smalltalk object by value, you need to define a two-way mapping between a Smalltalk class and an IDL typedef. However, you can have the option of passing by reference, also. The secret to having it both ways is to add some extras to the IDL that defines the interface.

Here's an example using DST: suppose you have a Smalltalk class called Customer. It has two instance variables, name and address, with accessors for each. The corresponding IDL definition, in module myModule, is:

```
module myModule {
interface CustomerInterface : ApplicationSem {
    attribute any name;
    attribute any address;
};
```

Remember that an IDL attribute declaration is just a shorthand way of defining a get and set accessor operations. It does not imply the existence of state variables, though this happens to be the case in this example.

If you declare a class pragma within the above interface that associates an IDL structure with a Smalltalk class, you can pass those classes' objects by value:

```
#pragmaclass byValue Customer
struct byValue {
    any name;
    any address;
};
```

Using `byValue` within the scope of `CustomerInterface` forces only the state of a Customer object to be passed. Ordinarily, an IDL struct maps to a Smalltalk Dictionary. However in DST, the class pragma,

```
#pragmaclass byValue Customer
```

associates the IDL type byValue with the Smalltalk type Customer. In Smalltalk-Broker, which does not use the class pragma, you would use the Binding Manager to accomplish the same thing.

You must also define a Smalltalk CORBAName instance method to make the mapping from Smalltalk to IDL, as was done in the section "For public consumption: the Interface."

If you want to pass a Customer object by reference as an argument or a return object, use Customer. If you want to pass a Customer object by value, use Customer::byValue.

There is one more useful "by value" technique. It enables you to get a local object value from a remote object reference. To do this, add the following method to your IDL interface:

```
byValue theValue();
```

This declares an operation called theValue that returns the object by value. You must also define a Smalltalk method that corresponds to this IDL operation. Add the following instance method:

```
theValue
^self
```

This answers the object itself. However, the IDL declaration for the corresponding operation automatically converts this remote object reference to a local object value.

With this technique, you don't even have to keep track of whether the object is remote or local. It does no harm to send a theValue message to a local object, because it simply answers itself.

The final IDL declaration looks like this:

```
module myModule {
interface CustomerInterface : ApplicationSem {
    attribute any name;
    attribute any address;
    // define byValue, to return objects by value
```

```
#pragmaclass byValue Customer
struct byValue {
    any name;
    any address;
};
// define theValue, to answer us by value
byValue theValue();
};
```

The Naming Service

The Naming Service is the CORBA service that binds names to objects. This service enables distributed objects to be located by a simple, programmer-friendly name. The union of a name with an object is called a name binding.

In this book, I use the Naming Service in a pretty simple way, but it's actually quite sophisticated. It lets you create an arbitrarily complex hierarchy of name bindings. You could, for example, map and represent the entire directory structure of a disk using the Naming Service. All the necessary messages are present in the Naming Service to navigate through this structure.

Name bindings and names

A **name binding** is defined relative to a naming context. A naming context is an object that contains a set of unique name bindings. These name bindings can be any combination of terminal objects and naming contexts. You can think of the naming contexts as all the non-terminal nodes of a tree. While it's not required according to the CORBA 2.0 specification, both CORBA-complaint distributed Smalltalks make the Naming Service itself an object that is a naming context. This is very handy, because it places the Naming Service as the root node in an ORB's naming tree. A Naming Service can then understand all messages for a naming context, and if you don't need to create additional naming contexts, you don't have to.

A Name is actually a special object, a CORBA Sequence of name components. It's not a Smalltalk String, though it's easy to make a CORBA Name from one. CORBA 2.0 doesn't specify how to do this, but here's how it's done in DST:

DSTName onString: aString

and in STB:

CosNamingContext nameFrom: aString

Single and multiple naming services

In DST, there can be only a single Naming Service over all the communicating object spaces. You must decide where the Naming Service is to reside when setting up your DST ORBs. The other ORBs are set up to point to and utilize this common naming service.

STB is more flexible. You can have more than one Naming Service, and refer to any Naming Service at run-time. You just need the particular Naming Service's host name and port number. To get a reference to a Naming Service, you send your local ORB the namingService:port: message:

aNamingService := CorbaORB default namingService: <aHost> port: <aPort>.

Binding objects

There are four messages you can send to a naming context to create and attach a name binding to it. One is:

bind: aName obj: anObject

that binds the CORBA Name aName to any CORBA object of your choosing. There is also:

rebind: aName obj: anObject

which is similar, but allows aName to be already bound to the context. If aName were already bound to the context and the bind:obj: message were used, an AlreadyBound exception would be raised.

The message:

bindContext: aName nc: aNamingContext

is just like bind:obj:, except that the second argument must be another naming context. To round out this set of messages, there is:

rebindContext: aName nc: aNamingContext.

Unfortunately, DST does not follow the CORBA 2.0 standard for naming its Naming Service messages, so here is a table that shows the equivalent messages:

CORBA 2.0 Standard	DNS SmalltalkBroker	ObjectShare DST
bind:obj	bind:obj:	contextBind:to:
rebind:obj:	rebind:obj:	contextReBind:to:
bindContext:nc:	bindContext:nc:	contextBindContext:to:
rebindContext:nc:	rebindContext:nc:	contextReBindContext:to:

Resolving names

A single message, resolve:, is sent to a naming context with a Name to look up the object bound to that name. If the Name could not be found in the naming context, the NotFound exception is raised.

CORBA 2.0 Standard	DNS SmalltalkBroker	ObjectShare DST
resolve:	resolve:	contextResolve:

Unbinding names

Once a name is bound to a context, it may be unbound using the unbind: message. You must be sure that the name is bound to the context, or a NotFound exception is raised.

CORBA 2.0 Standard	DNS SmalltalkBroker	ObjectShare DST
unbind:	unbind:	contextUnBind:

Creating and deleting naming contexts

Naming contexts are objects that belong to a particular Smalltalk class. In STB, this class is called CosNamingContext ("Cos" for Common Object Services). In DST, it is called DSTNameContext. So one way to create a new naming context is by sending the message "new" to the naming context class.

Another way, the CORBA way, is to send the message newContext to an existing naming context object. The resulting naming context has no relation to the existing naming context other than it is implemented by the same Naming Service.

There is one more context creation message defined by CORBA: bindNewContext:, which takes a Name as the argument. This is a combination of newContext. and bind:. It creates a new naming context, and then binds a Name to it.

To delete a naming context, you send it the message destroy. The naming context must not contain any bindings, or the NotEmpty exception is raised.

CORBA 2.0 Standard	DNS SmalltalkBroker	ObjectShare DST
—	CosNamingContext new	DSTNameContext new
newContext	newContext	newContext
bindNewContext:	bindNewContext:	bindNewContext:
destroy	destroy	destroyContext

Listing and iterating over a naming context

Here are the messages for listing and iterating over a naming context. The first one is sent to a naming context, and has one input variable followed by two output variables. The input variable is the maximum number of bindings to return. The outputs are a Binding List, which is the sequence of bindings returned, and a Binding Iterator, which holds any additional bindings. The next two messages are sent to the Binding Iterator returned by the first message, and allow you to iterate through the additional bindings, either one at a time or N at a time.

CORBA 2.0 Standard	DNS SmalltalkBroker	ObjectShare DST
list:bl:bi:	list:bl:bi:	listContext:bindingList:bindingIterator:
nextOne:	nextOne:	nextOne:
nextN:bl:	nextN:bl:	nextN: bindingList:

Dynamic Invocation Interface and Deferred Synchronous Operations

The standard way to invoke CORBA operations in Smalltalk is by sending messages to transparent CORBA proxies, which look just like local Smalltalk objects. This implies synchronous operation—the thread of the local Smalltalk program execution is blocked until the remote CORBA operation is executed, after which control is passed back to the local Smalltalk program.

This may not always be the best thing to do. If the CORBA operation is time-consuming, your Smalltalk program is unresponsive until it is finished. The remote operation could, for example, access a database with a complex query, perform a very long calculation, or have to ask other networked computers for information. An unresponsive Smalltalk program is definitely a problem when it is supporting a GUI. At best, you can change the cursor to a special shape that indicates to the user that he must twiddle his thumbs. But this is a far from ideal solution.

Deferred synchronous

A better way is to use a CORBA deferred synchronous operation. This is a remote operation that can execute without necessarily blocking your Smalltalk program. When you perform a deferred synchronous operation, using a "send" message, the Smalltalk program does not wait for a response from remote object, but simply sends the request to it. This is still not asynchronous communication, because you have to explicitly check for a response. For true asynchronous communication, you need to use the CORBA Event Service, discussed in Chapter 7 in the section "Events and Asynchronous Communication."

To find out if the deferred synchronous request is complete, you have two choices. One is to issue the message "getResponse" or "getNextResponse" when you are ready. This causes the Smalltalk program to wait until the request has completed. The request is still synchronous, but waiting for it is simply deferred to a later time; hence the term "deferred synchronous."

The other choice—the more flexible one—is to issue the message "pollNextResponse." This message answers true if the request has completed, and false if it has not. This option gives you pseudo-asynchronous capability, albeit by polling. True asynchronous operation requires multiple execution threads, which most languages (including Smalltalk) do not have. You could, for example, create a polling loop in a separate Smalltalk process, set it up to poll every second, and have it set a semaphore when the request has completed.

But there is a catch when making a deferred synchronous request. Instead of letting your CORBA-based distributed Smalltalk software automatically create a dynamic invocation request for you when you send a message to a CORBA proxy, you have to work at a lower level and build the dynamic invocation request yourself.

Dynamic invocation request

In order to build a dynamic invocation request, you must create versions of all the message arguments as CORBANamedValues. A CORBANamedValue is a CORBA protocol that corresponds to a class of the same name in a CORBA-based distributed Smalltalk. Well, almost. In SmalltalkBroker this class is called CorbaNamedValue, while in DST it is called DSTNamedValue.

A CORBANamedValue has three attributes: name, value, and flags. The "name" is a String associated with the instance. The "value" is the CORBA object associated with the instance. The "flags" describe how the argument is to be passed.

CORBANamedValue looks just like CORBAParameter (CORBA's version of a value holder, described in the section "Operations do all the work" earlier in this chapter), with the addition of "name" and "flags." In fact, just as with CORBAParameter, there is a convenient message you can send to any Smalltalk object that answers a CORBANamedValue for the object. This message is:

    asCORBANamedValue: aName flags: argModeFlags

In general, you should use an argModeFlags of 0 in Smalltalk, because it is a bitmask for low-level information required by some programming languages, such as the memory allocation mechanism for the argument.

The CORBANamedValues that you create for your operation arguments are passed to another object, the CORBARequest. Again, there are some name differences. In SmalltalkBroker this class is called CorbaClientRequestEvent, and in DST it is called ORBRequest.

But the actual class name is not very important, because just as with a CORBANamedValue, you can create an instance of a CORBARequest by sending a standard message to another object. For a CORBARequest, you send the following message to a proxy (a CORBA object reference that you have typically get from the Naming Service):

```
createRequest: aCORBAContext
operation: aSymbol
argList: anOrderedCollectionOf CORBANamedValues
result: aCORBAParameter
request: aCORBAParameter
reqFlags: flags
```

The arguments for this message require some explanation. The argument aCORBAContext should be the empty array #(). CORBAContexts haven't been discussed because they are not used in the CORBA Smalltalk language mapping. But for generality, the above message contains a CORBAContext so that it corresponds exactly to the create_request operation that other CORBA language mappings implement. Similarly, the flags should in general be set to 0. As with the argModeFlags for a CORBANamedValue, the flags holds memory allocation information not required for Smalltalk.

The "operation:" argument, aSymbol, is the CORBA operation to be invoked in the receiver. Remember that this is *not* identical to the Smalltalk method name invoked in the receiver.

A simple example makes this clear: suppose you want to invoke a Smalltalk method named jump:howHigh:, where the first argument is the number of times to jump, and the second argument is a number giving how high to jump, in inches. The method answers a boolean that indicates if the jumps were successful.

One IDL declaration for this method would be:

```
boolean jump(in short numberOfTimes, in short howHigh);
```

The "operation:" argument would then be "#jump", not "#jump:howHigh:" because it must refer to an IDL operation, not a Smalltalk method.

This example also illustrates why CORBANamedValues are necessary for arguments. The name that a CORBANamedValue is the same as its identifier in the IDL. To create a CORBANamedValue with a value of 5 and the name 'numberOfTimes', you use:

```
nv := 5 asCORBANamedValue: 'numberOfTimes' flags: 0.
```

The "argList:" argument, anOrderedCollectionOf CORBANamedValues, is just that. You create an OrderedCollection of CORBANamedValue objects, in the order required for the operation.

The "result:" argument is an output. It is the answer that is returned by the remote Smalltalk method. You must first create a CORBAParameter to hold the output. This can be done simply by sending the asCORBAParameter message to nil.

The "request:" argument, aCORBAParameter, is an output argument that sets the value for the resulting CORBARequest. You must first create a CORBAParameter to hold the CORBARequest object.

Example Smalltalk code

Here the complete Smalltalk code for a dynamic invocation request and simple asynchronous polling using the above example.

```
request := nil asCORBAParameter.
result := nil asCORBAParameter.
nvList := OrderedCollection
        with: (5 asCORBANamedValue: 'numberOfTimes' flags: 0
        with: (12 asCORBANamedValue: 'howHigh' flags: 0.
theRemoteObject
        createRequest: #()
        operation: #jump
        argList: nvList
        result: result
        request: request
        reqFlags: 0.
request value send.
...
request value pollNextResponse ifTrue: [
        result value
            ifTrue: [ ... ]
            ifFalse: [ ... ].
    ].
```

≡Chapter 6≡

Choosing an Implementation

The four distributed Smalltalks are very diverse in their approaches to distribution and to the platforms they support.

ObjectShare Distributed Smalltalk

ObjectShare Distributed Smalltalk has some advantages. It is a mature product with a track record. It is CORBA 2.0-compliant, just like DNS SmalltalkBroker. It is supported by the oldest Smalltalk vendor company.

ObjectShare was formerly named ParcPlace-Digitalk, Inc. It changed its name to ObjectShare (cutting off its deep Smalltalk roots in the process) in September 1997. ParcPlace-Digitalk, Inc. was formed by the merger of ParcPlace Systems, Inc. with Digitalk, Inc. in August of 1995. ParcPlace Systems, Inc. was organized in 1988 in cooperation with Xerox Corporation to commercialize the Smalltalk language. It acquired ObjectShare Systems, Inc. in 1996 and Polymorphic Software, Inc. in 1996.

As of the first quarter of 1998, ObjectShare had 112 full-time employees. A total of 23 people were in product development and 15 were in customer support. As of 1998, it was a 20 million dollar company, down from over 50 million dollars in 1995.

If inter-language operability is important, ask ObjectShare for specific technical information on which ORBs it has been tested with. Because this product was bought already developed from HP, it remains to be seen how much technical resources ObjectShare will put devote to keeping it current.

The sophisticated CORBA Services may be important to you. ObjectShare is about equal to its competition, DNS, in implementing specific CORBA Services. It supports five: Naming, Event, Life Cycle, Concurrency Control, and Transaction

Services. That may change, however, depending on ObjectShare's commitment to DST, or on DNS's success in the marketplace.

The current version of ObjectShare Distributed Smalltalk has an important new feature: an Implicit Invocation Interface. This enables developers to create distributed applications without defining IDL interfaces. This makes partitioning an application much easier. If you use this feature, though, you sacrifice the inter-language interoperability of CORBA.

Like virtually all the object-oriented tool companies, ObjectShare has re-hitched its wagon to Java. ObjectShared has been faced with financial problems—due in part to the sudden scene-stealing of Java and partly its own doing in being complacent with superior technology and performing inadequate marketing and sales of its products (the Apple Computer syndrome).

Like other previously Smalltalk-only companies, including GemStone and DNS, it is devoting a major portion of its resources to Java. You will see this if you visit its Web site. But there is a considerable installed base of Smalltalk customers to support. ObjectShare is faced with walking the line between embracing "new" technology and supporting its existing customers.

As described in Chapter 4, "Case Study: The LLNL Data Warehouse," a powerful Web browser technology exists as an add-on, third-party tool for ObjectShare VisualWorks—and it doesn't required ObjectShare Distributed Smalltalk. It is called Classic Blend, and it's from Applied Reasoning Systems Corporation in Raleigh, North Carolina. Classic Blend does not use CORBA technology, but runs its own proprietary "mini-ORB" to link standard Web browser Java to a VisualWorks client on a server machine. The Web browser runs just a thin user interface layer. The result is the ultimate Web-based thin Smalltalk client.

While it is not technically distributed Smalltalk, because the client is running Java instead of Smalltalk, you do all your coding in Smalltalk. The Java user interface gets created on the fly, so it is as if you are using Smalltalk throughout. The Smalltalk image can also be run "fat," meaning, directly from the server. This is particularly useful during development. In this mode, you can readily develop and debug your Smalltalk program without the added complications of a Java client.

Classic Blend is an extremely useful, relatively mature technology that is available now. While a standard CORBA ORB-based product would be nicer architecturally, giving the client more flexibility, Classic Blend finesses the partitioning issues of distributed Smalltalk. Partitioning of the UI tier is done automatically.

And Classic Blend does not preclude the use of distributed Smalltalk. In fact, as Lawrence Livermore Labs proved, the addition of distributed Smalltalk makes the entire system quite flexible. You combine the Web browser deployment of Classic Blend with the scalability and power of distributed Smalltalk. To do this, you need a powerful application server, because every concurrent Web user must have a dedicated

VisualWorks image. But this puts the burden on the server, where it belongs. And your VisualWorks server image has its choice of distributed Smalltalk strategies. It can go the CORBA route, via ObjectShare Distributed Smalltalk or DNS Smalltalk Broker. Or it can go the GemStone route, by being a Smalltalk client of a GemStone server. It can even do both at once, as was done by Lawrence Livermore Labs.

IBM VisualAge Distributed Feature

If you are using IBM VisualAge for Smalltalk, its Distributed feature is an obvious choice. It is probably the most painless and transparent of all the distributed Smalltalks.

One advantage to trying the IBM Distributed feature is that it is relatively easy to evaluate. It's contained on IBM's standard evaluation and distribution CD-ROM, which provides a free 60-day trial. It is necessary to install the professional version of IBM VisualAge because the distributed feature requires the integrated ENVY support in this version.

With the IBM Distributed feature, you're committing to IBM VisualAge Smalltalk 100 percent. IBM will not be inter-operating its Distributed feature with other Smalltalks; it is relying on the separate CORBA route to achieve this.

IBM VisualAge runs only under Windows, OS/2, and the major UNIX boxes. If you need Macintosh support, you are out of luck.

IBM MVS Smalltalk

IBM also has a related technology that provides client/server Smalltalk. This is IBM MVS Smalltalk. It has also been called **VisualAge for Smalltalk Server (VSS)**. The idea is that you can develop a Smalltalk application that can be deployed on a central IBM MVS mainframe.

Clients connected to this server via the special VisualAge for Smalltalk Enablement component. This communicates with the server to replicate Smalltalk objects on the client. The client computer also contains the user interface. Client/server interactions occur within an MVS transaction processing environment, which is either CICS or IMS. The latter is an important consideration if you already run in such an environment.

To develop a MVS Smalltalk application, you initially had to use the OS/2 version of VisualAge for Smalltalk via an add-on called the Server Workbench feature. Oh, how IBM tries with OS/2! It have since provided the Server Workbench feature for Windows NT, as well.

IBM MVS Smalltalk is based on transactions in either CICS or ISM. A transaction executing on a single CICS or ISM thread starts up a Smalltalk image on the server. After developing your application on a workstation, you can test it using one of the transaction processing simulators available, such as CICS for OS/2, or the IMS Option of AD-MVS Micro Focus Workbench.

An application is deployed by **packaging** it, which creates an image for the Smalltalk Server. This image is then uploaded to the mainframe. You then build an executable load module by linking this image with the MVS virtual machine.

Debugging a deployed MVS Smalltalk application is difficult, because there is no client-side Smalltalk development environment. The client image is passive, designed only to be downloaded and run. You have to resort to a low-level debugger or a stack dump for clues about your bug.

DNS Technologies SmalltalkBroker

If CORBA 2.0 compliance and interoperability with other ORBs and languages is important, SmalltalkBroker is a likely candidate. It promises a high degree of standardization because of its availability for multiple Smalltalk dialects. Because it is also available for GemStone, Smalltalk classes that utilize SmalltalkBroker on a client can be readily moved to GemStone's server Smalltalk, and vice versa.

Currently, Smalltalk broker supported five CORBA Services: Naming, Event, Life Cycle, Collection, and Transaction. Relationship, Query, and Security Services were in the planning stage. The Transaction Service was key to supporting GemStone. When used with GemStone, it is integrated into the GemStone locking mechanism. It is fully X-Open compliant, and has thread a sub-thread support.

According to Jeff Eastman, who architected both ObjectShare Distributed Smalltalk (DST) and SmalltalkBroker, "As far as its relationship with DST, I think of SmalltalkBroker as 'the daughter of DST: smaller, lighter, faster, and better looking.' Customers who have evaluated both agree with this, only somewhat parental, observation."

DNS Technologies is the smallest of the companies providing distributed Smalltalk, so this could be a factor if your management insists on doing business with large firms only. CORBA technology is developing fast and furiously, so DNS's status might well change.

DNS Technologies is a privately held corporation founded in 1991. In 1997, DNS merged with Synergistic Software. It has other, unrelated products besides Smalltalk-Broker, and currently, they appear to be promoted more heavily by DNS than its SmalltalkBroker product.

GemStone Client/Server Smalltalk

If you need an object database, you should strongly consider GemStone. That's the major reason for its existence. GemStone has what is probably the most sophisticated and flexible OODBMS.

If you tend to be conservative on new technology, GemStone is a good bet. It's a veteran in distributed Smalltalk. Companies were doing distributed Smalltalk with GemStone before GemStone realized that it was providing powerful distributed Smalltalk technology via its shareable object database. The majority of distributed Smalltalk applications deployed in the world have been built with GemStone. Florida Power and Light, for example, has a large GemStone information system, as do several Fortune-500 companies.

GemStone also runs on a variety of platforms. On the server side, Sun SPARC, HP 9000, and IBM RS6000 are all supported, running their particular versions of UNIX. The fourth supported server platform is an Intel PC running Windows NT.

For clients, all three major Smalltalk dialects, ObjectShare VisualWorks, Object-Share VisualSmalltalk, and IBM VisualAge, are supported. You can run your clients on any supported platforms for the dialects of your choice. And you can mix and match these, of course.

Another advantage to GemStone is that it also supports CORBA on the server. DNS SmalltalkBroker can be purchased for GemStone as the "GemORB" product. It runs on Smalltalk Gems, the GemStone server processes. So you are not locked out of future CORBA distributed Smalltalk technology.

Typically, you would use the basic features of GemStone to communicate between client Smalltalk machines and a local server. The servers would then be interconnected via SmalltalkBroker CORBA ORBs to provide a high level of scalability. You might, for example, put business logic relevant for a particular site on a local Gem. This Gem could access objects at other corporate sites whenever it needs to via CORBA.

An alternative to linking GemStone servers via CORBA is to use GemStone's GemEnterprise product. This enables multiple GemStone servers to work together, and appear to clients as a single server. Using GemEnterprise, a GemStone server can have multiple remote "views" on objects in other GemStone servers. GemEnterprise can also act as a replication server for fault tolerant operation.

GemStone Systems Inc. has been a privately held company since its incorporation in 1990. Previously, it had been operated by Servio Logic Corporation. In 1997, GemStone Systems had total revenues of 18.7 million dollars—up from 13.7 million in 1996. As of the middle of 1998, GemStone had 43 people in their product development organization, out of a total of 132 employees. GemStone Systems applied to the SEC to go public in July of 1998.

Specs

Specification sheets are probably not in themselves sufficient to determine your choice of a distributed Smalltalk implementation. But comparisons of specs can be worthwhile.

DNS SmalltalkBroker

	Smalltalk Dialect	Minimum Memory	Recommended Memory

Intel PC
  MS Windows 3.1, 3.11, 95
  MS Windows NT 3.51/4.0
  OS/2 3.0, Warp
	VisualWorks
	VisualSmalltalk
	VisualAge
		unspecified	unspecified

Power Macintosh	VisualWorks	unspecified	unspecified
HP9000/700 & 800 HP-UX 10.1010.20	VisualWorks	unspecified	unspecified
IBM RS/6000 AIX 4.1.3, 4.1.4, 4.2	VisualWorks	unspecified	unspecified
SUN SPARC Solaris 2.4/2.5.1	VisualWorks	unspecified	unspecified
GemStone Server (all platforms via GemORB)	GemStone Smalltalk	unspecified	unspecified

ObjectShare Distributed Smalltalk

	Smalltalk Dialect	Minimum Memory	Recommended Memory

Intel PC
  MS Windows 3.1, 95
  MS Windows NT 3.51/4.0
	VisualWorks	8 MB additional	8 MB additional

Power Macintosh	VisualWorks	8 MB additional	8 MB additional
HP9000/700 & 800 HP-UX 10.10, 10.20	VisualWorks	8 MB additional	8 MB additional
IBM RS/6000 AIX 4.1.3, 4.1.4, 4.2	VisualWorks	8 MB additional	8 MB additional

SUN SPARC
  Solaris 2.4, 2.5.1
  Sun OS
	VisualWorks	8 MB additional	8 MB additional

IBM Distributed Feature

	Smalltalk Dialect	Minimum Memory	Recommended Memory
Intel PC MS Windows 3.11, 95 MS Windows NT 3.51,4.0 OS/2 Warp 3.0, 4.0	VisualAge	unspecified	unspecified
HP9000/700 & 800 HP-UX 10.10	VisualAge	unspecified	unspecified
IBM RS/6000 AIX 4.1.4, 4.2.0	VisualAge	unspecified	unspecified
SUN SPARC Solaris 2.5.1	VisualAge	unspecified	unspecified

GemStone

	Smalltalk Dialect	Minimum Memory	Recommended Memory
Client			
Intel PC MS Windows 3.1, 3.11, 95 MS Windows NT 3.51,4.0 OS/2 3.0, Warp	VisualWorks VisualSmalltalk VisualAge	16 MB	32 MB
Power Macintosh	VisualWorks	16 MB	32 MB
HP9000/700 & 800 HP-UX 10.10, 10.20	VisualWorks	32 MB	32 MB
IBM RS/6000 AIX 4.1.3, 4.1.4, 4.2	VisualWorks	32 MB	32 MB
SUN SPARC Solaris 2.4/2.5.1	VisualWorks	32 MB	32 MB
Server			
Intel PC MS Windows NT 3.51	GemStone Smalltalk	32 MB	64 MB
HP9000 HP-UX 10	GemStone Smalltalk	32 MB	64 MB
IBM RS/6000 AIX 4.1	GemStone Smalltalk	32 MB	64 MB
SUN SPARC Solaris 2.4/2.5	GemStone Smalltalk	32 MB	64 MB

A (Discordant) Note on the Macintosh

The Macintosh has definitely been a second-class citizen in the world of distributed Smalltalk. IBM doesn't support it, because IBM VisualAge isn't available for the Mac OS. ObjectShare VisualSmalltalk Enterprise doesn't run on a Mac, either. And ObjectShare VisualWorks runs on a Macintosh, but only recently has its Distributed Smalltalk been able to run on it.

The reason? Fundamentally, the original Macintosh TCP/IP system software, **MacTCP**, didn't have an **application programming interface (API)** that looked at all like standard Berkeley sockets. It's not stream oriented. On the other hand, the IBM PC-compatible TCP/IP system software, Winsock, is similar to Berkeley sockets. There is a single set of socket classes provided with VisualWorks that talk to the TCP/IP API of the native machine. This means it has been relatively easy for ObjectShare to support the PC once it had Berkeley socket communication. It also means that it was correspondingly difficult for them to support Macintosh MacTCP.

Who's to blame? You could say Apple, because MacTCP doesn't conform to either de-facto standard for its TCP/IP API. In fact, MacTCP was a quick TCP/IP "hack" for a large customer, using an undocumented package called "mdev," which accidentally turned into the Macintosh's TCP/IP software. You could also point the finger at ObjectShare, because it has not devoted the resources to supporting TCP/IP on the Mac.

Fortunately, there's a new Apple technology that provides a way out of this stalemate. This is **Open Transport**, Apple's latest networking software that supports TCP/IP, and is far superior to MacTCP. It has API calls that map readily to Berkeley sockets. The VisualWorks Socket library relies on socket primitives to bind, accept, connect, close, and listen for socket connections, and Open Transport has all of these. Open Transport is included with the latest versions of the Mac OS, and it will gradually replace MacTCP.

ObjectShare now has VisualWorks Distributed Smalltalk working on the Mac. It uses a new software component: Winsock for Mac. Support for it was put into the version 2.5.2 release. It is supported only for the PowerPC, not the older 680x0 processors. This shouldn't be a problem for most Macintosh users, because they will probably require the greater power of the PowerPC in order to run Smalltalk.

═══ Chapter 7 ═══

How to Partition an Application

Smalltalk takes message sending for granted. In ordinary Smalltalk, messages are cheap. And good object-oriented design encourages fine-grained objects, with lots of messages passing between them. Good design also encourages collaborations of classes—groups of objects of different classes that work together toward common goals.

With distributed Smalltalk, objects are partitioned across object spaces. You cannot ignore the overhead of messages sent between them. This overhead can easily become the performance bottleneck for your distributed application.

Minimizing Network Traffic

If your classes are not well designed, you may pay a heavy price in network traffic when you try to partition the classes over different object spaces. An illogical tangle of classes will undoubtedly cause difficulties in partitioning. Classes that work closely together should be placed in the same object space.

Improving your class design

You should not, in general, retrieve an object from a remote object space, use it to create a result object, and move that object back to the remote object space. If you think you have to do this, take a harder look at your classes. You may find that the method that does this processing really belongs in one of the remote object classes.

You may also find that you are putting some computation in the wrong place. Localize all your business rules that belong in a particular domain to a single object space.

For example, suppose you have a proxy for a Customer object called aCustomer. Consider the following code:

```
(aCustomer address country = 'USA') ifTrue: [
    stateAbbrev := aCustomer address stateAbbreviation.
    (stateAbbrev = 'AL' | stateAbbrev = 'HA') ifFalse: [
        ...
    ].
].
```

A great deal of business logic is performed locally to determine if aCustomer lives in the USA, but not in Alaska or Hawaii. This not only causes a lot of network traffic, but it is probably the wrong place to make this decision. Why not ask aCustomer directly? This is this a cleaner design, and you have to send the remote object only a single message:

```
aCustomer livesInContinentalUSA ifTrue: [
    ...
].
```

Collecting objects to send as a group

When you send objects to a remote object, try to see if you can group them together in some logical way. If you can send the objects grouped as a single one, it reduces traffic, even though the same amount of information is sent. This reduction is because a certain amount of overhead is associated with sending a message between object spaces, no matter how many objects it contains. A single message containing several objects is typically much cheaper than sending each object in its own message.

Sometimes, grouping objects to send to an object space is just a matter of looking at your code carefully. In the following case, we iterate over a local collection, adding each element to a remote collection:

```
localCollection do: [ :each |
    remoteCollection add: each.
].
```

Now consider the following Smalltalk code:

```
remoteCollection addAll: localCollection.
```

If localCollection had 1000 objects, you would save 999 message sends!

The IBM Object Visualizer tool

The IBM distributed feature has a tool called the Object Visualizer that can provide valuable information about message traffic. It has a Cluster View that gives a dynamic representation of object relationships.

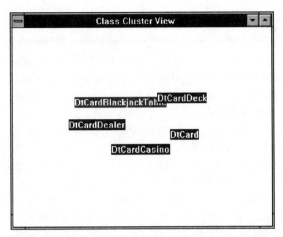

Figure 7-1. Blackjack game Cluster View after initialization

The Cluster View technology has been patented by IBM. You will not find it in any other distributed Smalltalk tool. The Cluster View displays each class (or instance of a class) as a colored rectangle. As the message traffic between classes increases, the rectangles move closer together. As message traffic drops, the rectangles drift apart. In addition, objects that are "hot" with message traffic turn increasingly brighter shades of red.

You can watch the cluster view in real time. If classes cluster together, this is a strong hint that they should be in the same object space.

The Distributed feature for IBM VisualAge for Smalltalk comes with a demo program, a simple multi-user blackjack game. Figure 7-1 shows the interaction between some of the game's classes after initialization, but before play has begun. There is no clear pattern at this point.

A more important view of the game, though, is during play, when message traffic patterns are not necessarily the same. Figure 7-2 shows that the classes DtCardDealer and DtCardBlackjackTable have so much traffic between them that they are coincident. DtCardDeck is just above, very nearby. Both DtCard and DtCasino have little traffic to them, so they are off to the side and bottom.

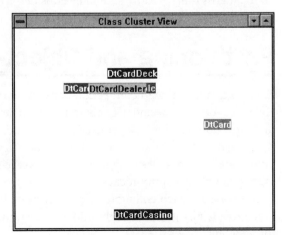

Figure 7-2. Blackjack game Cluster View during play

Think "Scalability"

The previous strategies have a common theme: scalability. You should consider the level at which objects exist and function in your application. Is an object a broad, high-level entity, like a "ledger" or an "inventory"? Or is it a smaller, more specialized unit, such as a "sell order" or a "stock item"?

A common problem that stands in the way of good distributed application design is a lack of recognition for the scale for objects. You may not be paying sufficient attention to exactly who is sending messages to whom. High-level objects should, in general, talk to other high-level objects, and they should do so through a well-designed, public message interface. These high-level objects simply the complexity of large programs. The concept of partitioning is therefore a generic one and is not confined to the practical matter of partitioning a distributed program over object spaces. And there is a vital connection between partitioning and interfaces:

> *"The act of partitioning a program into individual components can reduce its complexity to some degree. ... Although partitioning a program is helpful for this reason, a more powerful justification for partitioning a program is that it creates a number of well-defined, documented boundaries within the program. These boundaries, or interfaces, are invaluable in the comprehension of the program."*[4]

Once you have identified and architected high-level objects, you can make sure that they reside in particular object spaces rather than being smeared across multiple object spaces. This naturally improves both distributed application design and performance.

Sometimes the high-level objects aren't immediately apparent. It's very easy to concentrate on making good Smalltalk objects and messages and assume that once you have done this, everything else will fall into place. But you should also take a look at how groups of objects collaborate. Such collaborations may reveal higher level patterns that logically should be considered objects.

Partitioning and Object-Oriented Design

There is actually a deep connection between partitioning a distributed application and object-oriented design. Collaborations help define the high-level objects discussed in the previous section. The collective noun "a collaboration of classes," seems like a very natural term, like "a pack of dogs" or "an exaltation of larks." Such collaborations are in themselves useful, as they reveal the boundaries of objects and the messages that will be communicated between them.

But what are such collaborations in terms of formal object-oriented design? Can they provide any greater insight and architectural guidelines in the building of distributed Smalltalk systems?

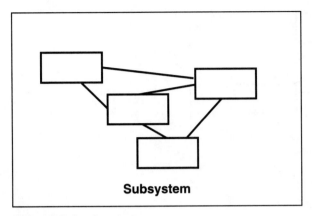

Subsystem

Figure 7-3. A subsystem

Subsystems

A collaboration of classes is generally termed a **subsystem** (see Figure 7-3). We have been thinking of such an entity from a "bottom-up" perspective.

Bottom-up design is done in the Responsibility-Driven Design methodology of Rebecca Wirfs-Brock et al.[5] They describe the discovery of subsystems in the analysis phase:

> *"As you begin to decompose the application, you might immediately identify classes. But you might also find other things: pieces that have a certain logical integrity, but that are themselves decomposable into smaller pieces. We will refer to these pieces as subsystems. A subsystem is a set of classes (and possibly other subsystems) collaborating to fulfill a set of responsibilities."*

Rumbaugh et al.'s OMT methodology describes subsystems in somewhat different, broader terms:

> *"A subsystem is not an object nor a function but a package of classes, associations, operations, events, and constraints that are interrelated and that have a reasonably well-defined and (hopefully) small interface with other subsystems.*
>
> *... Each subsystem has a well-defined interface to the rest of the system. The interface specifies the form of all interactions and the information flow across subsystem boundaries but does not specify how the subsystem is implemented internally. Each subsystem can then be designed independently without affecting others.*
>
> *Subsystems should be defined so that most interactions are within subsystems, rather than across subsystem boundaries, in order to reduce dependencies among subsystems."[6]*

Defining subsystems has other advantages. Subsystems reduce complexity by allowing you to think of a complex system in high-level terms. And in addition to

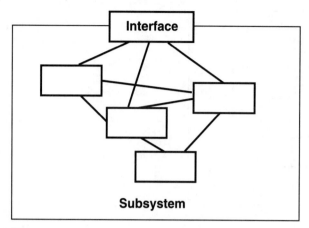

Figure 7-4. A subsystem with an interface

minimizing dependencies, the correct identification of subsystems automatically maximizes communication within each subsystem while minimizing communication between subsystems.

So is a subsystem itself also a class? It doesn't have to be. However, for distributed Smalltalk, requiring a subsystem to be a class makes a lot of sense.

The interface to a subsystem

Consider the interface of a subsystem, as described by Rumbaugh et. al. It is very desirable to have this interface defined in a single class, so that access to that subsystem is via the public methods of that class.

This has been recognized as a common theme, or **design pattern,** in object-oriented software. Gamma et al.[7] call this design pattern the Facade pattern. This design pattern is prescribed when you want to provide a simple interface to a complex subsystem. The Facade shields client objects from the entire set of subsystem objects, thereby limiting the size of the interface.

The Facade pattern deals with the issue of object **coupling**. Coupling can be defined as the use of methods in one object by another object. There is no widely accepted metric for object coupling, but in general, weak coupling occurs when there is a minimum of such inter-object dependence.

Using a Facade, weak coupling between the subsystem and its client objects is substituted for strong coupling. This lets you change the objects in the subsystem without affecting the client objects. We will term this facade the **interface** to the subsystem (see Figure 7-4).

High coupling between two subsystem objects makes it harder to understand one of them in isolation. On the other hand, low coupling leads to self-contained and thus easy-to-understand, maintainable subsystem objects. High coupling also increases the probability of remote effects, where errors in one object cause erroneous behavior of other objects. Loose coupling makes it easier to track down errors, which in turn improves testability and eases debugging.

If you implement your distributed system using a CORBA-complaint distributed Smalltalk, you will be faced with creating CORBA interfaces for your distributed objects. Remember that a CORBA interface maps to a Smalltalk class. If you want your distributed subsystem to be accessible via a single interface, then it should be implemented by a single Smalltalk class.

So, making a subsystem a class solves two distribution problems at once. It creates a partitioning of objects that is indivisible and therefore resides in a single object space. And it provides a public interface to that subsystem, cleanly defining its boundaries with other subsystems.

Vertical subsystems

So far, subsystems have been described in horizontal terms. That is, subsystems have been thought of as all at the same level, and composed of simple classes. Such subsystems can be accessed via their facades. But a single level of subsystem limits the amount of complexity that can be put into such a subsystem. Before long, as a subsystem grows more complex, we are faced with the same problem we had in organizing our original, non-partitioned system.

Subsystems composed of other subsystems create a vertical subsystem architecture. A vertical "stack" of subsystems constitutes a layered architecture.

A classic and highly successful example of a layered architecture can be found in the telecommunications world. This is provided by the Open Systems Interconnection (OSI) Reference Model (see Figure 7-5). It was developed in the late 1970s by the ISO international standard organization.

This model describes seven architectural layers that form a network communication protocol stack. Each layer uses and builds upon the services provided by the layer below it. The physical layer, at the bottom of the OSI Reference Model, was originally meant to be implemented by copper telephone wires. But because of the clean layering, the physical layer can be implemented by any other means, such as fiber-optic cables. All it needs to do is preserve the same interface to the layer above it—in this case, the data link layer.

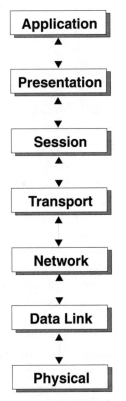

Figure 7-5. OSI Reference Model

This layering is an effective means for reuse and implementation-independence. Different upper-layer protocols, such as application services, may use the same set of primitives supplied by a lower-layer protocol. Conversely, different lower-layer protocols may be transparently substituted and not effect the operation of the higher-layer protocols.

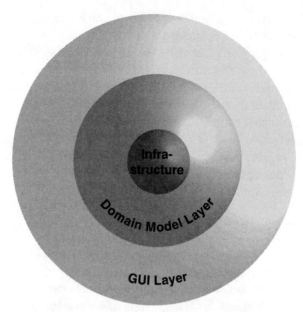

Figure 7-6. Three-tiered architecture

An important principle of layering is that any one layer should have no specific knowledge of any layer above it. Layered architectures may be in one of two forms: closed or open.

In an open layered architecture, a subsystem may directly utilize any layer below it, to any depth. In a closed layered architecture, a layer may only communicate with the layer or layers directly below it. This reduces dependencies between layers and properly encapsulates each. Put another way, a closed layered architecture utilizes only the public interface of a subsystem.

A well-designed object-oriented layered architecture is of the closed type. Although one can argue that an open layered architecture is less restrictive and may be implemented more efficiently, such an architecture is also less robust and actually less flexible than a closed layered architecture.

Of course, we have dealt with layered architectures before in this book. A client/server architecture and a three-tiered architecture are both examples of layered architectures. A tier is the same thing as a layer. As we saw in the discussion of three-tiered architectures, they are more flexible than two-tiered ones. This is because in designing such a system, the top and bottom tiers are typically specified as requirements. The user (ultimately) tells us what she wants her user interface to be. And the physical constraints of our system, such as a relational database server, specify the bottom layer.

Creating a middle layer results in the top and bottom layers not being "hardwired" together. This provides, among other things, implementation flexibility down the line. Without this flexibility in the OSI Reference Model, for example, telephone companies would have a much more difficult time switching to fiber-based physical layer (see Figure 7-6).

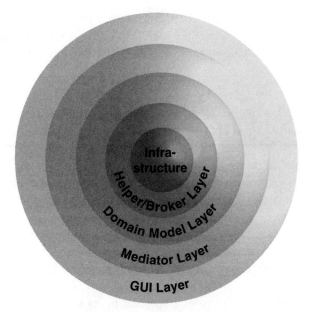

Figure 7-7. Five-tiered architecture

Other layering architectures are possible besides the three-tiered "middle tier" ones. As we saw in the LLNL Data Warehouse, a middle tier is not just a single thing. The middle tier is the domain model tier of a three-tiered architecture. But another layer can be defined between the middle layer and the inner, "infrastructure" layer. This is a **helper** or **broker layer**.

This layer was implemented by the LLNL Middleware Services team for their "helper" classes. Here, the middleware services, such as printing and scheduling, were part of the inner, and the helper layer was responsible for communicating to and coordinating these services.

On the client side, it is also possible to split out another layer. This is the **mediator layer**. [8] It is responsible for the details of communication between a **GUI layer** and the domain model layer. ObjectShare's VisualWorks uses subclasses of ApplicationModel to form this layer. In this case, it mediates between the GUI widgets and the domain model.

However, a mediator layer can also be put to good use in a distributed system. An example of this is in the Classic Blend product. Here, the mediator layer forms the mini-ORB distribution mechanism that links the Java GUI with its Smalltalk domain model (see Figure 7-7).

So we have added two more layers, to come up with a five-tiered architecture! This may sound imposing and as if we are adding extra layers that will just create additional overhead and complicate an overall design. But layering adds flexibility and can be well worth the extra cost down the line. Your system will be more agile in responding to growth and new requirements. And you will be better able to deal with performance issues by having the flexibility to move functionality between layers.

You may actually already have these layers—you just don't know it because you haven't done enough analysis to make them explicit. In this case, once you "mine" the layers that you had all along, you will gain additional insight and potential control over your application.

Object Copying

Another technique to minimize network traffic is to make local copies of remote objects. This is also called **caching**. Do this when you must send lots of messages to an object, but the object's state should logically be kept elsewhere—at a central server, for example.

You have to do this judiciously, though. When you copy a remote object so that it also resides locally, you must distinguish between messages sent to the local or remote object. If you change the state of the local object, you must not forget to (eventually) update the remote object as well.

Making local copies of objects requires fetching **by value**. This will be discussed at length in the Stock Market Project example. See also Chapter 4.

Events and Asynchronous Communication

When a Smalltalk program is confined to a single object space, the time it takes to execute a single method to execute is generally not an issue. But distributed Smalltalk changes this.

The standard model for distributed Smalltalk uses a local proxy object that forwards its message to a remote object, waits for the remote method to finish executing, and then returns its result to the sender. This works well most of the time. But what if the remote method is very time consuming? Perhaps it spawns other messages to other, far-flung distributed objects. Or what if it encapsulates a large legacy application, which could take many seconds to produce an answer?

The solution is to use events to communicate. An event permits uncoupling the invocation of a method on a remote object, and the execution of that method.

One of the most important features that events can provide is the ability to do asynchronous communication. Events themselves do not imply asynchronous communication. But all event facilities are designed to allow asynchronous communication as an option.

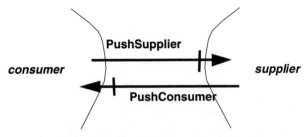

Figure 7-8. Push-style communication

How asynchronous communication works

At the level of a computer's hardware, true asynchronous communication requires interrupts. The computer program needs to be interrupted from its normal flow of execution in order to asynchronously execute code that processes the reply.

This typically happens via one of two mechanisms. The reply from the remote object can itself trigger a hardware interrupt, and this interrupt does a "callback" of a particular object's method. The second mechanism is more indirect: A task scheduler in the operating system takes periodic control (generally, by a clock interrupt) and polls to see if anything besides the currently executing program needs to be run. In the case of an asynchronous reply, it changes the execution context to run the reply-processing code.

CORBA-compliant asynchronous events

CORBA-Complaint Event Service is provided by the two CORBA-based distributed Smalltalks and by the IBM Distributed feature. It is not supported between GemStone clients and servers; however it is supported with CORBA via GemORB.

Asynchronous events provided by CORBA Event Service go by the arcane name of "typed push model." This name is due to the fact that CORBA Event Services allows both suppliers of events and consumers of events to operate in either a "push to the other object" or "pull from the other object" fashion. Although this is conceptually symmetrical in that it generates various combinations, some more useful than others, this generality can also be quite confusing.

In the push model, suppliers "push" event data to consumers; that is, event suppliers communicate event data by invoking push operations on the *PushConsumer* interface (See Figure 7-8). To set up a push-style communication, consumers and suppliers exchange *PushConsumer* and *PushSupplier* object references.

In the pull model, event consumers "pull" event data from suppliers; that is, consumers request event data by invoking pull operations on the *PullSupplier* interface (See Figure 7-9). To set up a pull-style communication, consumers and suppliers must exchange *PullConsumer* and *PullSupplier* object references.

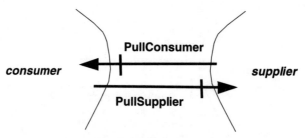

Figure 7-9. Pull-style communication

To do asynchronous communication using CORBA, you need to use two events—one from the local object to the remote object, and another from the remote object to the local object.

The first event is the easy one. Here, the local object sends an event, which contains a parameter, to the remote object. The local object "pushes" the event that it supplies to the remote object, which acts as the event consumer, hence it uses the CORBA Event Services *PushConsumer* interface. This interface uses the push: message, which has as its argument the parameter. The push: message has no return value, so execution on the local object is not blocked.

The second event is more complex, because it must operate asynchronously. The typed push model is used in CORBA to asynchronously return a result from a remote object to a local object. In the typed push model, a supplier (the remote object) calls an operation on the consumer (the local object) using some mutually agreed interface. The interface is defined in IDL and may contain any operations subject to the following restrictions:

- All parameters must be *in* parameters only.
- No return values are permitted.

This form of communication is designed to return results only—hence the requirement for in parameters. These parameters are where the result are supplied. Since there is nothing more to do at the remote object after the results are returned to the local object, no return value to that remote object can be sent.

To set up typed push-style communication, a consumer (local object) and supplier (remote object) exchange *TypedPushConsumer* and *PushSupplier* object references. The remote object then invokes the getTypedConsumer method of the *TypedPushConsumer* interface, which returns an object reference supporting the interface, *I*, referred to as an *I-reference*.

The particular interface, *I*, that the reference supports is dependent on the particular *TypedPushConsumer* and must be mutually agreed by both sides. Once the remote object has obtained the *I*-reference, it can call operations in interface *I* on the local object.

≡Chapter 8≡

AN EXAMPLE:
The Stock
Market Project

The Stock Market Project is a Smalltalk program designed to illustrate writing a full application in distributed Smalltalk. It allows a user to buy and sell a stock on a particular stock exchange. A simple user interface lets you select an exchange, and then any stock on that exchange (see Figure 8-1).

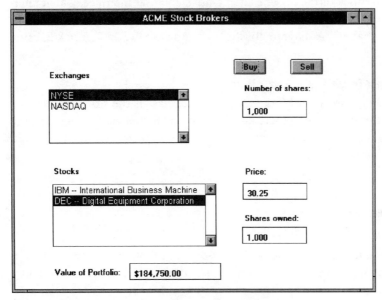

Figure 8-1. The Stock Market Project user interface

The current price for a selected stock is displayed, and you can buy or sell shares of that stock. Your holdings for the stock are updated on the screen, as well as the total value of your portfolio. As a result of each buy or sell transaction, a stock price can shift, simulating a real stock market.

This example will be implemented in all four distributed Smalltalks. This gives us an opportunity to compare how the different distributed environments would accommodate the identical program.

The Design

This program was intentionally written first as a stand-alone application. Just to see the architectural impact of distribution, no consideration was given to the fact that objects would later reside in separate places. We see later what we have to do to distribute it efficiently.

This strategy is useful exercise for a couple of reasons. Sometimes, you don't have the luxury of designing a distributed program as such from scratch. And it's also good to separate out overall design considerations from distribution-specific ones so you understand them better. You can always go back and iterate the design.

This example is presented first in ObjectShare VisualWorks, and later in IBM VisualAge. As you'll see, there is little difference beyond the user interface class.

The classes

There are six classes that comprise this example: Market, Exchange, Stock, Portfolio, StockHolding, and StockTerminal. The latter class is the user interface, which interacts with the other objects. It allows the user to simulate the buying and selling of stocks on stock exchanges. A diagram for these classes is shown in Figure 8-2, using OMT notation.

Making a killing in the Market class

I first introduce the class called Market. The Market class is the stock market as a whole. It is a singleton, meaning there can only be one instance of it. Sending the "new" message to the class always answers the same single instance, which is kept in the class variable MarketSingleton.

Class:	Market
Superclass:	Object
Instance variables:	exchanges
Class variables:	MarketSingleton

Here are the instance methods that are accessors. The first, exchanges, answers a Dictionary of Exchange objects. It uses lazy initialization to create an initially empty

single object space

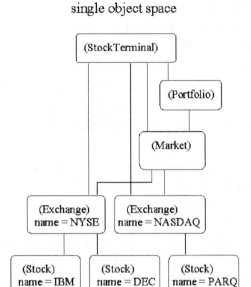

Figure 8-2. The object diagram for the Stock Market Project

Dictionary. The keys into this Dictionary are the names of the exchanges, and the corresponding values are the Exchanges themselves.

```
exchanges
    exchanges isNil ifTrue: [ exchanges := Dictionary new ].
    ^ exchanges
```

The next instance method answers a particular Exchange, given its name. It looks up the name in the exchanges dictionary, and if it doesn't already exist, it creates a new Exchange by this name.

```
exchangeNamed: aString
    ^self exchanges at: aString ifAbsent: [
        self exchanges at: aString
        put: (Exchange new name: aString)
    ]
```

An Exchange object knows how to answer true if it includes a stock named by a particular ticker symbol. The following method determines which Exchange a given stock ticker symbol is on:

```
exchangeForStock: aSymbol
    ^self exchanges detect: [ :exchange |
        exchange includesStock: aSymbol
    ] ifNone: [ nil ]
```

Finally, the following accessor method uses exchangeForStock: to get a quote for a particular stock ticker symbol. It does this by sending the message quoteForStock: to the correct Exchange for the stock.

```
quoteForStock: aSymbol
    ^(self exchangeForStock: aSymbol) quoteForStock: aSymbol
```

There is one "action" method in the Market class. It sets a particular price for a Stock on a particular Exchange. It uses the putStock:price:name: message implemented by the Exchange class.

```
putExchange: exString stock: aSymbol price: aNumber
        name: nameString
    (self exchangeNamed: exString) putStock: aSymbol
        price: aNumber name: nameString.
```

The Market class has is an instance initialization method called initialize. It sets up a few Stocks on two Exchanges. You could, of course, substitute whatever exchanges and stocks you prefer.

```
initialize
    self putExchange: 'NASDAQ' stock: #PARQ price: 10
        name: 'ObjectShare'.
    self putExchange: 'NYSE' stock: #IBM price: 95
        name: 'International Business Machine'.
    self putExchange: 'NYSE' stock: #DEC price: 35
        name: 'Digital Equipment Corporation'.
```

On the class side, Market has a class initialization method, initialize, which resets its only instance to nil:

```
initialize
    MarketSingleton := nil
```

The new method answers the market singleton object.

```
new
    ^self marketSingleton
```

Finally, the class method marketSingleton answers the singleton object, creating a one if it doesn't already exist.

```
marketSingleton
    MarketSingleton isNil ifTrue: [ MarketSingleton := self
        basicNew initialize ].
    ^ MarketSingleton
```

The Exchange class

There is one Exchange object for each stock exchange. It has a name, and a Dictionary of Stock objects.

Class:	Exchange
Superclass:	Object
Instance variables:	name stocks

The accessors for the two instance variables are as follows. The stocks variable has no "setter" method, because its "getter" method does lazy initialization to set the stocks as an IdentityDictionary.

```
name
    ^name
name: aString
    name := aString
stocks
    stocks isNil ifTrue: [stocks := IdentityDictionary new].
    ^stocks
```

The following methods take a stock ticker symbol as their argument. The first answers the current price for the stock. The next method answers true if the stock is included in the Exchange; false if it's not.

```
quoteForStock: aSymbol
    ^( stocks at: aSymbol ifAbsent: [ ^0 ] ) price

includesStock: aSymbol
    ^self stocks keys includes: aSymbol
```

To buy a stock on an exchange, you send that exchange the message *buyStock:shares:account*:

```
buyStock: aSymbol shares: aNumber account: anAccount
    self fakeStockPriceMovement: aSymbol shares: aNumber.
```

Because this is a simulation, no record is made of the transaction, and anAccount is ignored. However, to make this program do something entertaining, the stock price is moved according to a simple-minded algorithm:

This following method sends putStock:price: to the exchange.

```
fakeStockPriceMovement: aSymbol shares: shares
    | price adjust |
    price := self quoteForStock: aSymbol.
    adjust := shares * price / 100000.
    adjust abs < 0.125 ifTrue: [ ^self ].
    price := price + adjust.
    price < 1 ifTrue: [ price := 1 ].
```

```
"round price to nearest 8th"
price := ( ( ( price * 8 ) asInteger ) / 8 ) asFloat.
self putStock: aSymbol price: price.
```

This method, in turn, sends putStock:price:name: with an empty string for the stock name:

```
putStock: aSymbol price: aNumber
    self putStock: aSymbol price: aNumber name: ''.
```

If this stock was not already on the exchange, it would be added with the given name. But the method putStock:price: is only called if the stock already exists on the exchange, so we can be assured that the name string will be ignored. So putStock:price:name: does a double duty: it puts the given stock into the exchange at the given price. If it doesn't exist, it is added. Otherwise, its price is updated.

```
putStock: aSymbol price: aNumber name: aName
    | stock |
    stock := self stocks at: aSymbol ifAbsent: [
        stocks
            at: aSymbol
            put: (Stock new tickerSymbol: aSymbol; name: aName).
    ].
    ^stock price: aNumber
```

To sell a stock, you send the exchange the message sellStock:shares:account:. This looks the same as buyStock:shares:account:, except that the number of shares is negated. This will subtract, rather than add shares.

```
sellStock: aSymbol shares: aNumber account: anAccount
    self fakeStockPriceMovement: aSymbol shares: aNumber negated.
```

Finally, an Exchange knows how print itself by implementing the standard Smalltalk printOn: method. This simply prints the exchange's name.

```
printOn: aStream
    aStream nextPutAll: self name.
```

Maintaining the Portfolio class

A single Portfolio is held by an instance of the user interface class, StockApplication. A Porfolio maintains a Dictionary of StockHoldings.

Class:	Portfolio
Superclass:	Object
Instance variables:	account market stockHoldings

Here are the accessors for the instance variables for a Porfolio object:

```
account
    ^account
```

```
account: anAccount
    account := anAccount
```

Answer the holding for the stock ticker symbol. If there is none, try to create it.

```
holdingForStock: aSymbol
    ^self stockHoldings at: aSymbol ifAbsent: [
        self newHolding: aSymbol.
    ]
```

The market is the single instance of the Market object, which we can get from the StockTerminal class that is defined later.

```
market
    market isNil ifTrue: [ market := StockTerminal
    marketSingleton].
    ^ market
```

Answer the number of shares owned for the given stock ticker symbol. If this stock is not in the holdings, answer 0.

```
sharesForStock: aSymbol
    | holding |
    holding := self stockHoldings at: aSymbol ifAbsent: [ ^0 ].
    ^holding numberOfShares
```

```
stockHoldings
    stockHoldings isNil ifTrue: [ stockHoldings :=
    IdentityDictionary new ].
    ^stockHoldings
```

Answer the value of this Portfolio by adding all the values of the stockHoldings, using the current prices for the stocks.

```
value
    | value price |
    value := 0.
    stockHoldings keysAndValuesDo: [ :symbol :holding |
        price := ( self market exchangeForStock: symbol )
    quoteForStock: symbol.
        value := value + ( price * (self sharesForStock: symbol)
    ).
    ].
    ^value
```

The following instance method adds a given number of shares to the stock holding identified by a given ticker symbol. It answers "nil" if there is no such ticker symbol on any Exchange, or it answers with the number of current shares for this holding.

```
addToHolding: aSymbol shares: aNumber
    | holding |
    holding := self holdingForStock: aSymbol.
    holding isNil ifTrue: [ ^nil ].
    ^holding addShares: aNumber
```

This method subtracts a given number of shares to the stock holding identified by a given ticker symbol. It answers "nil" if there is no such ticker symbol on any Exchange, or if there are not enough shares in this StockHolding from which to subtract. Otherwise, it answers with the new number of shares for this holding.

```
subtractFromHolding: aSymbol shares: aNumber
    | holding |
    holding := self stockHoldings at: aSymbol ifAbsent: [ ^nil ].
    ^holding subtractShares: aNumber
```

This method buys shares of a given stock. If the stock doesn't exist, it answers #noSuchStock. Otherwise, it adds these shares to our holdings, and informs the appropriate exchange of the transaction. It answers the current number of shares of the stock owned.

```
buyStock: aSymbol shares: aNumber
    | exchange newShares |
    exchange := self market exchangeForStock: aSymbol.
    exchange isNil ifTrue: [ ^#noSuchStock
    ] ifFalse: [
        newShares := self addToHolding: aSymbol shares: Number.
        exchange buyStock: aSymbol shares: aNumber
            account: self account.
    ].
    ^newShares
```

This method sells shares of a given stock. If the stock doesn't exist, it answers #noSuchStock. Otherwise, it removes these shares from our holdings and informs the appropriate Exchange of the transaction. If we don't have enough shares to sell, it answers #notEnoughShares. Otherwise, it answers with the current number of shares of the stock owned.

```
sellStock: aSymbol shares: aNumber
    | exchange newShares |
    exchange := self market exchangeForStock: aSymbol.
    exchange isNil ifTrue: [ ^#noSuchStock
```

```
] ifFalse: [
    newShares := (self subtractFromHolding: aSymbol shares:
Number).
    newShares isNil ifTrue: [ ^#notEnoughShares ].
    exchange sellStock: aSymbol shares: aNumber
        account: self account.
].
^newShares
```

The newHolding: method creates a new StockHolding for a stock ticker symbol. It first makes sure the stock exists on some exchange, and if not, it answers "nil." Otherwise, it answers the new StockHolding object, which it has placed into the stockHoldings IdentityDictionary as the value for the ticker symbol key.

```
newHolding: aSymbol
    | holding |
    ( self market exchangeForStock: aSymbol ) isNil ifTrue: [ ^nil
    ].
    holding := StockHolding new.
    self stockHoldings at: aSymbol put: holding.
    ^holding
```

A Portfolio knows how print itself by implementing the Smalltalk printOn: method. It passes the printOn: message down to its account instance variable.

```
printOn: aStream
    self account printOn: aStream
```

There is one instance initialization method, initialize, which gives a default name to the account.

```
initialize
    self account: 'My Account'.
```

On the class side, there is one instance creation method, which follows the common Smalltalk "super new initialize" form. This invokes the previous instance initialization method.

```
new
    ^super new initialize
```

Taking stock of the Stock class

A Stock object encapsulates the knowledge for a particular stock. It has a name, a ticker symbol, and a current price.

Class: Stock
Superclass: Object
Instance variables: name tickerSymbol price

Here are the accessors for a Stock's instance variables.

```
name
    ^name

name: aString
    name := aString

price
    ^price

price: aNumber
    price := aNumber

tickerSymbol
    ^tickerSymbol

tickerSymbol: aSymbol
    tickerSymbol := aSymbol
```

A stock knows how print itself by implementing the Smalltalk printOn: method. It first prints its ticker symbol, and then its name. When the list of stocks is shown in the window's list widget, each stock in the list is automatically asked by the VisualWorks to print itself.

```
printOn: aStream
    aStream
        nextPutAll: self tickerSymbol asString;
        nextPutAll: ' -- ';
        nextPutAll: self name.
```

How much do you have? The StockHolding class

Instances of the StockHolding class are what allow a Portfolio to maintain the shares of all stocks in the Portfolio. A Portfolio instance has a dictionary called stockHoldings that associates stock ticker symbols with StockHolding instances.

Class:	StockHolding
Superclass:	Object
Instance variables:	numberOfShares

The StockHolding class has one instance variable—number of shares—so all its method are concerned with maintaining these shares.

```
numberOfShares
    numberOfShares isNil ifTrue: [ numberOfShares := 0 ].
    ^numberOfShares

numberOfShares: aNumber
    ^numberOfShares := aNumber
```

The following method adds a given number of shares and answers the new number of shares for the holding.

```
addShares: aNumber
    ^self numberOfShares: self numberOfShares + aNumber
```

This method subtracts a given number of shares, and answers the number remaining. If there are not enough shares, it answers "nil."

```
subtractShares: aNumber
    self numberOfShares < aNumber ifTrue: [ ^nil ].
    ^self numberOfShares: self numberOfShares - aNumber
```

The user interface: the StockTerminal class

This is the Smalltalk dialect-specific user interface class, called StockTerminal. The following is for VisualWorks 2.5.

```
Class: StockTerminal
Superclass:   ApplicationModel
Instance variables:    exchanges stocks price portfolio
    numberOfShares
    sharesOwned portfolioValue
Class variables: MarketSingleton
```

Here are the accessors for the value model instance variables. They all perform lazy initialization, so that the first time a model is accessed, it is created. Value models all respond to the message value to get their value, and value: to set their value. The VisualWorks user interface uses value models for all the objects that correspond to the information for screen widgets.

Because there is just one market, let's make it a class variable, called MarketSingleton, that can be readily accessed by the instance method called market:

```
market
    ^self class marketSingleton
```

```
marketSingleton (class)
    MarketSingleton isNil ifTrue: [MarketSingleton := Market new
    ].
    ^ MarketSingleton
```

```
portfolio
    portfolio isNil ifTrue: [ portfolio := Portfolio new ].
    ^portfolio
```

```
numberOfShares
    numberOfShares isNil ifTrue: [ numberOfShares := 0 asValue ].
    ^numberOfShares
```

```
portfolioValue
    portfolioValue isNil ifTrue: [ portfolioValue := 0 asValue ].
    ^portfolioValue

price
    price isNil ifTrue: [ price := 0 asValue ].
    ^price

sharesOwned
    sharesOwned isNil ifTrue: [ sharesOwned:= 0 asValue ].
    ^sharesOwned
```

The exchanges object is a VisualWorks SelectionInList, a value model for a list of items from which one item can be selected. Its visual counterpart is a widget that displays a list, and selects an item by highlighting it when the user clicks it with the mouse button.

During lazy initialization, after the SelectionInList is created, it is initialized with a list of exchanges gotten from the market instance variable. Also, the dependency message onChangeSend:to: is sent to the newly created exchanges value model, so whenever the user changes the selection, the message changedExchange is sent to the StockTerminal instance.

```
exchanges
    exchanges isNil ifTrue: [
        exchanges := SelectionInList new.
        exchanges list: self market exchanges values.
        exchanges selectionIndexHolder
            onChangeSend: #changedExchange to: self
    ].
    ^exchanges
```

The same thing is done with the stocks instance variable, except it does not need to be initialized with a list. When the changedExchange message is received, it sets the list of stocks for the selected exchange.

```
stocks
    stocks isNil ifTrue: [
        stocks := SelectionInList new.
        stocks selectionIndexHolder
            onChangeSend: #changedStock to: self.
    ].
    ^stocks

setPortfolioValue
    self portfolioValue value: self portfolio value.
```

```
setSharesOwned: aSymbol
    self sharesOwned value: (self portfolio sharesForStock:
    aSymbol).
```

The following method is called when the user chooses a new stock exchange. It sets all the stocks in the chosen exchange so they are displayed on the screen.

```
changedExchange
    self exchanges selection isNil ifTrue: [
        stocks list: OrderedCollection new.
    ] ifFalse: [
        stocks list: self exchanges selection stocks values.
    ].
```

When the stock selection has been changed by the user, the changedStock message is sent. The method first sees if a stock is selected by sending the selection message to the stocks. If no stock is selected, the "buy" and "sell" buttons are disabled, and the price and shares owned are set to 0. If there is a stock selected, you get the ticker symbol by sending the message tickerSymbol to the selected stock. This symbol is sent as the argument to the showStockPrice: and setSharesOwned: methods. Finally, the "buy" and "sell" buttons are enabled.

```
changedStock
    | tickerSymbol |
    self stocks selection isNil ifTrue: [
        self disableButtons.
        self price value: 0.
        self sharesOwned value: 0.
    ] ifFalse: [
        tickerSymbol := self stocks selection tickerSymbol.
        self showStockPrice: tickerSymbol.
        self setSharesOwned: tickerSymbol.
        self enableButtons.
    ].
```

These methods do the disabling and the enabling of the "buy" and "sell" buttons.

```
disableButtons
    (self builder componentAt: #buy) disable.
    (self builder componentAt: #sell) disable.

enableButtons
    (self builder componentAt: #buy) enable.
    (self builder componentAt: #sell) enable.
```

This method is invoked when the user presses the "buy" button. It adds the number of shares shown on the screen to the Portfolio, and informs the Exchange for this stock of the transaction. It then calls methods that update the numbers displayed on the screen.

```
buy
    | exchange tickerSymbol |
    tickerSymbol := self stocks selection tickerSymbol.
    exchange := self market exchangeForStock: tickerSymbol.
    self portfolio
        addToHolding: tickerSymbol
        shares: self numberOfShares value.
    exchange
        buyStock: tickerSymbol
        shares: self numberOfShares value
        account: self portfolio account.
    self setSharesOwned: tickerSymbol.
    self showStockPrice: tickerSymbol.
    self setPortfolioValue.
```

This method is invoked when the user presses the "sell" button. It subtracts the number of shares shown on the screen to the Portfolio, and informs the Exchange of this stock of the transaction. It then calls methods that update the numbers displayed on the screen.

```
sell
    | exchange tickerSymbol result |
    tickerSymbol := self stocks selection tickerSymbol.
    exchange := self market exchangeForStock: tickerSymbol.
    result := self portfolio
        subtractFromHolding: tickerSymbol
        shares: self numberOfShares value.
    result isNil ifTrue: [
        ^Dialog warn: 'You don''t have enough shares of this stock
    to sell.'
    ].
    exchange
        sellStock: tickerSymbol
        shares: self numberOfShares value
        account: self portfolio account.
    self setSharesOwned: tickerSymbol.
    self showStockPrice: tickerSymbol.
    self setPortfolioValue.
```

This method displays the stock price for the given ticker symbol by asking the market object for a quote on the stock:

```
showStockPrice: tickerSymbol
    self price value: (self market quoteForStock: tickerSymbol).
```

StockTerminal has one class method, windowSpec. All VisualWorks application models have a class method by this name. It is automatically created by the Canvas Tool, the VisualWorks facility, which the programmer uses to visually build a user interface. It specifies exactly how the application's window is to be laid out by the VisualWorks component—called the UIBuilder—when the window is opened.

```
windowSpec
    "UIPainter new openOnClass: self andSelector: #windowSpec"
    <resource: #canvas>
    ^#(#FullSpec
        #window:
        #(#WindowSpec
            #label: 'ACME Stock Brokers'
            #bounds: #(#Rectangle 146 148 698 545 ) )
        #component:
        #(#SpecCollection
            #collection: #(
                #(#SequenceViewSpec
                    #layout: #(#Rectangle 54 97 270 178 )
                    #name: #exchanges
                    #model: #exchanges
                    #useModifierKeys: true
                    #selectionType: #highlight )
                #(#LabelSpec
                    #layout: #(#Point 53 65 )
                    #label: 'Exchanges' )
                #(#SequenceViewSpec
                    #layout: #(#Rectangle 59 239 311 333 )
                    #name: #stocks
                    #model: #stocks
                    #useModifierKeys: true
                    #selectionType: #highlight )
                #(#LabelSpec
                    #layout: #(#Point 59 209 )
                    #label: 'Stocks' )
                #(#InputFieldSpec
                    #layout: #(#Rectangle 352 238 452 263 )
                    #name: #price
                    #model: #price
```

```
                    #tabable: false
                    #isReadOnly: true
                    #type: #number )
            #(#LabelSpec
                    #layout: #(#Point 354 210 )
                    #label: 'Price:' )
            #(#InputFieldSpec
                    #layout: #(#Rectangle 352 115 452 140 )
                    #name: #numberOfShares
                    #model: #numberOfShares
                    #type: #number
                    #formatString: '#,##0;-#,##0' )
            #(#LabelSpec
                    #layout: #(#Point 353 85 )
                    #label: 'Number of shares:' )
            #(#ActionButtonSpec
                    #layout: #(#Rectangle 338 51 390 76 )
                    #name: #buy
                    #flags: 40
                    #model: #buy
                    #label: 'Buy'
                    #defaultable: true )
            #(#ActionButtonSpec
                    #layout: #(#Rectangle 426 51 478 76 )
                    #name: #sell
                    #flags: 40
                    #model: #sell
                    #label: 'Sell'
                    #defaultable: true )
            #(#InputFieldSpec
                    #layout: #(#Rectangle 351 304 451 329 )
                    #name: #sharesOwned
                    #model: #sharesOwned
                    #tabable: false
                    #isReadOnly: true
                    #type: #number
                    #formatString: '#,##0;-#,##0' )
            #(#LabelSpec
                    #layout: #(#Point 353 280 )
                    #label: 'Shares owned:' )
            #(#InputFieldSpec
                    #layout: #(#Rectangle 178 358 318 383 )
                    #name: #portfolioValue
```

```
              #model: #portfolioValue
              #tabable: false
              #isReadOnly: true
              #type: #number
              #formatString: '$#,##0.00;-$#,##0.00' )
        #(#LabelSpec
              #layout: #(#Point 60 361 )
              #label: 'Value of Portfolio:' ) ) ) )
```

The Strategy to Distribute the Program

Before I attempt to distribute the program, let's see how the objects look when they're all in one object space. This is shown in Figure 8-2, in OMT notation. The figure shows an object diagram, not a class diagram. Individual objects, which are instances of a particular class, are given by round-cornered rectangles. The class of which each is an instance of is shown in parentheses. If you executed the Stock Market Project as defined by the previous classes and methods, you'd get these objects.

Note that I have omitted instances of the StockHolding class. These instances are purely local, and do not have a role in distributing the application.

To distribute the Stock Market Project, we must decide where to put its objects. We need to partition the program. There are several considerations in partitioning, as I discussed in Chapter 7. A very important one is minimizing network traffic.

How not to get stuck in the GUI

One fundamental issue when we try to distribute the Stock Market Project is that certain objects interact directly with the Graphical User Interface, the GUI. If there are many such objects that must be displayed all at once, as in a list, then consider what would happen if these objects were in another object space. We would have only local proxies for them, and would have to send messages to them over a network in order to get their names, for example.

Simply selecting different groups of such objects for display would generate a lot of network traffic, and could result in an annoying delay when updating the screen. Even such a trivial thing as scrolling the list would be slow and costly if all the objects in the list were remote. The GUI should not span the computer network!

Consider the Exchanges objects. The exchanges instance variable in the StockTerminal class holds Exchange objects, which display themselves in a list box of the screen display. When a particular Exchange is selected by the user, the stocks on that Exchange need to be displayed. This is done when the StockTerminal object receives the changedExchange message. The method of the same name sets the stocks screen display list by asking the selected Exchange for its list of stocks.

So the stocks that generate the list should probably be local objects. Exchanges hold Stocks, and because the same mechanism is used to display both exchanges and stocks, it would be simplest to keep both kinds of objects local. That way, we have a simple two-level hierarchy that is locally held.

However, both the exchanges and their stocks cannot only be local. The obvious idea in distributing this application is to allow potentially many client programs to access the same exchanges and stocks, and have transactions centrally coordinated. A single current price for each stock can be "negotiated" and maintained in one server object space.

The answer: get objects "by value"

So what we really want to do is get local copies of the data for the Exchange and Stock objects. This means fetching the objects "by value," so we have their states locally. But then what about the stock prices, which we want to be handled by a single server object space?

Clearly, we need to use both local and remote versions of these objects. We only need the local versions for the direct interactions with the GUI. They mirror the Market, Exchange, and Stock objects on the server machine, so that list display can be performed efficiently. All messages for buying and selling stocks should be sent to the remote, server object space versions. The stock prices are not maintained locally. Buying and selling of stocks, and the resulting price movements, takes place only on the objects of the server.

This is easily done, because our single Market object contains the exchanges, which in turn contain the stocks. If the Market object were itself remote, then all buy and sell messages to it would be invoked in the server object space. So we must always send messages via a proxy for the remote Market. Our application is already well-designed to do this, because all buy, sell, and pricing operations initiated from the GUI go through the Market object.

Have another look at the buy and sell methods of the StockTerminal class. They first send the market message, which answers the remote Market object on the central server. An Exchange object is received from this, so that it too resides on the server. A buyStock:shares:account: message is sent to this remote Exchange object to buy shares, while the sellStock:shares:account: message is set to buy shares.

To get the local versions of the Exchange and Stock objects, we could choose to fetch the objects on demand and only then keep local copies. That way, we would effectively cache the objects if they need to be subsequently accessed.

A simpler strategy is to fetch all the objects on initialization. This is practical if there are not an unreasonable number of objects to deal with. Even then, if the image was saved after the objects were fetched, it wouldn't have to be done each time. I'm going to choose this method for the Stock Market Project, and get all in the objects when the lazy initialization for the exchanges instance variable is done.

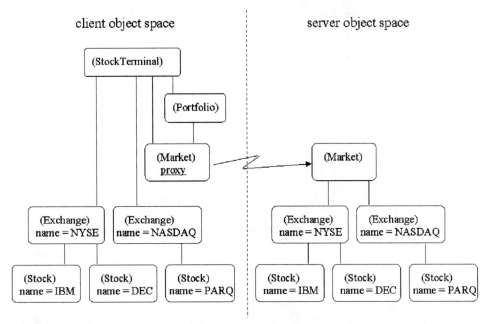

Figure 8-3. The distributed object diagram for the Stock Market Project

Here's what the fully-partitioned application looks like as an object diagram (see Figure 8-3). Compare it with Figure 8-2.

Implementation with CORBA-Compliant Distributed Smalltalks

As I discussed in the previous section, there are two keys to the distributed implementation of the Stock Market Project. One is to use a local proxy for the Market object. Doing this is implementation-specific, so I discuss it later, for each of the two CORBA-compliant distributed Smalltalks.

The second is to create local exchanges and stocks for display in the GUI. This can all be done in the lazy initialization for the exchanges instance variable.

Here's how the original, non-distributed exchanges method looks:

```
exchanges
    exchanges isNil ifTrue: [
        exchanges := SelectionInList new.
        exchanges list: self market exchanges values.
        exchanges selectionIndexHolder
            onChangeSend: #changedExchange to: self
    ].
    ^exchanges
```

Now, here is what must be done in the distributed version:

```
exchanges
    exchanges isNil ifTrue: [
        exchanges := SelectionInList new.
        exchanges list:
        "get exchanges byValue"
            (self market exchanges values collect: [:each |
                each theValue]).
        exchanges list do: [ :each |
            | localStocks |
            "get stocks for each exchange by value"
            localStocks := IdentityDictionary new.
            each stocks keysAndValuesDo: [ :key :stock |
                localStocks at: key put: stock theValue
            ].
            each stocks: localStocks.
        ].
        exchanges selectionIndexHolder
            onChangeSend: #changedExchange to: self
    ].
    ^exchanges
```

This method gets both the exchanges and the stocks for each exchange by value. Look at the line below the comment line, "get exchanges byValue":

```
(self market exchanges values collect: [:each | each theValue]).
```

First, this sends the message exchanges to the Market object proxy. The proxy passes the message on to the "real" Market object, which answer the Dictionary of Exchange objects in the remote object space. This, in turn, is sent the message values, which answers the values for the Dictionary, which is a collection of Exchange objects. Finally, we send this collection the collect: message, with a block argument that sends the message theValue to each Exchange object, and answers a new collection made from the results. Remember, this message creates a local "by value" copy of each remote object, so we have a collection of local Exchange objects that are assigned to the exchanges list.

So the instance method theValue must be added to the Exchange class, with an appropriate IDL definition that has a byValue return type.

```
theValue
    ^self
```

But we're not done yet. These Exchange objects, although local, still contain Dictionaries of remote Stock objects, which are proxies. We would like them to contain local Stock objects. So the code following the comment line "get stocks for each exchange by value" changes this Dictionary of proxies to a Dictionary of local objects:

```
localStocks := IdentityDictionary new.
each stocks keysAndValuesDo: [ :key :stock |
    localStocks at: key put: stock theValue
].
each stocks: localStocks.
```

A new IdentityDictionary is created, and populated with local "by value" copies of each Stock object, which you get by sending the proxy the theValue message. A theValue instance method must be added to the Stocks class.

Implementing it with
ObjectShare Distributed Smalltalk

The ObjectShare Distributed Smalltalk implementation requires you to use the CORBA Naming Service in order to get proxy objects. You must also be careful to subclass the distributed object classes from the correct Distributed Smalltalk abstract superclasses.

A proxy for the Market object

Getting a proxy for the Market object held by the StockTerminal class is somewhat specific to the particular CORBA-compliant distributed Smalltalk. This is because it uses the Naming Service to find the distributed object bound the single Market object named 'Market.' As described earlier, the Naming Service is done differently in the two distributed Smalltalks. There's not much difference, but because STB (Smalltalk Broker) is up to date in following the CORBA 2.0 standard, I'll defer a detailed discussion of name binding for this method until that section. Here's how it is done in DST:

```
marketSingleton (class)
MarketSingleton isNil ifTrue: [
        self namingService class notFoundSignal handle: [:ex |
            self namingService
                contextBind: (DSTName onString: 'Market')
                to: (MarketSingleton := Market new)
        ] do: [MarketSingleton :=
    self namingService contextResolve: (DSTName onString: 'Market')
        ]
    ].
^ MarketSingleton asRemotable
```

The method namingService sends the same message to the ORBObject class:

```
namingService
^ORBObject namingService
```

Remember, in DST there can be only a single Naming Service over all the communicating object spaces. Every ORBObject knows how to get to the single Naming Service. So there's no need to worry about which ORB, local or remote, is being called upon.

The Market object should be installed on the desired server ORB using its class install method. This binds a new instance of a Market to the name "Market" in the Naming Service:

```
install
^ self namingService
    contextReBind: (DSTName onString: 'Market')
to: self new
```

Subclassing from DST classes

To distribute the Market class within DST, it must be made a subclass of DSTapplicationObject. This class provides the CORBA machinery to distribute the class.

In VisualWorks, the StockTerminal class would normally be a subclass of ApplicationModel, which gives it all the behavior it needs to be a VisualWorks GUI. But because this class also needs DST-specific behavior, it must be made a subclass of DSTPresenter, which is a subclass of ApplicationModel. It is the GUI class equivalent of DSTapplicationObject.

asRemotable

The "asRemotable" message in the marketSingleton method is not strictly necessary, but is extremely useful for debugging. It enables you to test your distributed Smalltalk application in a single object space by simulating distribution. This mode is called "local RPC," (Remote Procedure Calls) and can be turned on for an ORB in both DST and STB.

Local RPC mode causes the ORB to intervene in any message sent to a potentially remote object. How does an ORB know which objects are to be treated as remote? You have told it, of course, by adding the message "asRemotable" to the object. This causes the object, in this case a Market object, to be tagged as remotable.

When your object is distributed to a remote object space, the asRemotable tag is signored because you will not have not turned on local RPC mode. But when you are testing in this mode, the asRemotable tag forces the ORB to marshal all messages sent to this object, and then unmarshal them, exactly as though they were sent from a different object space. It exercises all the machinery of the ORB in the process, so your distributed Smalltalk program can be debugged on one machine, in a single object space.

The CORBAName method

As described earlier, each distributed Smalltalk class also needs a special instance method called CORBAName. This method maps the Smalltalk class to its corresponding CORBA interface. It answers a symbol that is the scoped name that identifies the IDL interface to this class.

For the Exchange class, the CORBAName method looks like this:

```
CORBAName
    ^#'::StockApplication::ExchangeInterface'
```

And for the Market and Stock classes:

```
CORBAName
    ^#'::StockApplication::MarketInterface'
```

```
CORBAName
    ^#'::StockApplication::StockInterface'
```

Factory Finders and UUIDs

In DST's implementation of the CORBA spec, each CORBA Smalltalk class is required to have a unique identifier registered with the Factory Finder. A Factory Finder is part of the Life Cycle Service CORBA specification. Because a Smalltalk class knows how to generate instances of itself (via the standard "new" class method), it is technically a factory. It manufactures objects of its own kind.

To register with the Factory Finder, a distributed Smalltalk class corresponding to an IDL interface must have an instance method called abstractClassId. This method returns a special object, a UUID, which uniquely identifies the class. For example:

```
abstractClassId
    "return the abstract class Id of the receiver"
    ^'76a69f6f-ef38-0000-02ac-10103f000000' asUUID
```

The "asUUID" messages encodes a hexadecimal string as a **Universally Unique Identifier (UUID)** definition. A UUID is a 16-byte quantity that is guaranteed to be unique. It encodes the local network IP address and a time stamp value, the elapsed time since January 1, 1980. UUIDs are used extensively in OSF's (Open Software Foundation's) DCE (Distributed Computing Environment), the major non-object oriented distributed computing standard. But UUIDs actually date back to the earlier Network Computing System (NCS) standard developed by Apollo Computer, before it was bought out by HP. This distributed computing business is very incestuous!

So where do you get a UUID string? You can ask DST for a UUID by typing the following in a worksace, and then selecting "print it" from the operate menu:

```
ORBObject newId
```

The IDL

Here is the DST interface definition for the StockMarket project. Many IDL (Interface Definition Language) declarations are possible because attributes and return values may be either typed with the IDL type corresponding to a specific Smalltalk class, or as the wildcard type, "any." Because Smalltalk is untyped, it is in the spirit of distributed Smalltalk to make everything of type "any."

This is a matter of philosophy in a purely Smalltalk distributed environment. When inter-operating with other languages, it's better to type. With "any," runtime type errors become a possibility, and extra overhead a certainty, using a strongly typed language. But because this is Smalltalk-to-Smalltalk, we can use "any" everywhere using DST. This preserves Smalltalk polymorphism across the distributed interface.

```
module StockApplication {
    interface MarketInterface : SmalltalkObject {
        attribute any name;
        attribute any exchanges;

        #pragma class byValue Market
        struct byValue {
            any name;
            any exchanges;
        };
        any exchangeForStock (in any aSymbol);
        any quoteForStock (in any aSymbol);
        void putExchange(in any exString, in any stock, in any
            price, in any name);
        byValue theValue();
    };

    interface ExchangeInterface : SmalltalkObject {
        attribute any name;
        attribute any stocks;

        #pragma class byValue Exchange
        struct byValue {
            any name;
            any stocks;
        };
        any quoteForStock(in any tickerSymbol);
        void buyStock(in any tickerSymbol, in any shares, in any
            account);
        void sellStock(in any tickerSymbol, in any shares, in any
            account);
        void putStock(in any tickerSymbol, in any price, in any
            name);
        byValue theValue();
    };

    interface StockInterface : SmalltalkObject {
        attribute any name;
        attribute any price;
```

```
        attribute any tickerSymbol;

        #pragma class byValue Stock
        struct byValue {
            any name;
            any price;
            any tickerSymbol;
        };
        byValue theValue();
    };
};
```

Also notice the #pragma class declarations. These are required in DST to connect a Smalltalk class with a corresponding CORBA type.

Implementing it with DNS SmalltalkBroker

As with ObjectShare Distributed Smalltalk, you must also go to the Naming Service to get object proxies.

Getting a proxy via the Naming Service

A proxy for the Market object for a StockTerminal is gotten in a similar way as DST, though the messages and classes are somewhat different:

```
StockTerminal>marketSingleton (class)
    MarketSingleton isNil ifTrue: [
        CosNamingContext NotFoundSignal handle: [:ex |
            CorbaORB default namingService
                bind: (CosNamingContext nameFrom: 'Market')
                obj: (MarketSingleton := Market new)
        ] do: [ MarketSingleton :=
self namingService resolve: (CosNamingContext nameFrom: 'Market')
        ]
    ].
^MarketSingleton asRemotable
```

Let's consider the first message in this method. It uses lazy initialization code for the market instance variable, which has the form:

```
CosNamingContext NotFoundSignal handle: [ <exception code> ]
    do: [ <normal code> ]
```

The normal code is the following:

```
MarketSingleton := self namingService
    resolve: (CosNamingContext nameFrom: 'Market')
```

This asks the Naming Service on which the Market object is located (see upcoming code) to resolve the name 'Market'; that is, to answer the object that is associated with this name. It assigns this object to the market instance variable.

If in the process of running the normal code, the Naming Service raises the NotFoundSignal, indicating that the name 'Market' could not be found, then the exception code is run. The exception code block is:

```
[:ex |
    CorbaORB default namingService
        bind: (CosNamingContext nameFrom: 'Market')
        obj: (market := Market new)
]
```

This code instructs the Naming Service for the default CORBA ORB (the local one) to create a binding for the name 'Market.' A new Market object is created, and used as the object to bind the name 'Market' to. Unlike DST, STB permits multiple Naming Services.

The bind:obj: and resolve: messages sent to the naming service exactly follows the CORBA 2.0 standard–DST uses contextBind:to: and contextResolve: messages, which are the same in function, but are not named according to the latest standard.

How does a Market object get associated with any other Name Service than the one used by the StockTerminal's ORB? Simple: the Market class has an install method that binds a new instance of itself to the local ORB's Naming Service. The Market object should be installed on the desired server ORB using this class method:

```
install
^CorbaORB default namingService
    rebind: (CosNamingContext nameFrom: 'Market')
    obj: self new
```

The rebind:obj: message is used, rather than bind:obj, just in case the name is already bound.

The STB namingService method in the StockTerminal class is:

```
namingService
^self class namingService
```

This is different from DST. Though both versions support the CORBA Naming Service (with DST using many non-standard method names), STB lets you have a Naming Service on each ORB. So it also provides you with ORB methods for finding Naming Services on other ORBs. The class CorbaLocation aids in this. Here are the methods on the class side of StockTerminal for the STB example:

```
namingService
^CorbaORB default
    namingService: self marketLocation host
    port: self marketLocation port
```

```
marketLocation
    ^MarketLocation isNil
        ifTrue:[CorbaLocation thisLocation]
        ifFalse:[MarketLocation]

marketLocation: aCorbaLocation
    MarketLocation := aCorbaLocation
```

MarketLocation must then be a class variable in the StockTerminal class. This class variable allows you to specify the location of the Market object. If it is not explicitly set, then it defaults to the local ORB.

The marketLocation message answers an instance of class CorbaLocation. This is an object that holds host and port information. Sending the message thisLocation to CorbaLocation answers an instance of CorbaLocation, which describes the local location. You can also create CorbaLocation objects for other locations via the messages locationForSocketAddress: and locationFor: port:. Whatever location is set for the MarketLocation, the corresponding Naming Service will be used by StockTerminal.

Remember, in DST, we had to make the Market a subclass of DSTapplicationObject, and StockTerminal a subclass of DSTPresenter. STB, on the other hand, has no such requirements. It hooks objects that need distributed behavior to its CORBA ORB more transparently, without the need to inherit from specific superclasses. In STB, then, the Market class is simply a subclass of Object, and StockTerminal, because it maintains a GUI, is a subclass of the standard VisualWorks ApplicationModel.

The CORBAName method

STB also uses the CORBAName method to map Smalltalk classes to IDL interfaces:

```
CORBAName
    ^'StockApplication::Exchange'

CORBAName
    ^'StockApplication::Market'

CORBAName
    ^'StockApplication::Stock'
```

In DST, the CORBAName methods looked a lot like the previous example. The interfaces were also kept in a module called StockApplication. However, in DST, the Exchange class had an interface called ExchangeInterface rather than Exchange, and Market's interface was called MarketInterface, etc. It is certainly more obvious to give the interface the identical name as its Smalltalk class. However, if you tried to do this in DST, you'd get a namespace collision. In DST, you are forced to give the interface a different name, which, by convention, is the class name with "Interface" appended to it. STB fixes up this limitation by letting you use the same name for both class and interface. This is an advantage of SmalltalkBroker.

The IDL

SmalltalkBroker is better at inter-operating with other languages, but this comes at the cost of a stricter IDL definition compared to DST. DST takes liberties that make it possible to use the "any" type everywhere, but that may cause problems with other languages.

For example, consider passing a Smalltalk Symbol as an input parameter. There is no unique CORBA type to map this to. So if a different language wants to send this, it needs to use an IDL interface that contains the definition of a Smalltalk Symbol. But the only way for it to know how to do this is by specifically referencing it in the interface that wants a Smalltalk Symbol sent to it.

In STB, a Smalltalk Symbol is defined in the module "::Smalltalk". So, to properly declare an input parameter "foo" as a Symbol, you must use,

```
in ::Smalltalk::Symbol foo
```

Why didn't we have to do this in DST? Because DST is more forgiving (or sloppy, depending on your viewpoint). If you're not careful, you can create IDL in DST that will not inter-operate with other languages. So, in the following STB IDL declaration for the Stock Market interface, I made everything an "any" that it would allow me to.

Also, notice that all the interfaces inherit from the CosLifeCycle::LifeCycleObject interface. This gives them formal access to the Life Cycle Service, in accordance with CORBA 2.0. The DST version of the Stock Market interface used SmalltalkObject to inherit from. This gives it Smalltalk-specific debugging capabilities, such as a remote object inspector.

```
module StockApplication
{
    interface Market : CosLifeCycle::LifeCycleObject {
        attribute any name;
        attribute any exchanges;
        struct byValue {
            any name;
            any exchanges;
        };
        Exchange exchangeForStock(in ::Smalltalk::Symbol
tickerSymbol);
        any quoteForStock(in ::Smalltalk::Symbol tickerSymbol);
        void putExchange(in string exString, in
::Smalltalk::Symbol stock, in any price, in any name);
        byValue theValue();
    };

    interface Exchange : CosLifeCycle::LifeCycleObject {
        attribute any name;
        attribute any stocks;
```

```
    struct byValue {
        any name;
        any stocks;
    };
    any quoteForStock(in ::Smalltalk::Symbol tickerSymbol);
    void buyStock(in ::Smalltalk::Symbol tickerSymbol, in long
shares, in any account);
    void sellStock(in ::Smalltalk::Symbol tickerSymbol, in
long shares, in any account);
    void putStock(in ::Smalltalk::Symbol tickerSymbol, in any
price, in any name);
    byValue theValue();
};
interface Stock : CosLifeCycle::LifeCycleObject {
    attribute any name;
    attribute any price;
    attribute any tickerSymbol;
    struct byValue {
        any name;
        any price;
        any tickerSymbol;
    };
    byValue theValue();
};
};
```

Implementing It with GemStone

GemStone is a rich, complex system. There are different ways to implement a distributed system in GemStone, but I chose a method that is the least intrusive to our
Smalltalk code.

GbsObject

Objects of class GbsObject are the best match to the proxy objects on which the Stock
Market distributed example was architected. That is what we will use to distribute it
in GemStone.

Remember, sending remote messages via GbsObjects is a bit clumsy. In standard
GemStone, you have to prefix each message by the letters "gs."

This is not in keeping with the spirit of distributed Smalltalk, and is a holdover
from the days when GemStone was thought of as only an object database.
Fortunately, it's easy to remedy. All we have to do is change one method in the

GbsObject class. Messages from GbsObjects are forwarded to the server is via the "doesNotUnderstand:" method. The last statement in this method is:

```
^super doesNotUnderstand: aMessage
```

This sends "doesNotUnderstand:" to GbsObject's superclass, which is the Object class. To get the message sent on to the server object instead, replace this line with the following:

```
^self remotePerform: sel withArgs: aMessage arguments
```

I highly recommend that you create a new instance method category for GbsObject, and call it "Survival Guide." Put the old "doesNotUnderstand:" method in there, and rename it "originalDoesNotUnderstand:". Here is that method in GemStone 5.0:

```
originalDoesNotUnderstand: aMessage
    "This overrides Object's behavior by checking for selectors
    that begin with 'gs'.
    If this is the case, the 'gs' part is stripped from the
    selector and it is sent to
    the GemStone for remote execution"
    | sel newSel |
    sel := aMessage selector.
    ('gs*' match: sel)
        ifTrue: [
            newSel := sel asString copyFrom: 3 to: sel size.
            ^self remotePerform: newSel withArgs: aMessage
    arguments ]
        ifFalse: [
            ('priv*' match: sel) ifTrue: [
                newSel := '_' , (sel asString copyFrom: 5 to: sel
    size).
                ^self remotePerform: newSel withArgs: aMessage
    arguments ].
                ^super doesNotUnderstand: aMessage ]
```

Here is the new "doesNotUnderstand:" method, which you should also put in the "Survival Guide" category:

```
doesNotUnderstand: aMessage
    "This is the same as the original doesNotUnderstand, except
    that we remote perform everything by default so we don't need
    the 'gs' prefix."
    | sel newSel |
    sel := aMessage selector.
    ('gs*' match: sel)
```

```
ifTrue: [
    newSel := sel asString copyFrom: 3 to: sel size.
    ^self remotePerform: newSel
        withArgs: aMessage arguments ]
ifFalse: [
    ('priv*' match: sel) ifTrue: [
        newSel := '_' , (sel asString copyFrom: 5
            to: sel size).
        ^self remotePerform: newSel
            withArgs: aMessage arguments ].
    "^super doesNotUnderstand: aMessage"
    ^self remotePerform: sel
        withArgs: aMessage arguments ]
```

One other method is useful. Since we have been using the message "theValue" to get a local (a "by value" copy) of a remote object in the CORBA-compliant distributed Smalltalks, we can define the same method in the "Survival Guide" category of GbsObject:

```
theValue
^self asLocalObjectCopy
```

Methods

Here is how the MarketSingleton class method for StockTerminal is implemented in GemStone:

```
marketSingleton (class)

"Answer the remote GSObject."
MarketSingleton isNil ifTrue: [MarketSingleton :=
    Market new asGSObject ].
^MarketSingleton
```

You also have to use the following "exchanges" method for the StockTerminal class. Any changes from the CORBA-compliant version of this method are shown by commenting out the relevant lines and adding the appropriate code for GemStone.

```
exchanges

    | values keys |
exchanges isNil ifTrue: [
exchanges := SelectionInList new.

"make sure that GemStone has initialized its market singleton"
        self market exchanges theValue isEmpty ifTrue: [
            self market initialize.
        ].
```

```
exchanges list:
    "get exchanges byValue"
    "for GemStone, get a local copy of exchanges, and ask
        for its values"
    "(self market exchanges values collect: [ :each |
        each theValue])."
    self market exchanges theValue values.
exchanges list do: [ :each |
    | localStocks |
    "get stocks for each exchange by value"
    localStocks := IdentityDictionary new.
    each stocks keysAndValuesDo: [ :key :stock |
        localStocks at: key put: stock theValue
    ].
    values := each stocks values.
    keys := values collect: [ :value |
        each stocks keyAtValue: value ].
    keys with: values do: [ :key :stock |
        localStocks at: key put: stock
    ].
    each stocks: localStocks.
].
exchanges selectionIndexHolder
    onChangeSend: #changedExchange to: self
].
^exchanges
```

One other method needs to be changed. GemStone does not automatically return simple objects, such as numbers, "by value" as the answer to a GbsObject message. This differs from CORBA implementations. Furthermore, GemStone likes to use Doubles rather than Floats as its default floating point class. This means that two additional messages need to be added to the "showStockPrice:" method of the StockTerminal class:

```
showStockPrice: tickerSymbol
    "For GemStone, get a local copy of the price, and convert it
        to a float."
    self price value: (self market quoteForStock: tickerSymbol)
        theValue asFloat.
```

Implementing it with the IBM Distributed Feature

IBM defines a different dialect of Smalltalk than ObjectShare VisualWorks. Fortunately, the fundamental classes are identical, since both Smalltalks conform to the proposed ANSI standard Smalltalk (put forth by IBM).

Therefore, five out the six classes that define the Stock Market Project can remain exactly the same. They remain subclasses of Object. The one class that must be modified is, predictably, the user interface class: StockTerminal. VisualWorks and VisualAge have very different models of the GUI, and there is a corresponding difference in the GUI classes. VisualAge GUIs are all subclassed from AbtAppBldrView.

Another difference in the StockTerminal class, beyond just dialect, is how a proxy for the Market object is gotten. This differed just between CORBA-complaint distributed Smalltalks, so it's not surprising that IBM has its own means for getting proxies to remote objects.

A non-distributed version

To make things simpler, I first discuss a port of a non-distributed version of the Stock Market Project to IBM VisualAge; then I add distribution.

A fundamental difference between VisualWorks and VisualAge is VisualAge has an event mechanism built right in, which is essential to its high-level visual programming paradigm. This port makes minimum use of VisualAge's visual programming. The visual programming capabilities are limited to building the GUI screen and simple functions, such as enabling and disabling buttons. VisualAge visual programming makes it possible for a non-Smalltalker to construct very simple applications with little or no textual programming—simply by placing components and establishing connections between them. VisualAge emphasizes this visual application construction, often at the expense of ease of development for the "real" Smalltalk programmer. So bear with me if things seem a bit confusing at first.

The exchanges and stocks list boxes are instances of AbtListView, which is VisualAge's name for a list viewing widget. VisualAge widgets begin with the letters "Abt," which stands for "Application Builder Technology," the original name for IBM's VisualAge for Smalltalk software. An AbtListView, as is true of all VisualAge widgets, is held in a subpart of the GUI class. It is normally accessed programmatically by sending the message subpartNamed:, with a subpart name string as the argument, to self. Fortunately, though, an instance variable can be created that corresponds to each subpart, so you don't have to be constantly sending the subpartNamed: message in order to access a widget. You just send the get message for the instance variable.

But this also means that lazy initialization cannot be done in the "getter" method. Remember, I used lazy initialization for the exchanges instance variable in order to set up the values of the exchanges. Initialization of VisualAge widgets needs to happen elsewhere. A good place for this to occur is as an instance method called "finalInitialize."

This is called when VisualAge has created all the widgets and established their connections. Here is the way finalInitialize looks in the StockTerminal class:

```
finalInitialize
    super finalInitialize.
    self exchanges items: self market exchanges values.
```

Compare this to the non-distributed VisualWorks initialization of the exchanges variable:

```
exchanges
    exchanges isNil ifTrue: [
        exchanges := SelectionInList new.
        exchanges list: self market exchanges values.
        exchanges selectionIndexHolder
            onChangeSend: #changedExchange to: self
    ].
    ^exchanges
```

Because VisualAge automatically initializes the exchanges to an AbtListView, there is no need for the equivalent of "SelectionInList new." And there is also no need to set up a change message to be sent when the selected exchange changes. This, too, is handled automatically by VisualAge. The only thing left is to initialize the values in the list widget. The VisualAge message that is equivalent to sending "list:" to a VisualWorks SelectionInList is sending "items:" to an AbtListView. Note the argument to this message is exactly the same in both Smalltalks.

Unlike VisualWorks, VisualAge instance variables that hold widgets are not value models. They do not understand the message "value," for VisualAge does not use value models. Instead, they have getter and setter pair methods such as these:

```
exchanges
    ^exchanges

exchanges: anExchange
    exchanges := anExchange.
    self signalEvent: #exchanges
        with: anExchange.
```

The setter method always sends the signalEvent:with: message, which is the hook into VisualAge's event mechanism. The instance variables for screen widgets, which are exchanges, numberOfShares, portfolioValue, price, sharesOwned, and stocks, have getter and setter methods with the identical form. VisualAge can be instructed to automatically generate such accessor methods for widgets.

The exchanges and stocks widgets are list boxes, so what about the others, which display simple numeric values? These are of class AbtTextView. Because VisualAge does not use value models, how do you get at the values for these widgets? It may sound confusing, but you send each the message "object." This is because an

AbtTextView inherently displays a string (which you get by sending it the message "string"), but holds an object of a different underlying type, such as a Number or Date. To get this "raw object," you send it the "object" message.

Two instance variables that don't correspond to widgets remain: portfolio and market. In the non-distributed version, the get accessors to these variables do not change from VisualWorks.

Some minor changes to action methods are required. We don't need the methods "enableButtons" and "disableButtons" because these actions can be done more conveniently visually, from VisualAge's Composition Editor, which I discuss in a moment.

There are one-line changes to the "buy" and "sell" methods. The first line of code in each method:

```
tickerSymbol := self stocks selection tickerSymbol.
```

is changed to:

```
tickerSymbol := self stocks selectedItem tickerSymbol.
```

This is because the stocks object in VisualAge is an AbtListView, and the message to get its selection happens to be "selectedItem," not "selection." The "sell" method has one more change. If the result is "nil," a warning message is placed on the screen, and VisualAge has a different class to handle such things:

```
result isNil ifTrue: [
    ^CwMessagePrompter warningMessage: 'You don''t have enough
    shares of this stock to sell.'
    ].
```

Since the value protocol is not used to get and set values for widgets, some other minor changes are necessary. The method

```
setPortfolioValue
    self portfolioValue value: self portfolio value.
```

becomes:

```
setPortfolioValue
    self portfolioValue object: self portfolio value.
```

Similarly,

```
setSharesOwned: aSymbol
    self sharesOwned value: (self portfolio sharesForStock:
    aSymbol).
```

becomes:

```
setSharesOwned: aSymbol
    self sharesOwned object: (self portfolio sharesForStock:
    aSymbol).
```

And,

```
showStockPrice: tickerSymbol
    self price value: (self market quoteForStock: tickerSymbol).
```

becomes:

```
showStockPrice: tickerSymbol
    self price object: (self market quoteForStock: tickerSymbol).
```

There are two methods left to modify: changedExchange and changedStock. The activation of these methods is slightly different, because in VisualAge it's quite easy to do it visually, with a connection from the exchanges and the stocks widgets. The method:

```
changedExchange
    self exchanges selection isNil ifTrue: [
        stocks list: OrderedCollection new.
    ] ifFalse: [
        stocks list: self exchanges selection stocks values.
    ].
```

becomes:

```
changedExchange
    self exchanges selectedItem isNil ifTrue: [
        stocks items: OrderedCollection new.
    ] ifFalse: [
        stocks items: self exchanges selectedItem stocks values.
    ].
```

This uses messages I've previously mentioned.
Similarly,

```
changedStock
    | tickerSymbol |
    self stocks selection isNil ifTrue: [
        self disableButtons.
        self price value: 0.
        self sharesOwned value: 0.
    ] ifFalse: [
        tickerSymbol := self stocks selection tickerSymbol.
        self showStockPrice: tickerSymbol.
        self setSharesOwned: tickerSymbol.
        self enableButtons.
    ].
```

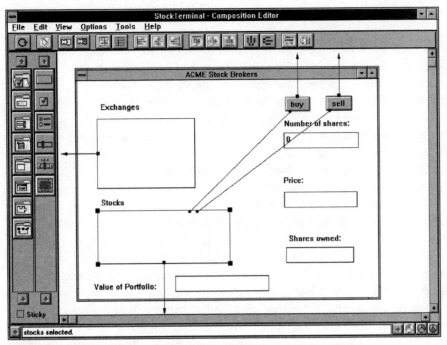

Figure 8-4. IBM VisualAge Composition Editor for the StockTerminal

becomes:

```
changedStock
    | tickerSymbol |
    self stocks selectedItem isNil ifTrue: [
        self price object: 0.
        self sharesOwned object: 0.
    ] ifFalse: [
        tickerSymbol := self stocks selectedItem tickerSymbol.
        self showStockPrice: tickerSymbol.
        self setSharesOwned: tickerSymbol.
    ].
```

The button enabling and disabling methods have disappeared in favor of a simpler, visual approach using the Composition Editor.

The Composition Editor and visual parts

VisualAge uses a tool called the Composition Editor to create and maintain the user interface. It provides both visual and non-visual "parts" that can be dragged and dropped, and then interconnected. Each connection is shown in the Composition Editor as an arrow or line between two parts.

A Composition Editor view of the Stock Market Application GUI is shown in Figure 8-4. This GUI is part of the StockTerminal class. There are only visual parts used to construct this GUI, so the connection arrows are either between visual parts, or between visual parts and an instance of the StockTerminal class. The latter connections show as arrows that point outside the GUI window, to the edges of what IBM calls the "free-form surface," an area that would hold any non-visual parts.

Look at the "buy" and "sell" buttons at the upper right. There is an arrow going straight up from each, into the free-form surface. These particular connections are "event-to-action" connections. Each connects the "clicked" event of a push button to an instance method in the StockTerminal class. The "clicked" event of the buy push button connects to the "buy" instance method, and the "clicked" event of the sell push button connects to the "sell" instance method.

Notice that there are also lines with filled dots at each end connecting the "buy" and "sell" buttons to the "stocks" widget. These are called "attribute-to-attribute" connections. They are an extremely convenient means for propagating value changes from one part to another. These lines happen to connect the Boolean "selectionIsValid" attribute of the stocks AbtListView to the "enabled" attribute of each button's AbtPushButtonView, which is also a Boolean. The effect is to enable the buttons only if the user has selected a stock from the stocks list. If no stock is selected, or the list is empty, the "buy" and "sell" buttons will be dimmed.

There's also an arrow leading away from the stocks widget, onto the free-form surface. This is another "event-to-action" connection. It connects the event "selectedItemChanged" in the stocks AbtListView to the "changedStock" instance method of the StockTerminal. The "selectedItemChanged" event is issued whenever the user changes what is selected from the stocks list.

Finally, there is a similar "event-to-action" connection arrow from the exchanges AbtListView. It connects the same event in the exchanges list to the "changedExchanges" instance method in StockTerminal.

These visual connections make the function of the program less obvious, because one can only see what each does by selecting and inspecting it in the Composition Editor. But it eliminates the "grunt work" of programming the low level actions of a GUI, and the results are a few less lines of Smalltalk code to write and maintain.

The distributed version

To distribute the Stock Market Project using VisualAge, only two methods in the StockTerminal class need to be changed. But why should any need to change? You are supposed to be able to partition a program in VisualAge using a distribution matrix, so that absolutely no source code change is required.

There is one catch, though. The Stock Market Project uses pass "by value" to create a local copy on the client of the Exchange objects (and, in turn, their Stock objects) held by the Market object. The distribution matrix approach passes objects by reference unless you add some specialized code. Specifically, there are three methods in VisualAge distributed that support pass by value. So special code is required in order to pass by value whether or not you use a distribution matrix.

One of the two methods I am changing is required to fetch these objects by value. The other method would not require any change with a distribution matrix. It is a useful demonstration of how to use a VisualAge distributed feature Naming Server, which is not used for a distribution matrix. On the theory that in a book such as this, it more useful to illustrate a feature than to *not* illustrate one, I will not use the distribution matrix for this example.

Without distribution, a single line of code was used in the finalInitialize method to initialize the exchanges object. But as we saw in the other distributed versions, more code is required to do this initialization "by value," from the server.

As I mentioned earlier, there are three methods that support pass by value. These methods are extensions to the Object class, so they can be sent to absolutely any object. You don't have to make sure that the "by value" passing actually moves an object between object spaces. They attempt to pass by value, and if this is not possible, they do no harm.

To pass an object value as an argument to remote object's message, you send that argument object the message asDsByValueObject. Another message, asDsByValueArray, is used when the argument object is an array. The third method is dsPerformWithLocalResult:. This method performs another method remotely, but returns the result as a local object. It is just like the standard Smalltalk method perform:. You pass it a keyword message symbol as its argument. There are also forms of this message that allow passing one or more arguments. They are completely analogous to their non-distributed counterparts. These are:

- dsPerformWithLocalResult:with:

- dsPerformWithLocalResult:with:with:

- dsPerformWithLocalResult:with:with: with:

- dsPerformWithLocalResult:withArguments:

In the Stock Market Project, we need to get local copies of remote objects. But this is not explicitly provided for in the "by value" messages. What do we do?

It's very simple. Every object in Smalltalk understands the message "yourself," which answers the object itself. So if a remote object is passed the following message and argument:

```
dsPerformWithLocalResult: #yourself
```

it will answer with a local copy of itself.

Here's the distributed version of finalInitialize, which gets "by value" copies. Compare it to the lazy initialization of the exchanges instance variable in the CORBA-compliant versions.

```
finalInitialize
    super finalInitialize.
        exchanges items:
        "get exchanges byValue"
```

```
            (self market exchanges values collect: [:each |
each dsPerformWithLocalResult: #yourself
]).
        exchanges items do: [ :each |
            | localStocks |
            "get stocks for each exchange by value"
            localStocks := IdentityDictionary new.
            each stocks keysAndValuesDo: [ :key :stock |
                localStocks
at: key
put: (stock dsPerformWithLocalResult: #yourself)
            ].
            each stocks: localStocks.
        ].
```

As in CORBA-compliant distributed Smalltalks, a Naming Service is used to locate a reference to the remote Market object. With the IBM distributed feature, the Naming Service is called a NameServerList.

```
market
    | marketRef remoteMarket |
    market isNil ifTrue: [
        marketRef := (NameServerList default)
    referenceAtFirstIdentifier: 'Market'
        ifAbsent: [
            CwMessagePrompter warningMessage: 'No Market found in
name server. ',
                'Defaulting to local Market.'.
            market := Market new.
            ^market
        ].
        remoteMarket := marketRef shadow.
        market := remoteMarket new.
    ].
    ^market
```

≡Chapter 9≡

Building Complex Distributed Systems

Because distributed object technology is still in its infancy, building complex distributed object systems remains a complex engineering task requiring considerable iterative development and tuning.

But what high-level concepts will enable distributed objects to scale up and work correctly in arbitrarily large systems?

We know of two such concepts. One is **component** technology, and the other is **transaction** technology. Interestingly enough, they are related in a fundamental way. Components assure object integrity over large "blobs" of space; that is, over multiple object instances. Transactions assure object integrity over large blobs of time.

You can think of transaction technology as providing yet another important dimension of integrity: **concurrency control**. In this dimension, many users access objects in parallel. Not only are the users unaware of each others' existence; concurrency control technology assures that the distributed objects have a single, consistent state, despite what individual users are doing with these objects.

Components

com·po·nent (kəm-'pō-nənt, 'käm-) *n.*

1. a constituent part; element; ingredient.

—The Random House Unabridged Dictionary, Second Edition

In Chapter 7 we introduced the concept of a subsystem as a collaboration of classes. This was expanded to a new level with the addition of a public interface. A subsystem with an interface used to be commonly called a component, at least when it played the role of a building block in a system. Here, reuse was a key feature of a component.[9] In the past, the term subsystem and component have often been used interchangeably.

However, in recent years, a more sophisticated and precise definition of a component has emerged. A component is more than just a subsystem with an interface. Yes, it is designed for reuse. But *key* to the reuse is the possession of **metadata**. See Figure 9-1. We encountered metadata previously, in Chapter 4, in the context of the Lawrence Livermore Data Warehouse. Metadata provides information about a system that is at a higher level than the system itself.

Components are playing an increasingly important role in building complex systems. They go beyond objects and provide a simple paradigm to promote reuse. The metadata of a component provides plug-and-play capability. Components are a natural way to package classes for distributed Smalltalk.

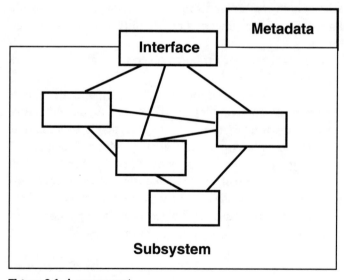

Figure 9-1. A component

Introspection

One category of metadata is **self-description**. This is also termed **introspection** (or, like we need yet another name, "reflection") and is a property of the Java components called JavaBeans.

Smalltalk has always had the capability for introspection. One can ask an object its class by simply sending it the *class* message. This is not the case for languages like C++, which are compiled into object code that has been stripped of any metadata that might be extracted from the original program.

One basic but important capability of introspection is the public means by which attributes are accessed: the "getter" and "setter" methods. This may sound like a triviality, because in Smalltalk it is just a convention. To get the value of an attribute called "foo" we simply send the message "foo," and to set it, we send the message "foo:".

JavaBeans gives publicly accessible attributes the name **properties**. It prescribes that each be accessed by prefixing the letters "get" or "set," and by capitalizing the first letter of the property name. A JavaBean may explicitly provide introspection metadata by supplying a BeanInfo class. Or you can simply rely on the introspection naming rules.

Introspection provides the extra information necessary to easily interconnect components. Visual building tools that use components have enabled GUI construction in a revolutionary new way. They can also be used to assemble higher level components by simply interconnecting components. IBM VisualAge for Smalltalk has such a GUI component tool, called the Composition Editor, as we saw in Chapter 8. In fact, The VisualAge for Smalltalk's Composition Editor is very similar to a comparable editor in VisualAge for Java. But the latter directly uses JavaBeans as its components.

If visual connection between properties (as enabled by introspection) is not sufficient, you can use a scripting language. A scripting language does not need to have to full power of a language like Smalltalk in order to be useful. It is meant to be simple, programmatic "glue" to interconnect components.

Interaction and dependency

Another property of the modern component is that there is a mechanism for setting up dependencies, so that it a component automatically interacts with other components. The most sophisticated way to do this is via events. A component issues an event when something of possible interest to other components happens. Other components may choose to be "listeners" for a particular event. They will be automatically notified when the event occurs. If any parameters are necessary to provide specific useful information, they are sent along with the event.

As we've seen, CORBA has an Event Service that provides this type of facility. Three out of four distributed Smalltalks, namely IBM VisualAge Distributed, ObjectShare Distributed Smalltalk, and DNS SmalltalkBroker, support this CORBA service. Smalltalk images using Event Services send events to each other, which are objects that do not need answers.

CORBA provides the infrastructure for events. But it does not yet have a means for readily setting up dependencies between components—or for formally defining a component, for that matter.

In 1996, the OMG issued an RFP for a CORBA component model. The goal of this proposal is to implement true component technology in CORBA. It requires that a CORBA component model specify interfaces and mechanisms for generating component-events, and for installing arbitrary component-event handlers (listeners) for specific component-events generated by components. CORBA components will also have externally visible properties that can be connected to the event mechanism. When a property value changes, a component event may be generated.

Furthermore, CORBA components are required to map to JavaBeans. The mapping will permit a CORBA component to present itself as a JavaBean to Java programs and application building tools based on JavaBeans.

A CORBA component must have a standardized description, an "information model." This description captures all the salient features of components. These component descriptions will be stored in a repository.

These component descriptions will be mapped to Java BeanInfo structures, so that visual application building tools that rely on BeanInfo can be used to configure and assemble CORBA components and JavaBeans interchangeably.

Components and distribution

Some type of component-based technology has long been sought as a way to standardize software into reusable units. Nowhere is this need more critical than in distributed object-oriented software. What are the requirements of such a technology, and where can it take us?

The component as a black box

Jacobson[9] distinguishes between **white-box** components and **black-box** components. A white-box component requires you to look inside and customize it for your specific needs in order to reuse it. A black-box component can only be accessed through its interface. You may not look inside or change the implementation in any way. Certainly, the modern view of a component, and the type discussed here, is the black-box variety.

In order to distribute a component, it must be a black box. For example, if it is a CORBA distributed component, then you may use it only through its IDL interface. Distribution adds a new dimension for component reuse.

The modern component was born from a need to make GUI construction natural and easy. The idea is to lay out components by dropping them onto a window and literally wire them together via connecting lines. These lines represent dependencies that are implemented via events and automatically create event channels between components. The Composition Editor in IBM VisualAge for Smalltalk is one such GUI builder.

But the Composition Editor can work with non-visual as well as visual components such as combo boxes and text entry widgets. A non-visual component has no visual representation. So, components, whether visual or non-visual, are all component and can be interconnected using the same tools as were originally designed to address the issue of GUI construction.

JavaBeans were originally envisioned as visual components. They were meant to be used as building blocks in composing applications, for example. So a user may employ a builder tool to connect together and customize a set of JavaBeans to act as an application. Thus a button component could be a JavaBean. It was also seen that some JavaBeans will be more like whole applications, such as a spreadsheets, which may then be composed together into compound document. In either case, the JavaBean was seen as something GUI-centric operating monolithically.

Enter the Enterprise JavaBean. The Enterprise JavaBean takes the JavaBeans component architecture to the next level by providing an API optimized for building scalable business applications as reusable server components. With Enterprise JavaBeans, a developer can design and re-use non-visual remote objects to build corporate applications. These "componentized" applications are expected to run manufacturing, financial, inventory management, and data processing system on a platform that is Java-enabled. So what have Enterprise JavaBeans got to do with distributed Smalltalk? You'll see in a moment.

Enterprise JavaBeans can be used with a visual builder tool and be interconnected together just as ordinary JavaBeans. What happens when we interconnect ordinary, visual client-based JavaBeans with non-visual, server-based JavaBeans? We get a distributed object-oriented system! Obviously, the builder tool must support distribution, and automatically partition a program and generate the appropriate connections to the distributed object infrastructure, such as CORBA. This is the next logical step in visual builder tool evolution.

The CORBA component model is interoperable with the JavaBean component model. This means that any builder tool that supports distributed JavaBeans also supports CORBA components, and vice-versa. This opens up a brave new world of system building for distributed Smalltalk. CORBA-compliant distributed Smalltalk components will be available for use by JavaBean builder tools. The Java juggernaut can be leveraged for use by CORBA and CORBA-compliant distributed Smalltalk.

The "Software IC"

Components promise to make the holy grail of "Software ICs" (units of software that can be interconnected together like integrated circuits) a reality.

Components offer the "industrialization" of software development. When a manufacturing process evolves to the point where it can be based on pre-built components, product quality, quantity, and speed of delivery soar. This principle applies as well to software systems development. It promises unprecedented quality and speed of development. But a fundamental paradigm shift is necessary to usher in the industrial age of software development. The traditional custom, handcrafted approach to software will have to give way to component standardization.

But do not think for a minute that component technology will eliminate the job of the programmer! Did the IC eliminate the jobs of hardware designers? No. What it did was allow engineers to work at a higher level. It let them build more complex systems, more reliably, and in a shorter time.

In order to successfully use the IC analogy, perhaps a closer look is necessary. Integrated circuit technology did not emerge full-blown. It evolved from small ICs performing simple functions, like AND and OR gates, through large scale integration (LSI) that provided things like adders, to very large scale integration (VLSI), which delivers powerful CPUs on a single chip.

Smalltalk has powerful built-in classes, such as OrderedCollections, which do the low-level work that must be coded "by hand" and with custom solutions in other programming languages. Do these correspond to the early small, primitive ICs that provided the first integrated building blocks for digital hardware designers? If so, then software components correspond to higher levels of integration—to LSI and VLSI.

More complex systems will be buildable, but with no less expertise required. If we can extrapolate from the hardware world, skills will move from hand-crafted, special-purpose engineering to high-level, architectural design. In the era of the software IC, the programmer will not be out of a job. But her skills will need to evolve beyond those of even today's cutting-edge object-oriented developer. Smalltalk has had its own "small" software ICs for years. At least us Smalltalkers will have a head-start.

Components are the natural units of a distributed system. Can we learn anything from the IC analogy here? The answer is yes. And you have to look no further than your own personal computer.

The processor chip in your PC, be it Intel, PowerPC, or Joe's Semiconductors, works at very high rate of speed. It runs off an internal clock that may be more than 200 megahertz, or even more than 300 megahertz. Your 266 megahertz PC is executing 266 million processor cycles every second. That is the speed at which internal elements of the processor, such as the ALU (arithmetic logic unit) and the address bus, communicate.

But computer printed circuit boards and card sockets cannot practically communicate at such speeds. The effects of the electronic capacitance of printed circuits and their connectors cause digital signals to "smear out" at these high speeds. And if capacitance effects were somehow eliminated, printed circuit board paths tend to act like transmission lines rather than simple electrical connections. PC board layout would be enormously more complex at these speeds.

In practice, 30–40 megahertz is a typical limit for today's PC boards. The clock rate, the heartbeat to which everything in the PC is synchronized, is actually much less than the processor chip. So a 266 megahertz processor might communicate with the rest of the PC at only 33 megahertz, or 1/8 of its internal speed. That is nearly an order of magnitude slower. In order to communicate with its own RAM, the processor is slowed to a virtual snail's pace.

Does this sound familiar? It is exactly the same situation that occurs in distributed Smalltalk systems. Within the same object space, object communication is very fast, but between object spaces, much slower network communication speed limits are in effect.

You've probably heard the term "memory cache" with reference to your PC's processor. This is on-chip, and therefore full-speed, RAM that the processor can use for instruction execution and the reading and writing of data. It is a local cache, or duplicate, of portions of the ordinary RAM of the computer.

In the Stock Market Application, you saw that keeping a local copy of distributed objects was necessary in order to maintain GUI performance (see "How not to get stuck in the GUI" in Chapter 8). This local copy of objects was none other than a local cache, just as exists in your personal computer's processor chip! The solution of caching to overcome speed limitations between slowly communicating elements of a system is a common one. We see it here in two very different domains. And the practical issues, such as pre-fetching and maintaining cache consistency, are exactly the same. So there may be even more to learn from the IC analogy than you might guess when we talk about distributed software components.

Transactions

Transactions are fundamental to most large systems. They are required wherever the state of data changes needs to be kept consistent. It is particularly critical in concurrent, shared data systems, where more than one program might try to modify the same data at the same time.

The basics

Transactions solve two types of problems. One is concurrency. It is simply in the nature of concurrent systems that a data modification may fail. An example will illustrate this.

Consider the case where a couple, Steve and Edie, are trying to deposit money into the same bank account at the same time. Steve deposits $100, and Edie deposits $200. The following steps would need to be done for both Steve and Edie:

1. Read the current account balance from the database.

2. Add this to the deposit amount ($100 or $200) to get a new balance.

3. Write the new balance to the database.

There is obviously a problem here if the deposits are made simultaneously. Both Steve and Edie get the same current balance in step 1. But in step 3, the wrong amount will get written to the database, depending upon who gets there first. If it is Steve, the balance would reflect an additional $100. If Edie gets there first, the balance will have increased by $200. This is known as a **race condition**, and either way

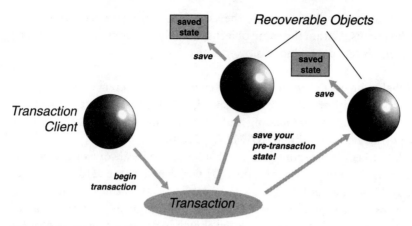

Figure 9-2. Start and object transaction

it is wrong, because the balance should have increased by $300. One deposit will get lost. This is not good for Steve, Edie, or the bank! Something needs to synchronize these deposits, and that something is a transaction.

The second problem that transactions solve is a failure condition. Consider what would happen if the above example were implemented by having two local databases at two bank branch offices. Steve makes his deposit at one branch office, and this updates the balance at the other branch office, too. Edie later makes her deposit at the other branch office, but this time a failure occurs, and the other office is not updated with Edie's deposit. The database is in an inconsistent state, and requesting the balance for Steve and Edie's account will yield a different result depending on which office you are at.

You may be familiar with relational databases management systems, such as Oracle or Sybase. Transactions are an essential feature of relational databases, which typically implement such systems as bank use for their accounts. And absolutely essential to correct transaction functionality is the **ACID** (Atomic, Consistent, Isolated, and Durable) set of characteristics. They are defined as follows:

- A transaction is **atomic**; if interrupted by failure, all effects are undone. This is termed a rollback. Either a transaction happens or it doesn't. There is nothing in between.

- A transaction produces **consistent** results; the effects of a transaction preserve invariant properties. In other words, the resulting state must be self-consistent, and not violate any constraints.

- A transaction is **isolated**; its intermediate states are not visible to other transactions. Transactions appear to execute serially, even if they are performed concurrently.

- A transaction is **durable**; the effects of a completed transaction are persistent; they are never lost (except in a catastrophic failure).

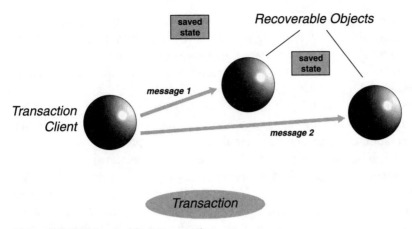

Figure 9-3. Within an object transaction

A transaction can be terminated in two ways: the transaction is either **committed** or **rolled back**. When a transaction is committed, all changes made by the associated requests are made permanent. When a transaction is rolled back, all changes made by the associated requests are undone.

Objects can engage in transactions, too. Figure 9-2 shows the start of a transaction involving a **transaction client** and two **recoverable objects**. At the start of the transaction, the recoverable objects are told to save their current, pre-transaction states. Within the transaction, the transaction client can send messages to the recoverable objects, which change their states as a result (see Figure 9-3). The transaction is ordered to roll back. In this case, the order is given by the transaction client (see Figure 9-4). The transaction propagates this rollback order to the recoverable objects, which then must restore their pre-transaction states. At this point, the transaction is complete.

Think of a transaction system as having two states: a **stable state** and a **volatile state**. The stable state is a self-consistent, agreed-upon state that the outside world sees; the "official" state of the system. While a transaction is in progress, any opera-

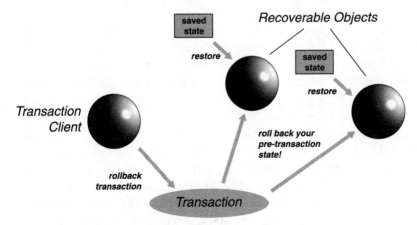

Figure 9-4. Roll back an object transaction

tions performed on the objects engaged in that transaction modify the volatile state. At the very start of the transaction, the volatile state is a carbon copy of the stable state. When the transaction is committed, the stable state gets updated to whatever was recorded in the volatile state. If the transaction is rolled back, the current volatile state is discarded and replaced by the pre-transaction stable state.

In practice, the volatile state can be implemented as a true duplicate of the stable state, or as simply a delta change or series of deltas on the original, stable state. This is an implementation decision that does not affect our conceptual model.

Transactions can be implemented at different levels of granularity. Fine-grained transactions (lots of small ones) allows more concurrency without conflict than course-grained transactions (a few large ones). On the other hand, coarse-grained transactions incur lower overhead, since fewer transactions are created or need to be committed. A coarse-grained strategy is likely to make a system simpler and easier to understand. But it also reduces concurrency, which may cause poor performance. In general, you should choose the coarsest-grained transaction granularity that meets your performance requirements.

CORBA Transaction Service

The CORBA Transaction Service is one way to apply ACID transactions to objects. It defines interfaces that allow multiple, distributed objects to cooperate in order to provide atomicity. These interfaces enable the objects to either commit all changes together or to rollback all changes together, even in the presence of a (non-catastrophic) failure. No requirements are placed on the objects other than those defined by the Transaction Service interfaces.

The CORBA Transaction Service synchronizes all the participating objects of a distributed client/server application. A transaction can involve multiple objects performing multiple requests. The scope of a transaction is defined by the single Transaction Context shared by the participating objects. There are no constraints placed on the number of objects involved, the topology of the application, or the way in which the application is distributed across a network.

Typically, a transaction client begins a transaction (see Figure 9-5). This creates a **Transaction Context**, transaction information associated with an execution thread. The Transaction Context gets propagated to all objects involved in a transaction.

The transactional client interacts with **Recoverable Objects**. These are objects whose data are affected by committing or rolling back a transaction. They are also **Resources**, which means that they have registered with the Transaction Service for involvement in a committing a transaction. When resources are registered, they become associated with the same Transaction Context as the transaction client.

Once a resource is registered, it is automatically notified of any transaction-related events for its transaction context. These include preparing for a commit, executing a commit, or rolling back a transaction. The Transaction Service uses a **two-phase commit** protocol. For the first phase of the two-phase commit, resources are asked

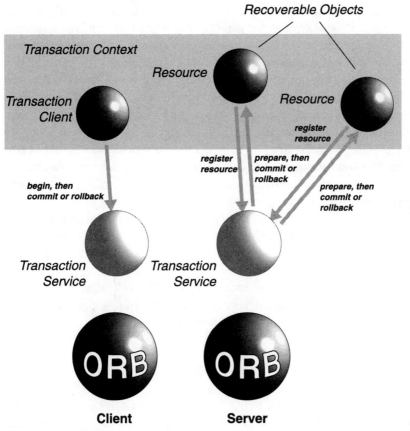

Figure 9-5. CORBA Transaction Service

to **prepare** for the commit. A transaction coordinator sends the prepare message, asking each resource if it believes that it is okay to go ahead and commit the transaction. A resource can respond to this order by either giving the go-ahead, or by voting no. Once a resource prepares a transaction, it cannot commit or rollback a transaction on its own. It must wait for the second phase to hear the final decision. In the second phase of the two-phase commit resources are ordered to either commit or rollback, depending on the voting results of the first phase. The second phase, whether a commit or a rollback, completes the transaction.

It is up to the resource to record its state at the start of the transaction. The beautiful thing is that a resource may implement this recording of state however it wants. This is none of the Transaction Service's business! The implementation of persistent state is safely encapsulated behind the Transaction Service CORBA interfaces. But the resource must be prepared to roll back its state to the original one if it should receive a rollback message rather than a commit message.

There is another type of server object that can participate in a transaction. This is a **TransactionObject** (not shown). It is just like a resource, except that it maintains no state. But it communicates with one or more resources. A TransactionObject has no methods in its CORBA interface. So what good is it? Its function is to implicitly pass its transaction context to resources "behind the scenes." This transaction context is the lifeline that connects the objects involved in a transaction together.

This is termed **implicit propagation** in CORBA. It makes use of the Transaction Service if not transparent at least, well, translucent. You can also choose to use **explicit propagation**. With explicit propagation, applications define their own mechanisms for sharing a common transaction.

The CORBA Transaction Service also supports **nested transactions** in addition to the single-level, **flat transaction model**. In nested transactions, a parent transaction spans one or more child **subtransactions**. An arbitrary number of levels of nested transactions can exist. However a transaction cannot commit unless all of its children have completed. Looking at this from the child subtransaction's point of view, when a subtransaction is committed, the changes remain contingent upon commit of all the subtransaction's ancestors. When a transaction is rolled back, all its children are rolled back.

Nested transactions are an optional feature of the CORBA Transaction Service. An implementation of the Transaction Service is not required to support the nested transaction model, but only the flat transaction model.

An example of a CORBA transaction

How does a CORBA transaction work in practice? Let's go through a simple example.

A client object called anATM desires to make a deposit to the object myBankAccount. The myBankAccount object is of a class BankAccount that has been declared in IDL as inheriting from the Transaction Service's Resource interface. This automatically makes myBankAccount a resource that can participate in a CORBA transactions.

Figure 9-6 shows an example of a CORBA transaction. There is a client object called anATM, and a server object called myBankAccount. The client object will interact with myBankAccount and also with one special pseudo-object called Current. Current is a CORBA interface that provides a convenient way to send messages to the Transaction Service without having to know about any specific object.

The client object knows that it needs to interact with myBankAccount inside a transaction. So it must first begin a transaction by sending the begin message to Current. Then, it sends the message makeDeposit: to myBankAcount with the argument of aDeposit object. This is all that it needs to do inside the transaction, so it sends a commit message to Current. To verify that the transaction was successful, it sends a getStatus message to Current.

Let's look at this in all its detail and see what goes on behind the scenes. The object anATM first sends the message begin to Current (1). This begins a new transaction. It then sends the message makeDeposit: to myBankAccount (2).

The myBankAccount makeDeposit: method was written so as to utilize transaction management. So, within this method, the message getControl is sent to Current, and this message answers a Control object (3). The makeDeposit: method now sends this

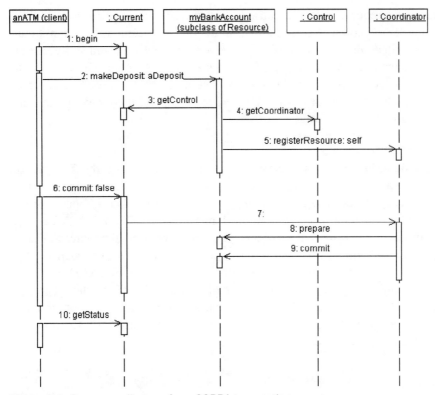

Figure 9-6. Sequence diagram for a CORBA transaction

Control object the message getCoordinator (4). This answers a Coordinator object. Finally within the makeDeposit: method, the message registerResource: method is sent, with the argument of self, to the Coordinator (5). This notifies the Coordinator that myBankAccount is a resource within the current transaction. The Coordinator places myBankAccount into a list of resources for the current transaction. Each of these resources must be notified when it is time to commit the transaction.

Next, anATM decides to commit the transaction. It sends the commit: message to Current (6). The argument false means that the client does not wish the Transaction Service to "report heuristics," special circumstances under which heuristic decisions about a rollback or commit are made. Current then notifies the Coordinator via a private message (7) that a commit has been requested. Now, the Coordinator must seek permission to do the commit from the transaction resources. It does this by sending the message prepare to its resources to get each resource's **vote**. In this case, there is just the one resource, myBankAccount (8). That object answer with the Vote (a CORBA enum) VoteCommit. This is the go-ahead signal. It could have answered with VoteRollback. It just takes a single resource to veto the commit. If any resource of a transaction votes VoteRollback, then the transaction is rolled back instead of committed.

In this case, of course, there is a consensus of one, so the Coordinator can tell the resource myBankAccount to commit the transaction by sending it the commit message (9). The client anATM's commit message has returned, so it can verify that the commit was successful by sending the getStatus message to Current. This answers the Status (a CORBA enum) StatusCommitted. Alternatively, it could have set up an exception handler to catch a rollback if it were to occur, and then it would not need to explicitly ask about the status.

The CORBA interfaces

I will now describe the most important CORBA interfaces of the Transaction Service. There are some other interfaces that perform specialized functions, such as for interoperating with the X/Open XA transaction protocol. The X/Open protocol is important because it defines a standardized interface to a TP monitor. A TP monitor is commercial software that provided transactions to control updates to shared resources. You will find TP monitors on large mainframe systems, such as IBM CICS. Popular TP monitors are Transarc's ENCINA and BEA's TUXEDO.

Current interface is designed to be supported by a pseudo-object whose behavior depends upon and may alter the transaction context. It is shared with other object services, such as security—you will encounter it again in Chapter 10. **Current** supports the following operations:

Message	Description
Begin	Begins a transaction
commit:	Commits the current transaction
Rollback	Rolls back the current transaction
rollbackOnly	Transaction is modified so only that the only possibility is to rollback
getStatus	Gets the status of the current transaction
getTransactionName	Answers a printable string name for the transaction
setTimeout:	Sets the number of seconds for the transaction to timeout—if phase 1 lasts beyond the timeout, then the Coordinator rolls back the transaction
getControl	Answers the Control object for the transaction context
suspend	Suspends the current transaction
resume	Resumes the current transaction after a suspend

The **TransactionFactory** interface lets you explicitly create a transaction. It is not needed in most situations, because transactions are implicitly created by the Current interface's begin method. This interface supports the following operations:

Message	Description
create	Begins a transaction, and answer a Control object
recreate	Used to import a transaction from outside of the CORBA Transaction service

The **Control** interface gives low-level access to managing a transaction context. It is implicitly associated with a specific transaction. **Control** supports the following operations:

Message	Description
getTerminator	Answers a Terminator object that can commit or roll back the transaction
getCoordinator	Answers a Coordinator object that provides transaction-handling methods for resources

The **Terminator** interface lets you commit or roll back a transaction. This interface is not needed in most situations, because transactions can be committed or rolled back by the Current interface. But if you need it, it's there. The Terminator interface supports the following operations:

Message	Description
commit:	Commits the current transaction
rollback	Rolls back the current transaction

The **Coordinator** interface is used by resources to get information about their transaction. It's the interface to the central coordinator for both phases of the two-phase commit. This interface supports the following operations:

Message	Description
getStatus	Gets the status of the current transaction
getParentStatus	Gets the status of the parent transaction in a nested transaction
getTopLevelStatus	Gets the status of the top level transaction in a nested transaction
isSameTransaction:	Answers true if the argument, a Coordinator object, refers to our transaction
isAncestorTransaction:	Answers true if our transaction is an ancestor of or the same as the transaction of the argument, a Coordinator object
isDescendentTransaction:	Answers true if our transaction is a descendent of or the same as the transaction of the argument, a Coordinator object
isRelatedTransaction:	Answers true if our transaction is a descendent of, ancestor of, or the same as the transaction of the argument, a Coordinator object
isTopLevelTransaction	Answers true if our transaction has no parent transaction
hashTransaction	Answers a hash code for our transaction
hashTopLevelTrans	Answers a hash code for our top level transaction
registerResource:	Registers the argument, a Resource, with our transaction
registerSynchronization:	Registers the argument, a Synchronization object (see Synchronization interface below)
registerSubtranAware:	Registers the argument, a SubtransactionAwareResource (interface below), to be notified when a subtransaction in a nested transaction has complete
rollbackOnly	Transaction is modified so only that the only possibility is to rollback
getTransactionName	Answers a printable string name for the transaction
createSubtransaction	Creates a nested subtransaction whose parent is the current transaction
getTxContext	Answers a PropagationContext object used to export the current transaction

The **Resource** interface is inherited by resources and provides all the messages they need to support transaction behavior. This interface supports the following operations:

Message	Description
prepare	Invoked to begin the two-phase commit protocol on the resource, which answers with a Vote
rollback	The resource should rollback all changes made as part of the transaction
commit	The resource should commit all changes made as part of the transaction
commitOnePhase	The resource should, if possible, commit all changes made as part of the transaction - can be used when there is just a single resource, for a one-phase commit instead of the standard two-phase commit
forget	Forget all knowledge of the transaction (used for special "heuristic outcome" exceptions)

More thoughts on CORBA transactions

Because CORBA transaction resource implementations are black boxes, the way a resource chooses to implement its persistent state is private. This creates some interesting possibilities. For example, a resource may implement its persistent state in the tables of a relational database. There could be multiple resources, all using different relational databases. If these multiple resources are involved in the same transaction, then the CORBA Transaction Service has in some sense wrapped relational database transactions in its own, higher level atomic transaction. Note, though, that the state stored in relational tables for the transaction resources must include the recoverable state *before* the start of the transaction. If the resource is called upon to rollback its transaction by the Coordinator, it must restore this pre-transaction state.

Because of its X/Open XA interface, the CORBA Transaction Service can be implemented in a TP monitor environment. It supports the ability to execute multiple transactions concurrently and to execute clients, servers, and transaction services in separate processes.

GemStone transactions

In GemStone, a client Smalltalk image talks to a server Smalltalk image. The server Smalltalk image provides an environment where many Smalltalk clients can share the same persistent objects. The GemStone server maintains a central repository of its shared objects. When a client Smalltalk image needs to view or modify its shared objects, it logs into the GemStone object server and starts a session.

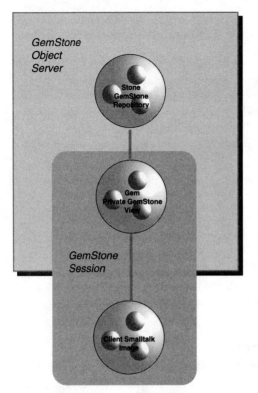

Figure 9-7. GemStone private view

When a GemStone session is begun, a private view of the GemStone repository is created (see Figure 9-7). This view contains shared objects for use by the client Smalltalk image. Don't confuse this private view with object replicates. This view does *not* consist of GemStone replicate objects. It exists regardless of your use of replicates or forwarders (as we used in the Stock Market Project). This view is managed by the Gem process on the GemStone object server.

GemStone uses transactions to maintain a consistent view of its shared repository. The operations that make up transaction happen within a client's private view of the repository. Only when you tell GemStone to commit the transaction does it try to merge the modified objects in your view with those of the repository.

When you log in to GemStone, a transaction is created for you. This is called **automatic transaction mode**. It is the default but may not be the best strategy, because you are working inside a transaction for the entire time that you are logged into GemStone. This is the coarsest possible granularity for a transaction. As such, it is the simplest transaction strategy but could yield poor performance with other concurrent users.

Alternatively, you can immediately set the transaction mode at the start of a GemStone session to **manual transaction mode**. This aborts the current transaction and leaves you outside a transaction. You are then free to start and end transactions whenever you want, giving you complete control over transaction granularity.

Concurrency Control

As we've seen, a primary reason to use transactions is to allow concurrent access to shared resources, such as a databases. So the subject of transactions is inextricably linked to the subject of concurrency control. A transaction provides the structure for access to shared resources. Concurrency control provides the underlying mechanics. So concurrency control provides an essential service for transaction processing.

Locks

A **lock** represents the ability of a specific single user, or **client**, to access a specific resource in a particular way. Concurrency control is not concerned with just who that client is. But because we are talking about concurrency control in the context of transactions, we can assume that in this case, the client is a transaction. But we are also talking about client objects for transactions. Because the lock that applies to a transaction also applies to the client object of that transaction (providing service for the client is, after all, the purpose of the transaction), we can be pretty loose in the definition of a client here. You can think of the client as either the client object of a transaction or the transaction itself. So purists be warned: We will be talking about a transaction acquiring a lock so that things don't get too confusing, even though in the general case, an anonymous client could acquire the lock.

The reason that the term *lock* is used is that in the simplest possible case, when a transaction accesses a resource, it locks it. Another transaction that wants to use the same resource must wait until the first transaction releases its lock on the resource.

But a concurrency control lock is actually more sophisticated than this. It's not just a Yale deadbolt that has just a single kind of key. You can think of a lock as the intelligent gatekeeper to a resource. The lock determines whether a transaction has access to a resource, and if so, exactly what **lock mode** of access. A lock may specify that a transaction can only read a resource, for example. That transaction may freely read and use the state of the resource. But it is not permitted to change the resource state in any way.

Each lock is associated with a single resource and a single client (and therefore transaction) of the resource. Concurrency control is responsible for creating and dispensing locks. It prevents multiple transactions from simultaneously having locks for the same resource if the activities of those transactions might conflict. A transaction must ask for an appropriate lock before accessing a shared resource, and the creation and management of that lock is the job of the concurrency control mechanism.

Typical lock modes for a resource are **read lock** and **write lock**. The read lock mode is also called a **shared lock**, because it's generally okay for more than one transaction to have a read lock on the same resource. But a write lock means that a transaction intends to write to the resource. In this case, nobody else may obtain a lock on that resource because two different writes on the same resource would put it in an inconsistent state (like Steve and Edie both writing a new account balance at the same time). This is why a write lock is also known as an **exclusive lock**, though this can sometimes designate a different lock mode. There can be more lock modes beyond read and write. GemStone distinguishes a more stringent kind of lock than a write lock, which it terms an exclusive lock (See "GemStone object locks" later in this chapter). And CORBA defines no less than five lock modes (See the section named "Lock modes" later in this chapter).

Two transactions are deemed to be in **conflict** if they each want a lock on the same resource, but the lock modes are incompatible. There can be a **read-write conflict** if one transaction has a write lock on a resource, and another transaction wants a read lock on that resource. If the read lock were granted, the information maintained by the resource could change out from under reading transaction because another transaction is writing it. Another type of conflict is the **write-write conflict**. We've already encountered this in explaining why a write lock is also known as an exclusive lock.

Two-phase locking

The most common algorithm used to implement concurrency control locks is called **two-phase locking**. Don't confuse this with the two-phase commit. They are entirely different things (sorry, I did not invent the terminology!).

In two-phase locking, there is a first phase during which a transaction may only acquire locks, and a second phase during which transaction may only release locks. These can be thought of as the **growing phase** and the **shrinking phase**.

Two-phase locking is sufficient to guarantee the serializability of transactions. This is an important concept in the theory of concurrency control. It means that although transactions happen concurrently, the outcome will be the same as executing them sequentially in some order. If such an order does not exist, then the transactions are not serializable. This is, in fact, a fundamental tenet of concurrency control. It is responsible for the important property that a programmer may deal with her individual transaction as if it were being executed alone.

Although two-phase locking is sufficient to guarantee serializability of transactions, it does not guarantee isolation. But hold on. This was the "I" in ACID. It is the property that declared that one transaction's intermediate states are not visible to other transactions. This had better be assured.

The reason that two-phase locking by itself does not guarantee isolation is as follows. Suppose that transaction A has modified some resource. It had a write lock on that resource while it modified it; but now it has released the write lock during the shrinking phase, making the changed resource visible to some other transaction B. Transaction B obtains a read lock on the resource, reading its state as updated from transaction A. But now, something nasty happens. Transaction A rolls back, causing the resource to revert to its previous state. Transaction B is now in trouble because it has observed an intermediate state.

In order to guarantee isolation, two-phase locking systems typically observe **strict two-phase locking**. This is when the locks acquired are held until the transaction either commits or rolls back. In other words, the shrinking phase does not begin until a commit or rollback has been declared. This synchronizes the locking phases with the transactions so that isolation is guaranteed. This is sometimes considered a special case for transactions, and given the name **transaction duration locking**.

Lock granularity

A resource object is to be locked, but so far, nothing has been said about the size of that object. Relational databases deal in tables that are composed of records, so it's not surprising that they can lock at either the whole table or the individual record level. An intermediate level, the page, is also a lockable unit for relation database management systems.

Just as for transactions, locking also possesses granularity. Fine-grained locks allow much more concurrency without conflict than do course-grained locks. In fact, the granularity of the resources locked by an application determines the degree of concurrency within the application. This is because with finer-grained resources, one is not as likely to conflict with someone else using the same resource. On the other hand, coarse granularity locks incur lower overhead, because there are fewer locks to manage. But they also reduce concurrency because conflicts are more likely to occur. Selecting an appropriate lock granularity is a balance between the lock overhead incurred and the degree of concurrency required.

Other concurrency control methods

Though locking in general and two-phase locking in particular are the most widely use concurrency control methods, others exist. There are timestamp-based techniques in which the start of each transaction is given a timestamp. All read and write operations within each transaction are processed so as to ensure that the timestamp order is enforced. The concurrency control mechanism allows a transaction to read or write a resource only if that resource has last been written by an earlier transaction (one with an older timestamp). Otherwise, the new transaction is rolled back.

There is a great deal of literature in the area of transaction processing. Once the domain of the stodgy mainframe, transaction processing is getting new life from distributed computing. The 1984 book *Distributed Databases: Principles and Systems*,[10] by Stefano Ceri and Guiseppe Pelagatti, is still a good reference.

One of the key recent contributors to transaction processing work is William Weihl, who was formerly a professor at MIT, and is now at Digital Equipment Corporation's Systems Research Center. To learn more about the details of modern transaction processing, see his "Transaction-Processing Techniques" chapter in the excellent collection of lecture notes for the ACM's Advanced Course on Distributed Systems entitled *Distributed Systems*.[11]

CORBA Concurrency Control Service

CORBA defines a powerful and flexible framework for concurrency control. It defines a set of lock modes, as well as a generic lock set mechanism that can be used with any desired resources.

Lock modes

The Concurrency Control service defines the standard **read** (R) and **write** (W) lock modes. As we've seen, read locks conflict with write locks, and write locks conflict with other write locks.

In addition, the Concurrency Control service defines an **upgrade** (U) lock. An upgrade mode lock is a read lock that conflicts with itself. Why is disallowing multiple read locks on a resource useful? Because it avoids a common form of deadlock that happens when two or more clients attempt to read and then update the same resource. If more than one client holds a read lock on the resource, a deadlock occurs as soon as one of the clients requests a write lock on the resource. If each client requests a single upgrade lock followed by a write lock, this deadlock does not occur because the second client will be denied the upgrade lock.

The Concurrency Control Service uses *strict two-phase locking* for transactions. When the service is signaled that all locks are to be released because of a commit or release, it considers the phase to have started. It releases the locks, and while it does this, it prevents any new locks from being acquired.

To support variable granularity locking, the Concurrency Control Service adds two more lock modes, **intention read** (IR) and **intention write** (IW). These additional lock modes are used to exploit the natural hierarchy between locks of different granularity.

Let's look at the hierarchical relationship inherent in a database. A typical "flat file" database consists of a collection of files, with each file holding multiple records. To access a record, a coarse-grain lock can be obtained for the whole database. But this isn't a good idea, because then other clients are restricted from accessing the database. However, only setting a lock on the record is also appropriate, because another client might set a lock on the file holding this record, and then delete or modify the file.

Using variable granularity locking, a client first obtains intention locks on the ancestor of a resource. To read a record in the database, for example, the client obtains an intention read lock (IR) on the database and then the file (in that order), before obtaining the read lock (R) on the record. Intention read locks (IR) conflict with write locks (W), and intention write locks (IW) conflict with read (R) and write (W) locks.

The following table summarizes the conflicts among all five lock modes.

Granted mode	Request mode				
	IR	R	U	IW	W
Intention Read (IR)					⊗
Read (R)				⊗	⊗
Upgrade (U)			⊗	⊗	⊗
Intention Write (IW)		⊗	⊗		⊗
Write (W)	⊗	⊗	⊗	⊗	⊗

The symbol ⊗ is used to indicate when locks conflict.

Lock sets

As we've seen, the Concurrency Control Service does not define the granularity of the resources that are locked. In fact, it does not, on its own, associated resources with locks. It defines a **lock set**, which is a collection of locks associated with a single resource.

The Concurrency Control Service does not define what a transaction is. Transactions are defined by the Transaction Service, described above in the section named "CORBA Transaction Service". The Concurrency Control Service is designed to be used with the Transaction Service to coordinate the activities of concurrent transactions.

The Concurrency Control Service can have two types of client: a transactional client and a non-transactional client. There are two parallel interfaces to lock sets for these types of clients. For a transactional client, a first argument is always supplied. This argument is the Coordinator of the transaction.

Because our primary concern is concurrency from the point of view of a transaction, I'll describe the **TransactionalLockSet** interface. The **LockSet** interface is identical, except that the *TransactionalLockSet* operations always have one additional first parameter, which is the *Coordinator* for the transaction. The *TransactionalLockSet* supports the following operations:

Message	Description
lock:mode:	Acquires a lock in the specified mode, and will block the called thread of control if a lock is held on the same lock set by another, client and that lock is in an incompatible mode
tryLock:mode:	Same as lock:mode:, but will not block—instead will answer false if the lock could not be obtained
unlock:mode:	Drops a single lock on the specified lock set in the specified mode
changeMode:heldMode:newMode:	Changes the mode of a single lock. If the new mode conflicts with an existing mode held by an unrelated client, then the changeMode operation blocks the calling thread of control until the new mode can be granted
getCoordinator:	Returns the lock coordinator associated with the specified transaction

So what exactly connects the Concurrency Control Service with the Transaction Service? A resource must be the common connection. Transactions know about resources, and Concurrency Control needs to lock resources.

But then why doesn't the Concurrency Control Service explicitly know about the Resource interface? There do not seem to be any arguments in the *TransactionalLockSet* operations that supply a resource, or even a generic object to which a lock applies.

That's because it is up to clients of the Concurrency Control Service to associate a lock set with each resource. And who is such a client? Typically, it would be a resource itself. The resource holds onto a unique lock set instance, not vice-versa. So the

Concurrency Control Service does not have to know anything about a resource, because it is a client. It's the resource that knows about its lock set.

On the other hand, the Resource interface does not have specific knowledge of a lock set. That is because to remain general-purpose, the Concurrency Control Service requires that the mapping between resources and lock sets remains completely up to the implementation of the resource. But the simplest and most common case is where a single lock is placed directly on a resource. Here, the CORBA object implementation of the resource would use the Concurrency Control Service to get a lock set, and to coordinate concurrent access to the object by multiple clients via that lock set.

A resource obtains a lock set by asking the **LockSetFactory** to manufacture a new one for it. The *LockSetFactory* interface has the following definition:

Message	Description
Create	Create and answer a new LockSet
createRelated:	Create and answer a new LockSet that is related to the argument LockSet—related LockSets drop their locks together
createTransactional	Create and answer a new TransactionalLockSet
createTransactionalRelated:	Create and answer a new TransactionalLockSet that is related to the argument TransactionalLockSet—related Transactional LockSets drop their locks together

So a resource that is starting a transaction would create a *TransactionLockSet* by sending the createTransactional message. The resource must hold onto that lock set instance until it is no longer needed. In the meantime, any message sent to that resource, which implements read or write behavior, must acquire an appropriate lock by sending a message to the lock set.

All of the *TransactionalLockSet* methods require a transaction Coordinator as a first parameter. Within the Transaction Service, a resource is needed to find its Coordinator in order to register itself as a resource within a transaction (see Figure 9-6). A resource gets its Coordinator object by first obtaining its Control object by sending the getControl message to its Current interface. Then, it sends the message getCoordinator to its *Control*, and this answers the necessary object to pass to its *TransactionalLockSet*.

What does a resource do when you are all done committing or rolling back a transaction, and it no longer needs a lock set? It would like to simply release all the locks of the lock set. It does this via a **LockCoordinator**. Send the getCoordinator: message to the TransactionLockSet object, and this answers the lock coordinator. The *LockSet* and *TransactionalLockSet* interfaces create an instance of the *LockCoordinator* for each transaction. The *LockCoordinator* interface provides a single operation:

Message	Description
DropLocks	Releases all locks held by a transaction

GemStone object locks

Because it was designed from the start to share database objects, GemStone also has concurrency control features. It has two basic concurrency policies, and a straightforward set of locking modes.

Optimistic and pessimistic concurrency control

There are two basic approaches to managing locks on GemStone distributed objects. One is called **optimistic concurrency control**, and it is very simple. It specifies that you don't bother to lock objects at all. You simply read and write objects as you please. GemStone detects conflicts with other transactions when you try to commit.

The alternative is termed **pessimistic concurrency control**. Here, you explicitly request locks on objects. You can use whatever granularity of locking you deem appropriate.

Running under optimistic concurrency control is only practical if you are not sharing objects, are reading but not writing, or are writing very often and don't mind being sometimes unable to commit your work.

If you do not lock an object that you are reading or writing, then you are implicitly using optimistic concurrency control. Under optimistic concurrency control, you can globally configure two modes of level checking. You can set the level of checking to either **full checks**, which is the default mode, or to **no read-write checks**. In *full checks* mode, either a read-write conflict or a write-write conflict is detected, and renders a transaction unable to commit. In *no read-write checks* mode, only a write-write conflict is detected.

Locking modes

Gemstone has three locking modes: **read**, **write**, and **exclusive**. These types of locks are acquired on distributed objects by sending the messages readLock:, writeLock:, and exclusiveLock: to GemStone. The argument in each case is the object you want to lock.

Holding a read lock on an object means that you are free to read the object's state and be assured that some other transaction has not changed its state out from under you. More than one read lock can be held on the same object. In fact, GemStone allows up to 1 million read locks on an object! This is not recommended, however, and GemStone documentation suggests that the practical limit is 2000 read locks on an object. If you hold a read lock, it guarantees that no other transaction will be able to:

- Acquire a write lock or exclusive lock on that object.
- Commit a transaction if that object has been written.

A write lock on an object guarantees that you can change it within a transaction and successfully commit the transaction. If you hold a write lock, this guarantees that no other transaction will be able to:

- Acquire any mode of lock on that object.
- Commit a transaction if that object has been written.

An exclusive lock is very similar to a write lock, except that it is even more restrictive. If you hold an exclusive lock, no other transaction will be able to:

- Acquire any mode of lock on that object.
- Commit a transaction if an object has been written *or read*.

You should use an exclusive lock if you intend to update an object's state and you want to guarantee that no other transaction will use the old state of the object. This is important if you want to make sure that the information in the old, soon-to-be-obsolete object state is not read and then propagated to other objects.

The following table summarizes the lock conflicts for GemStone.

Granted mode	Request mode		
	R	W	E
Read (R)		☹	☹
Write (W)	☹	☹	☹
Exclusive (E)	☹	☹	☹

When you send the messages readLock:, writeLock:, and exclusiveLock: to GemStone, the system attempts to acquire the desired lock for you immediately. If the lock is granted, the message answers the receiver object. If it is denied because of a lock conflict, an exception is raised, which you should handle via an appropriate exception handler. These messages do *not* block the execution of your code and force you to wait.

There is another form of the lock messages that is very convenient because it lets you provide a block to be executed if the lock is denied. Plus it handles a **dirty lock**. If another transaction has committed a change to an object since the beginning of your transaction, the lock is granted, but the lock is marked as dirty. A transaction with a dirty lock cannot commit. It must abort (roll back) its transaction to get the updated version of the object.

The following message form allows you to specify both an **ifDenied** block and an **ifChanged** block:

```
readLock: anObject ifDenied: ifDeniedBlock ifChanged: ifChangedBlock
writeLock: anObject ifDenied: ifDeniedBlock ifChanged: ifChangedBlock
exclusiveLock: anObject ifDenied: ifDeniedBlock ifChanged: ifChangedBlock
```

Reduced-conflict classes

Gemstone provides a very clever facility to reduce the need for locking. If you take a closer look at the semantics of object classes, it is possible to go beyond the simple notions of reading and writing. You can use the details of object modification messages to your advantage in not requiring a write lock in every case of altering the object.

For example, the bag is a standard Smalltalk collection that contains unordered objects and allows more than one occurrence of the same object. If two parties want to add an object to a bag (via the add: message), these operations do not logically conflict, even though they both involve writing to the object. How do we know this? Because the add: method is **commutative**; that is, it doesn't matter in what order two such methods are invoked for a bag. In this case, they can both succeed in either order and produce a single, consistent result.

GemStone defines some special classes that reduce conflict on the server by exploiting the semantics of such classes. These classes all have the prefix letters "Rc," for "reduced conflict." The following reduced conflict classes are defined:

- RcCounter
- RcIdentityBag
- RcQueue
- RcKeyValueDictionary

As a detailed example, let's look at the reduced conflict Bag class, RcIdentityBag. As we know, add operations are no problem for RcIdentityBag because they are commutative. It doesn't matter in what order adds from different transactions occur, because the result are the same regardless of the order in which the transactions commit.

But what about remove operations? Some additions and removals commute. If one transaction adds an object to the bag, and another transaction removes a different object, the result is the same regardless of who goes first. These operations commute, so there is no possibility for conflict. But if the object for addition and removal happens to be the same, things get more complicated.

Consider an RcIdentityBag with only one occurrence of one object in it. What happens when an addition or removal occurs within a single transaction? In this case, addition and removal are not commutative. If the addition occurs first, followed by the removal, then there is no conflict. But if the removal occurs first, then the operation fails because there is not yet any object to remove.

But what happens when the addition occurs in one transaction, and the removal occurs in another? In this case, because of the isolations of the two transactions, the removal operation will never be aware of the addition operation. The removal will always fail. But wait—in this case the operations are commutative. The final state of the database is unambiguous. There is a conflict, and one operation fails. So commutivity does not guarantee transaction success. Commutivity simply means that there is no **logical conflict**. It does not necessarily mean that there will be no read-write conflict, for example. The important thing is that the database remains in a consistent state, and that the locking mechanism has unambiguous rules for committing and rolling back transactions.

BOCA

A new CORBA standard addresses the needs of complex, enterprise-wide development. This is the **Business Object Component Framework (BOCA)**. It is a long-awaited and long-argued-over standard that provides the next higher level for defining CORBA distributed objects.

Common Business Objects

As of this writing, adoption of this specification was imminent. This spec provides for **Common Business Objects**, an important technological infrastructure to support "plug and play" business application components. Common Business Objects represent the business semantics that may be found in any enterprise, such as the concept of a "purchase." These objects are subclassed to create business objects in the business model.

The BOCA Meta-Model describes the constructs and types that are used to build a business object system. Among other things, BOCA extends CORBA IDL into a new **Component Definition Language (CDL)**. CDL is a meta-language for defining complex business objects. It can define complex relationships, constraints, pre and post-conditions, and an event model.

BOCA extends and interoperates with the **UML** modeling standard. UML, a unification of both the OMT and Rumbaugh standards, has been adopted by the OMG as its official model specification language. Models for systems can be described in UML, and maintained in a Meta-Object repository as defined by the CORBA **Meta-Object Facility (MOF)**. The MOF specifies how such models are stored and can be used to exchange models between different modeling tools. Given a UML design, the BOCA provides a way to express and realize the design as CORBA-based distributed business objects. This common repository facility is expected to become the standard, vendor-neutral component repository of the future.

BOCA Business objects are one type of component in the repository. They represent business entities and processes—the central elements of the business object specification. Business objects are specialized into Common Business Objects, among other object types.

For each kind of component, there is a **manager** object. The manager object contains information about the component as well as methods for maintaining component instances through their life cycles. There can be instance constructors, attributes and operations that effect the entire type, not just one instance. BOCA uses **type managers**. Type managers are CORBA objects that contain constructors, extents, attributes and operations that may affect the entire type, not just one instance. Features may be declared to be in the instance scope or in the manager scope. One of the jobs of managers is to be the instance factory and to manage the extent of instances.

Dependencies

One goal of BOCA is to promote loose coupling between components and to provide the ability for components to be added to a system on an ad-hoc basis. These components may have dependencies on other components that were not anticipated when those other components where implemented. Such a loosely coupled system requires that an event client drive event publication, not the event producer. It would be impractical for every instance to publish every event that happens to it. Instead, every **feature** of an object is considered a candidate event producer. These features includes all attributes, relationships, states, and operations of an object.

A feature only generates notifications when an interest has been registered for it due to a declared dependency. These events are typically simple messages from one instance to another. The declaration of a feature and the declaration of a dependency on that feature are both required to generate an event notification.

It's not reasonable to expect that all of the dependency requirements of future systems can be anticipated by a developer. The BOCA event/dependency system exposes all potential state changes and invocations as events, eliminating the need to guess at future requirements. **Implicit events** are provided so that objects or applications can be built that have unanticipated dependencies.

BOCA declares that standard implicit events be generated on actions that effect the overall "abstract state" of any component (all attributes, states, relationships and the object lifetime), and on operation invocations. These events are dynamically accessible to any object with a relationship or visibility to the component's definition through the use of the BOCA dependency/trigger mechanism.

The implicit events are:

- The change of any attribute
- The change of any relationship
- Any state transition
- Invocation, completion or failure of any operation
- Entering or leaving any particular state
- Insertion or removal of an element in any collection or relation
- The creation or destruction of any object
- The launching of any process

Appliances

BOCA also has a facility called an **appliance**. Appliances specify some semantic aspect of a business object, such as a business rule or database mapping. Appliances are a generic facility for "mixing in" functionality and specifications. Appliances allow new constructs to be defined and then "applied" to types.

Applying an appliance means that the semantics of the appliance now apply to the defined type. Applying an appliance is analogous to component assembly. The appliance is defined as an independent component and then "plugged into" a component. The component's behavior is then supported by, and partly defined by, the appliance. Appliances only affect the specification. They are a mechanism for defining some semantic aspect of the component. BOCA does not specify the implementation aspects of an appliance. Implementations of BOCA are free to assemble components that correspond to appliances, but this is not part of the standard. When the CORBA component specification is available, applying an appliance can be directly linked to component assembly.

A core set of appliances has been predefined and is part of the BOCA specification. These appliances are:

- **ECRule**: An abstract rule that is triggered by events, filters the events based on a guard condition, and then fires the rule. Subtypes of ECRule provide an action. All EC rules may defer action until transaction commit.

- **StateTransitonRule**: Defines a transition from one state to another based on events and conditions.

- **Invariant**: Defines a condition that must always hold for the type. The condition may always hold for the type or only in response to a given event.

- **Dependency**: Defines a dependency from one type to another. Dependencies are a declarative way to register interest in events.

- **Label**: Defines a natural language translation for symbols based on the user's choice of language locale.

≡Chapter 10≡

Whither the Internet?

The Internet is just a huge (*the* huge) TCP/IP network. In theory, any distributed piece of Smalltalk software could hook right up to it, because they all support TCP/IP (see Figure 10-1). For example, CORBA ORBs could freely use the Internet as a transport medium. The IIOP, which allows ORBs to talk to each other over TCP/IP, is all that is required.

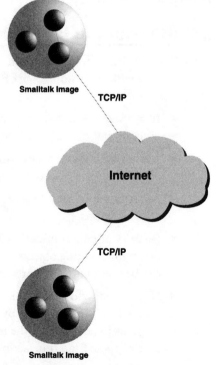

Figure 10-1. Distributed Smalltalk over the Internet

Distributed Smalltalk over the Internet: Security

In practice, there is one important real-world consideration: security.

It's fine to have privileged company information flying around within the confines of a private computer network. But the Internet is by nature public. Without security, a clever programmer could readily eavesdrop on sensitive information as it travels through the Net. A user could masquerade as someone else, so as to obtain access to information intended for the other person's eyes. Objects could also be tampered with. Information could be modified, inserted, or deleted. Or inadequate security controls could be bypassed altogether. Security must also require adequate identification of users, lest there be no accountability.

Security consists of the following elements:

- **Authentication**: Assuring that users are who they say they are.

- **Confidentiality**: Information is available only to those who are authorized to access it.

- **Integrity**: Information can be modified only by those who are authorized to do so.

- **Availability**: Access cannot be denied to authorized users.

- **Accountability**: Users of information are responsible for all security-relevant actions they take.

Different levels of security typically are available on any distributed computing system. For example, some communication may not need to be confidential, but authenticating the other party may still be vital. Security isn't free. There may be a noticeable performance penalty for the higher levels of security.

CORBA over the Internet

A CORBA Security Service has been adopted by the OMG. This service has become a top priority with the coming age of Internet distributed objects. CORBA Security provides:

- **Identification** and **authentication** of principals (the CORBA term for both humans and objects involved in security) to verify who they claim to be.

- **Authorization** and **access control**, which consists of deciding whether principals may access an object based on their identity and/or privileges.

- **Security auditing,** to assure that users are accountable for their security-related actions.

- **Security of communication** between objects, which includes authentication of communicating objects, as well as **integrity protection**. Optionally, there can be **confidentiality protection** for messages in transit.

- **Non-repudiation**, which is proof of the origins of data, as well as proof that a data was received by a particular recipient. This protects against attempts to falsely deny the receiving or sending of data, as in, for example, an electronic fund transaction.

- **Administration** of security.

The CORBA Security Service is a layer of software between an ORB and its objects. When a request to a client object is made, the request passes through the

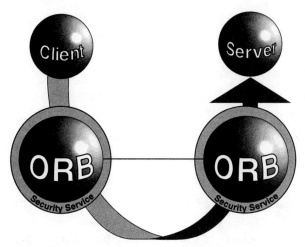

Figure 10-2. A request through the CORBA Security Service

Security Service of the client-side ORB, and also through the Security Service of the client-side ORB before reaching the client object (see Figure 10-2).

CORBA Security is not all-or-nothing. Security requirements vary from enterprise to enterprise. There is flexibility of security with regard to choice of access control policy. CORBA Security provides for two explicit levels of functionality. Level 1 is for applications that are to remain unaware to security, and those that have limited requirements to enforce their own security. Level 2 allows applications to control security in dealing with individual objects. They can also administer their own security policy in a portable way. All OMG-compliant ORBs supplying the CORBA Security Service must implement level 1 as a minimum.

CORBA Security is a very new service, so it may not be available yet on the Smalltalk ORB of your choice. However, the OMG has designed the Security Service so that an ORB can understand security messages but take no action yet. This way, security components of it can be slipped in, or **replaced**, at any later time.

Interceptors

A key feature of CORBA Security is its use of **interceptors**. An interceptor is software that snags a normal CORBA message, and forces it through the security system. An **Access Control Interceptor** determines whether an invocation (that is, a remote message send) should be permitted. After the Access Control Interceptor grants permission for the invocation, a **Security Invocation Interceptor** is used. This interceptor can utilize cryptographic services to provide message protection and verification. It can check and protect messages, both requests and replies, for integrity and confidentiality.

Interceptors use lower-level security functions to actually implement security using implementation-level security objects. These objects are the following:

- **Vault**: Responsible for establishing the security association between client and target, and creating a security context for this association.

- **Security Context**: Holds security information about the client-target security association and is used to protect messages.

- **Access Decision**: Used to decide if request should be allowed or not.

- **Audit Decision**: Used to decide if events are to be audited.

- **Audit Channel**: Used to write audit records to the audit trail.

Collectively, the objects and messages that security interceptors use are called the CORBA Implementor's Security Interface.

As of this writing, CORBA security does not mandate one particular cryptographic algorithm or interface with such an algorithm. This is because no specific interface has been agreed upon by other international standards bodies but are being activity discussed now.

However, the industry standard **Generic Security Services** GSS-API is used for security associations and for the majority of Credentials and Security Context operations. Several CORBA Security interfaces have been designed to map easily to GSS-API functions. CORBA Security defines an external Cryptographic Support Facilities so as to allow easy replacement of cryptographic algorithms.

The GSS-API defines an interface to security services at a generic level. It is independent of any particular underlying security mechanisms. GSS-API security is implementable (and has been implemented) over a range of underlying mechanisms based on secret-key and public-key cryptographic technologies.

The GSS-API uses something called a security context to determine the specific encryption implementation. The underlying implementation mechanism is called a mech_type in GSS-API lingo. The definition of a mech_type includes not only the use of a particular cryptographic algorithm (or a hybrid or choice among alternative cryptographic algorithms), but also definition of the syntax and semantics of data element exchanges that that mechanism will employ in order to support security services. In order to successfully establish a security context with a target peer, it is necessary to identify an appropriate mech_type that both initiator and target peers support. When one party desires to talk to another, he firsts requests a security context from the API. A token representing this security context is then sent to the other party.

So, users of the GSS-API still have to agree on a cryptographic algorithm. For example, services provided by GSS-API can be implemented by secret-key technologies, such as Kerberos, or a public-key approach. See the "Encryption" section below for more on cryptographic algorithms.

Security level 1

Level 1 provides the most basic level of security. It can provide security in a manner that is completely transparent to an application program.

Features

Security level 1 provides a number of features. The following are supplied, regardless of whether an application is security-aware:

- Allows user and other principals to be authenticated.

- Provides security of the invocation between client and target objects. This does not have to be provided at the ORB level if it can be implemented at a lower communications level. This security includes establishment of trust between the two parties, integrity and/or confidentiality of requests and responses between them, and control of whether a client can access an object.

- When there is a chain of message sends with an intermediate object, the ability to either delegate the incoming credentials, or use the credentials of the intermediate object.

- A required set of auditing capabilities.

For security aware applications, it must also

- make the privileges of authenticated principals available to applications.

Classes and messages

There is one object type, called **Current**, which implements level 1 security. It is in module SecurityLevel1, and it understands a single message:

getAttributes:

This message's single argument is an AttributeTypeList, which is from the Security module. The Security module must be supplied by any ORB that claims to be security-ready. An AttributeTypeList is an OrderedCollection of AttributeType objects. An **AttributeType** is a Smalltalk Dictionary with two entries:

Key	Value
attributeFamily	ExtensibleFamily
attributeType	SecurityAttributeType

An **ExtensibleFamily** is a Dictionary, also with two elements:

Key	Value
familyDefiner	Integer
family	Integer

Each SecurityAttributeType is one of a set of constants, defined in CORBAConstants. There are **SecurityAttributesTypes** for each set of attribute families. CORBA defines two standard families.

Family 1: Privilege	Attribute meaning
::Security::Public	The principal has no authenticated identity
::Security::AccessId	The identity of the principal used for access control
::Security::PrimaryGroupId	The primary group to which the principal belongs
::Security:: GroupId	A group to which the principal belongs
::Security::Role	The role the principal takes
::Security::AttributeSet	An identifier for a set of related attributes
::Security::Clearance	The principal's security clearance
::Security::Capability	A capability

Family 0: Other	Attribute meaning
::Security::AuditId	The identity of the principal used for auditing
::Security::AccountingId	The id of the account to be charged for resource use
::Security::NonRepudiationId	The id of the principal used for non-repudiation

So, to learn the values of any desired attributes, you send the message getAttributes: with the OrderedCollection of AttributeType objects. The answer to this message is an OrderedCollection of Attribute objects, each corresponding to a requested AttributeType.

The getAttributes: message answers an AttributeList object, also defined in the Security module. An AttributeList is an OrderedCollection of **SecAttribute** objects. A SecAttribute object is a Dictionary with the following keys and values:

Key	Value
attributeType	AttributeType
definingAuthority	Opaque
value	Opaque

The value of an attribute can be interpreted only with the knowledge of AttributeType.

In addition to adding a Current class, security level 1 adds one additional message that the ORB must understand:

getServiceInformation: serviceInformation:

This message replies with a Boolean, which is true if the service (namely, Security) is supported by this ORB.

The message's first argument is a ServiceType. A ServiceType is one of a set of constants, defined in CORBAConstants. There is currently only one such constant defined so far. This is the constant named Security:

ServiceType	Meaning
::Security	Use the CORBA Security Service

The getServiceInformation: serviceInformation: message is not specific to security, so it could be used to get information about other CORBA facilities and services. When this happens, more constants are defined for use as the first argument to the message.

The second argument is an output, so it is a value holder that conforms to the CORBAParameter protocol. If the message answered true, meaning that security is supported, then sending the value message to the value holder after the message is sent results in a **ServiceInformation** object. A ServiceInformation object is a Dictionary with the following possible elements:

Key	Value
serviceOptions	OrderedCollection of ServiceOption
serviceDetails	OrderedCollection of ServiceDetail

A ServiceOption is one of a set of constants, defined in CORBAConstants:

ServiceOption	Meaning
::SecurityLevel1	Implements Security Level 1
::SecurityLevel2	Implements Security Level 2
::NonRepudiation	Implements the optional Non-repudiation Service
::SecurityORBServiceReady	Does not provide any security functionality yet, but makes calls to high-level interceptors when security is available
::SecurityServiceReady	Does not provide any security functionality yet, but supports calls to the low-level CORBA Implementor's Security Interface when security is available
::ReplaceORBServices	Can replace security services, and uses calls to high-level interceptors
::ReplaceSecurityServices	Can replace security services, and supports calls to the low-level CORBA Implementor's Security Interface
::StandardSecureInteroperability	Supports secure communication between ORBs using the Secure Inter-ORB Protocol (SECIOP)
::DCESercureInteroperability	Supports secure communication between ORBs using the DCE Common Inter-ORB protocol (DCE-CIOP)

A ServiceDetail object is a Dictionary with two elements:

Key	Value
serviceDetailType	ServiceDetailType
serviceDetail	OrderedCollection of Byte

ServiceDetailType is one of a set of constants, defined in CORBAConstants. A ServiceDetailType specifies a service supported by the implementation. There are two such constants defined:

ServiceDetailType	Meaning
::SecurityMechanismType	Type(s) supported for secure associations
::SecurityAttribute	Privileged types supported in standard access policy

Security level 2

Level 2 provides additional, more stringent security features. It allows applications to manage their own security. With it, an application can turn its own security features on and off. Among other things, it supports a credentials feature to validate the identity of another party.

Features

Level 2 security adds the following features:

- Principals can be authenticated either inside or outside the object system.

- The security of message invocation between objects is enhanced:
  - The establishment of trust and message protection can be done at the ORB level, so that security at a lower level of communication is not required;
  - Further integrity options can be requested, such as replay protections and out of sequence message detection, though these need not be supported;
  - Objects can have selective auditing methods.

- Applications can control the options used on secure messages.

- Administrators can specify security policies using domain managers and policy objects.

- Applications can find out what security policies apply to them.

- ORBs can find out what security policies apply to them.

Classes and messages

Security level 2 adds several more messages, which are defined in the CORBA module called SecurityLevel2. I won't describe the messages in detail. Their names and descriptions should give you a good idea of what they do.

Security level 2 provides a class called PrincipalAuthenticator. If the user (or other principal) needs authentication, and has not been already authenticated, it must request credentials from an object of this class.

A PrincipalAuthenticator understands two messages:

authenticate:securityName:authData:privileges:creds:continuationData:authSpecific Data:

This message has as one of its arguments a CORBA value object that, if the authorization was successful, is set to a Credentials object that includes the required attributes. There is also:

continueAuthentication:creds:continuationData:authSpecificData:

This is used when authentication requires more than one step.

A Credentials object is a principal's current credentials for a session. It includes information such as privilege attributes and an audit id. The Credentials messages are:

Message	Description
copy	Creates a deep copy of the receiver
setSecurityFeatures:securityFeatures:	Turns specific security features on and off
getSecurityFeatures:	Gets the state of any desired security features
setPrivileges:requestedPrivileges: actualPrivileges:	Sets privileges, such as role and group
getAttributes:	Gets security attributes
isValid:	Checks if credentials are expired
refresh	Updates expired credentials

Under security level 2, CORBA object references inherit some extra messages. These are:

Message	Description
overrideDefaultCredentials:	Specifies a Credentials object to be used
overrideDefaultQOP:	Specifies a particular quality of protection
getActiveCredentials	Answers the active credentials to use for invocations via this object reference
getSecurityFeatures	Answers the quality of protection and other security features to apply to this object reference
getSecurityMechanisms	Answers the security association mechanisms available
overrideDefaultMechanism:	Allows a different mechanism to be requested
getSecurityNames	Answers the security names for the target

In the above, the security mechanisms and security names are defined as strings.

Non-repudiation

Non-repudiation is an optional service and is not part of security level 1 or 2. It is defined in the CORBA module NRservice. The Non-repudiation service provides evidence of application actions in a form that cannot be repudiated later. Such evidence is always associated with some data—for example, the amount of bank withdrawal.

Non-repudiation tokens provide the necessary "evidence." A token either includes the associated data or has a unique reference to the associated data. Tokens can be freely distributed. Any holder of a non-repudiation token can store it and use it later for proof. The holder can also verify the validity of the token by asking the Non-repudiation service.

Secure Inter-ORB Protocol (SECIOP)

Secure communication between ORBs is defined in the CORBA module SECIOP. ORBs communicating using SECIOP send each other messages to establish secure contexts, and send messages using these contexts. A protocol has been defined for guiding both ORBs through the necessary states to establish secure communication.

IBM Distributed on the Internet

The IBM Distributed feature offers two security features that make it practical for many users to use on the Internet. It has internal security, which allows authentication of object spaces. There is also GSS API security, which uses the IBM product NetSP. This provides security services that conform to the de-facto industry standard Generic Security Services.

Internal security provided three levels, which are summarized as follows:

Security level	Description
Basic	Access control without authentication
Password	Client object space must supply a password for authentication
MutualPassword	Both object spaces must supply passwords

For data integrity and encryption, you must use GSS API security:

Security level	Description
GssApi	Both object spaces must supply passwords with GSS sign-on
GssApiSigned	GSS sign-on, data integrity check via signed messages
GssApiSealed	GSS sign-on, signed messages, and encryption of messages

When a client object space connects to a server object space, the two must negotiate that level of security to use. First, the server tells the client what levels of security it supports. Then the client checks its own list of security levels. If there is no security level matched by both object spaces, the connection fails.

Gemstone: ready for the Internet?

Gemstone is not secure enough all by itself to be considered Internet-ready. It does support Kerberos authentication, but only for UNIX platforms. Kerberos was developed for MIT's Project Athena, a campus-wide network environment.

Gemstone does have security, but it is geared toward database access, not networking. However, GemStone can utilize CORBA via SmalltalkBroker ORBs. Then, CORBA security, as it becomes available, is automatically added to inter-GemStone communication. With this scenario, you need a local GemStone server to supply the GemStone "Gems." GemStone machines on the Internet can then securely communicate via CORBA.

What About Intranets?

An intranet is simply an internal company TCP/IP network that uses the tools and facilities, such as Web browsers and servers, developed for the Internet.

Intranets are becoming increasingly popular as a way to distribute applications to desktops within a corporation. Updating software becomes a non-issue. Clients are "thin" because all they need, in theory, is a Web browser. A three-tiered architecture is virtually automatic. This was the approach taken by the Lawrence Livermore National Laboratories Data Warehouse Project described in Chapter 4.

Security is generally not an issue in such an environment. Typically, a "firewall" protects an intranet from unauthorized access from the Internet (see Figure 10-3). Because of this, all the distributed Smalltalks should work quite nicely on an intranet, without having to wait for security features to become available.

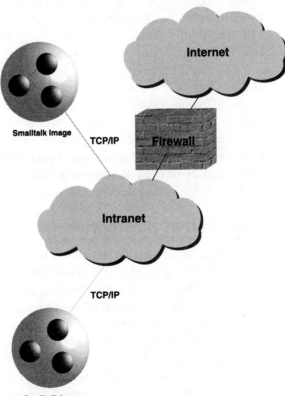

Figure 10-3. Distributed Smalltalk on an Intranet

Internet and Intranet Combined: Virtual Private Networks

The Virtual Private Network (VPN) is an emerging technology that combines the best features of the Internet and a company-wide intranet. A Virtual Private Network is a means for simulating a private network over the public Internet. Secure virtual connection are created that span portions of the Internet as necessary. VPNs are designed to provide the security, performance, and availability of a private network with the low cost and wide availability of the Internet.

The WAN

Traditionally, far-flung company networks have been interconnected by use of a leased line, which provides a Wide Area Network (WAN, see Figure 10-4). Such leased lines may range from single 56K-bps line up to a 1.5M-bps T1 line (or if money is truly no object, a 45M-bps T3 line). Fractional T1 lines are also available, where you can buy an integral number of the 24 64K-bps T0 lines that make up a T1. You then need a bit of extra multiplexing hardware to utilize the assigned T0 lines.

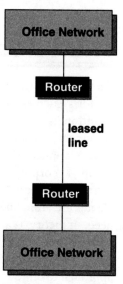

Figure 10-4. A Wide Area Network (WAN)

Packet-based frame relay technology extends to the low end, 56K-bps line. ISDN offers more bandwidth, 128K-bps for a single ISDN line. ISDN lines come in pairs, so you really get 256K-bps of possible bandwidth.

To connect the leased line to office networks at each end, routers are used. Each router examines packets on its LAN. If a packet has a destination address that indicates it is meant are for the partner office network, it sends it over the leased line.

The Internet alternative

VPNs leverage the Internet. So all you have to do is connect both ends of your network to the Internet, and you're in business. But how? Well, to connect your network to your ISP (Internet Service Provider), you are back to the same options as for a LAN, namely frame relay, ISDN, frame relay, T1, or fractional T1. So you still have to buy these lines, but they are much shorter, since they only need to get to your ISP.

But in addition, an ISP offers another option or two. The easiest, more familiar one is the traditional dial-up modem connection. This can give you 56K-bps of bandwidth on a good day, provided you are in a major metropolitan area where the telephone lines are of high enough quality to support these speeds.

There is another ISP technology that threatens to revolutionize networking and to shake up the entire rate structure of long-distance data communication: the cable modem. Cable television companies have realized that they have wired nearly all of

America with a very high speed wire that goes right into peoples' homes and offices. This "last mile" of wire is the most expensive to lay, which is why the existing telephone company infrastructure of twisted-pair, copper wire has been the limiting factor for everyday data communications.

Cable modem technology typically appropriates a couple of cable TV channels to carry TCP/IP traffic. These special channels can be out of the frequency range of the ordinary TV channels so that no TV channels have to be sacrificed. One channel carries data in one direction from the cable company Internet connection to you, and the other channel carries data in the other direction. Data communications speed is typically 1.5M-bps (the same as an expensive T1 line) from the Internet to you, and perhaps 300K-bps from you to the Internet.

The secret to achieving such high speeds over the same shared cable that supplies everyone in your neighborhood is to utilize the LAN model of network communication. Here, a "party line" works because not everyone is talking at the same time. Bursts of information need to flow, and packet technology can be optimally used. If two parties happen to send packets at the same time, a collision occurs, it is detected, and they try again. This is how Ethernet LANs work, and where the fundamental technology originated.

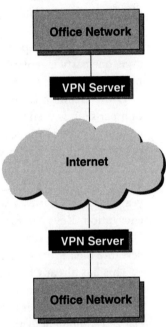

Figure 10-5. A Virtual Private Network (VPN)

What else you need

So given that you have an Internet connection, via ISDN, frame relay, cable modem, and so on, how do you link your company's network to it? You must purchase a VPN product, which can be hardware, software, or a combination of the two (see Figure 10-5). This product provides a secure link between peer networks over the public Internet. This is achieved through encryption, firewalls, and packet tunneling.

Encryption

Every VPN includes some sort of encryption technology to protect the private network traffic from "packet sniffing." Packet sniffing is when an unauthorized person connected to the Internet watches network traffic as it streams by. Potentially, someone could sniff traffic at your ISP, or at a major network access points that interconnect Internet backbone providers.

Sniffing your network is just a matter of somebody looking for packets whose header identifies one of your network's IP addresses. If the packet information is encrypted, though, packet sniffing does no good. The information is scrambled.

Encryption of data programmatically scrambles its bits so that a snooping party cannot make sense out of the data. The data is decrypted at the other end, using a mating algorithm.

Various encryption algorithms are available, with differing computing needs and levels of security. An older one, DES (Data Encryption Standard) was developed in the 1970s by the National Bureau of Standards. It was intended for commercial applications and low-security government communication.

DES is one of the "secret key" encryption systems. It requires that each end has private software keys to both lock (encrypt) and unlock (decrypt) the data. DES uses a 56-bit encryption key plus 8 parity bits.

Another secret key standard is called IDEA. Unlike DES, IDEA was designed for efficient software implementation. IDEA uses a 128-bit key.

A more modern class of encryption algorithms uses "public keys." Or rather, one of the two keys is made public, and the other is held as private. To send an encrypted message, one party is sent a public key by the other party. That key is used to encrypt the message. But once encrypted, nobody without the matching private key can decrypt it.

Diffie-Hellman is the oldest of the public key algorithms. It does not do encryption per se. It is used to generate keys by having two computers exchange the partial results of exponential calculations. The results can be exchanged over an insecure network, and yet the derived key at each end is secure.

The RSA algorithm was named for its inventors, Rivest, Shamir, and Adleman, who have a company that licenses this patented algorithm (the original patent expires in the year 2000). RSA uses a variable-length key; the longer the key, the more secure the encryption. Keys can range in size, typically between 512 bits and 4K bits. As with DES, cracking the keys for the RSA algorithm requires the factoring of very large numbers into their primes. This requires a vast amount of computation, but it can be done.

This has already been achieved for the 56-bit DES algorithm. A nationwide network of computers running around the clock cracked the DES code in 39 days. Later, the Electronic Frontier Foundation broke this code in a record 56 hours by adding specialized equipment to an ordinary PC, turning it into an encryption-cracking machine.

However, the longer the key, the more computation is required. Each additional bit roughly doubles the possible solutions for an encrypted message. So, as long as the key is large compared to current computation power, the algorithm is secure.

Firewalls

Firewalls guard a private network from unauthorized information packets. Firewalls control that computers, if any, can be seen from the external Internet. They also control what computers on the Internet an intranet user can see. Firewalls usually do their work by inspecting every packet that attempts to cross its boundaries. Any unauthorized packets do not get through. Specific IP addresses and port numbers are checked. This is known as **packet filtration**.

Because a firewall is the security boundary that separates a private network from the Internet, any VPN must be capable of bridging this wall without creating a security risk. A natural place to implement a VPN is right in a firewall. Cisco Systems, a major suppliers of network switches and routers, provides just this with its PIX firewall. In addition to be an effective packet filtration firewall, it provides a global pool of IP addresses that can be assigned. This pool automatically maps between internal IP addresses and external ones, which provides packet tunneling. The PIX firewall has an optional card for hardware encryption, which is necessary to use it as a true VPN.

Packet tunneling

The Internet exists within a single, global IP address space. From the viewpoint of the IP packet routers that manage the flow of information on the Net, each packet must have an IP address that is known to it. An ISP will typically be assigned a range of IP addresses that are dynamically assigned to a changing pool of dial-up users. Or the ISP will have corporate host machines that are permanently attached and have their own, fixed IP addresses.

But a private intranet has its own internal network addresses. These generally follow Internet standard for private addresses, which specifies that they be IP addresses in the range 192.168.n.n.

Packet tunneling consists of the following process. Take an IP packet on one network's internal network, and transform it in some way so that it now looks like it came from one of the assigned public Internet IP addresses. Also, set the destination address so that it, too, is a known Internet address and corresponds to the remote network that we are tunneling to. Feed this packet to the Internet, where it gets routed to the other private network. Then transform the packet received at the remote network, so that it is addressed to a machine within that network. Magically, the packet has tunneled through the Internet but appears to each private network to be contained within its private IP address spaces.

The IP address transformation can take place in a couple of ways. One way is to use **encapsulation**. For this approach, you simply take the entire original packet and enclose it within a new "public" Internet packet. Encapsulation is the approach taken by the Point-to-Point Tunneling Protocol (PPTP), which was jointly developed by companies including Microsoft and 3Com, which formed the PPTP forum. It looks like PPTP will merge into a common, Internet standard called Level 2 Tunneling Protocol (L2TP). Cisco had developed its own Layer 2 Forwarding protocol (L2F). L2TP combines the best features of PPTP and L2F. It allows interoperation between PPTP and L2F.

Another way to transform an IP packet is to change the source and destination addresses within the IP packet according to a mapping table. Then, at the other end of the tunnel, the addresses in the IP packet are mapped back. This is the approach taken by the Cisco PIX firewall.

VPNs, the next generation

IPsec is a newly emerging public standard for secure Internet communications right at the Internet packet (IP) level. It is being developed by the Internet Engineering Task Force (IETF). IPsec consists of a family of protocols that include the addition of an Authentication Header to an IP packet. This header supports authentication and data integrity. An additional header, the Encapsulated Security Payload header, provides for encryption of the packet contents.

The current generation of VPNs use host-based encryption schemes, which puts the encryption burden on desktop machines. Future VPNs are expected to rely on IPsec technology, so that this burden can be pushed out to the network packet routers.

Smalltalk and Web Browsers

Netscape Communications is making distributed, CORBA-based object technology a strategic part of its browser. Its current generation browser directly supports the Internet Inter-ORB Protocol (IIOP), the communication backbone between ORBs. And Netscape includes a full-fledged CORBA ORB, Visigenic Software's VisiBroker, within Netscape Communicator 4.0. This puts a CORBA ORB in an optimal place to work over the Internet—right in the browser. And matching server-side ORBs are also available via Netscape's SuiteSpot 3.0 servers.

This strategy deploys ORBs by the millions, ultimately placing an ORB into a large fraction of Web-aware computers. Rather than re-invent the distributed computing wheel, it leverages CORBA and makes it a commodity on the Internet.

Java has an important place in the picture, of course. In order to use a browser ORB, a Java applet gets downloaded. It talks to this ORB, which in turn talks to one or more ORB servers on the Web. All the CORBA services—Persistent Object, Transaction, Query, and importantly, the new Security Service, could become available to Java applets. And because they are speaking CORBA over the Net, the ORB servers could make use of any language they please, including, of course, Smalltalk.

Here is one way that distributed Smalltalk could work over the Internet or over a private Intranet. A Java ORB provides the GUI client interface within a Web browser and talks to server ORBs programs written in Smalltalk. Smalltalk servers could then freely cooperate in complex tasks. It's an ideal way to utilize Smalltalk's maturity and scalability, while plugging and playing with Java.

Why Smalltalk servers rather than a different CORBA-supported language? Smalltalk has some unique features among commercial languages that make it ideal for server side business objects. Smalltalk blocks can be used to encapsulate business rules. Blocks of code are not first-class objects in Java as they are in Smalltalk, necessitating ugly and idiosyncratic C-style control structures.

Because everything in Smalltalk is an object, including each and every class, Smalltalk has the built-in meta-capability of reflectivity—all Smalltalk objects know how to describe themselves. Smalltalk's unified object paradigm allows extending even the basic data types. Java does not have such a unified object view.

People complain about the steep learning curve for Smalltalk. However, much of this learning is required to embrace the pure object-oriented paradigm that Smalltalk utilizes. Without full acceptance and understanding of this paradigm, Java code is destined to be little more than C code with some object-oriented trappings. There are already horror stories of Java methods that run-on for hundreds of lines.

The C++ syntax for Java was chosen so that yet another new syntax would not be invented. This was an aid for those who already knew C or C++, which is a substantial fraction of the programming community. But tell that to a COBOL programmer! C/C++ syntax is horribly byzantine. In my experience, software departments that have used COBOL have an easier time migrating to Smalltalk than to C or C++ (or Java) because the syntax is so simple and in line with what they are used to.

The fact is that as of this writing, Java is not yet a viable production language in terms of stability, features, and support. Smalltalk is and continues to be such a viable language. But perception is everything, and Java is perceived as being superior to Smalltalk.

We believe that distributed Smalltalk is a stepping stone to distribute object technology as a whole; that ultimately, language will not matter. This is the model CORBA uses. It makes a lot of sense. If black-box objects are the correct way to do distributed objects, then it should not matter what language is used to implement the black box.

Today, relational databases form a large amount of the common infrastructure for enterprise computing. To require that a relational database be used with one particular language and one language only would be silly and unnecessary. All a computing language needs is an API to the relational database in order to utilize it. This is typically realized by a low-level library that converts SQL query character strings into SQL calls to the relational database and organizes the database results into data structures or objects appropriate to the language.

As multi-tiered architectures become the norm, distributed object computing will become a necessary infrastructure for its implementation. CORBA provides such an infrastructure. CORBA is destined (indeed, mandated) to interoperate with the Java environment and with Java's version of distributed components, JavaBeans. This means that distributed Smalltalk objects may live anywhere in the enterprise. Such objects may implement complex business logic behind the scenes, within layers of middleware. They may talk to their ilk across far-flung networks.

Web-based users may, unbeknownst to be them, be invoking distributed Smalltalk objects. After all, the computer user does not really know how the magic happens, nor should he. And distributed Smalltalk makes very powerful magic.

≡Notes≡

1. *CORBAservices: Common Object Services Specification.* Object Management Group, Framingham, MA. March, 1995.

2. *Smalltalk Portability: A Common Base.* ITSC Technical Bulletin GG24-3093, IBM, Boca Raton, FL. September 1992.

3. *The Common Object Request Broker: Architecture and Specification.* Object Management Group, Framingham, MA. July 1995.

4. Myers, G. (1978). *Composite/Structured Design.* New York, NY: Van Nostrand Reinhold, p. 21.

5. Wirfs-Brock, R., B. Wilkerson and L. Wiener. (1990). *Designing Object-Oriented Software.* Englewood Cliffs: Prentice-Hall, p. 30.

6. Rumbaugh, J., M. Blaha, W. Premerlani, E. Frederick, and W. Lorensen. (1991). *Object-Oriented Modeling and Design.* Englewood Cliffs: Prentice-Hall, pp. 199–200.

7. Gamma, E., R. Helm, R. Johnson, and J. Vlissides. (1995). *Design Patterns.* Reading, Massachusetts: Addison Wesley, pp. 185–193.

8. Brown, K. Remembrance of things past: Layered architectures for Smalltalk applications. The Smalltalk Report, 4(9), July/August 1995. pp. 4–7.

9. Jacobson, I., M. Christerson, P. Jonsson, and G. Overgaard. (1992). *Object-Oriented Software Engineering.* Reading, Massachusetts: Addison Wesley, pp. 289–312.

10. Ceri, S., and G. Pelagatti. (1984). *Distributed Databases: Principles and Systems.* New York, NY: McGraw-Hill, pp. 173-244.

11. Mullender, S., editor. (1993). *Distributed Systems.* Reading, Massachusetts: Addison Wesley, pp. 329–353.

≡Index≡